e

Futurology

Issues, contexts and conditions for contemporary art practice today

Edited by Andy Hewitt and Mel Jordan (Freee)

www.futurologybook.com

Published by The New Art Gallery Walsall
Distributed by Cornerhouse Publications (www.cornerhouse.org/publications)
Printed by Pinstripe Print
Design: 43°North

ISBN 978-0-946652-82-2
A catalogue record of this book is available from the British Library.

Artists acknowledgements
With thanks to all the collaborators of the Futurology project.
The young citizens and teaching staff from Castle School, Deansfield High School, The Kings
CofE School, George Salter High School and Tividale High School.
All photographs where not credited by Andy Hewitt and Roger Westwood.

Artists: Barby Asante, Dave Beech, Nick Crowe & Ian Rawlinson, Simon Poulter, Becky Shaw
Writers: Mark Hutchinson, Esther Leslie, Malcolm Miles, Charlotte Smith, Ruth Robinson
Speakers: Rasheed Areen, Tim Butler, Claire Fox, Charles Landry, Malcolm Miles, John Roberts
Facilitors and supporters: Rebecca Owen (Futurology Education Manager),
Nick Slater, Arts Council of England West Midlands, Black Country Tourism, University of
Wolverhampton, Roz Hall (Evaluation), Michelle Cotton (Futurology research), Ceri Hand, FACT
(observer), Pat Nesbitt (design and print). Martin Kelly (video documentation).
All the staff at The New Art Gallery Walsall and Creative Partnerships Black Country.

Thanks also to the speakers at the artist two-day event: James Heartfield, Sylvia King (the
pUBLIC), Sarah Middleton (Black Country Regeneration), Sophie Churchill (Regen West Midlands), Esther Leslie, Sian Lincoln, Matthew Biagetti (Walsall Borough Council).

Thanks to Ruth Robinson for her help in the production of this book.

  Black Country **Consortium**

Futurology

Issues, contexts and conditions for contemporary art practice today

Edited by Andy Hewitt and Mel Jordan (Freee)

www.futurologybook.com

Contents

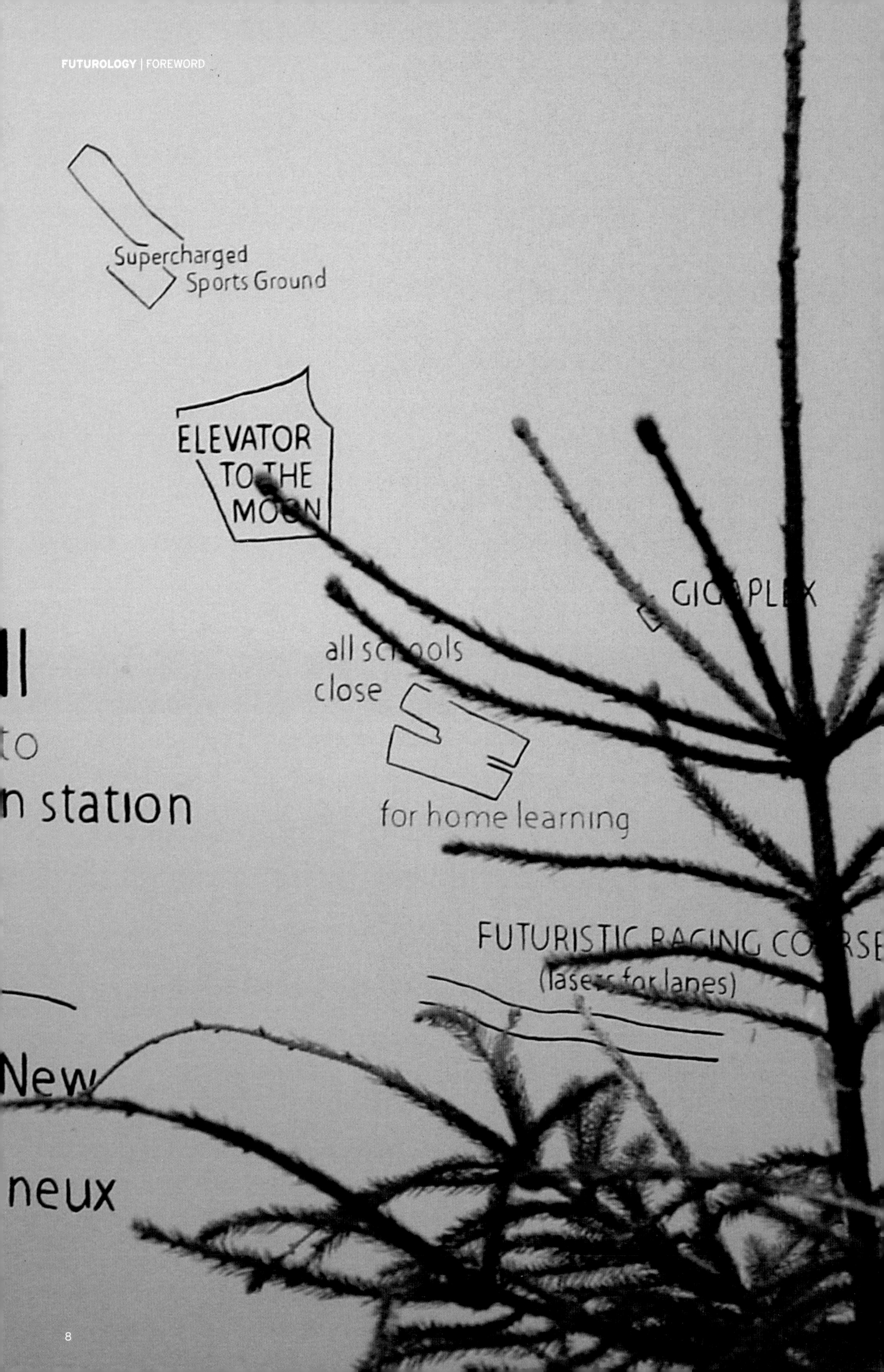

Supercharged
Sports Ground

ELEVATOR
TO THE
MOON

GIGAPLEX

all schools
close

to

n station

for home learning

FUTURISTIC RACING COURSE
(lasers for lanes)

New

neux

Foreword

The New Art Gallery Walsall is pleased to be able to publish this book; as well as documenting the project, **Futurology: The Black Country 2024,** the book offers an opportunity to extend the inquiry associated with the initial commissions and exhibition, inviting further contributors to comment and engage in the questions posed by the project and by the artists Hewitt and Jordan.

Hewitt and Jordan have been working together since 1999; their practice is consistently collaborative, challenging, provocative and importantly, in relation to this project, engaged with a wider social and political agenda. The object is rarely at the centre of their practice, which instead, focuses on consultation, research and communication. This project, proposed by them, in response to an invitation by The New Art Gallery Walsall and Creative Partnerships Black Country to work collaboratively with us on developing an exhibition, offered an opportunity for them to further explore the idea of functionality and autonomy within current art practice and commissioning.

The *Futurology* project focuses on the theme of regeneration and explores creativity in relation to issues of social change. It investigates what the economic, social and political landscape might look like for the next generation of Black Country citizens.

The artists invited to participate in the initial project all have a wealth of experience in working outside of studio or gallery models. An exhibition was always thought to be an important ingredient within the project in order to provide the kind of profile and visibility needed, but this inevitably provided tensions and contradictions. Artists whose approach was essentially non-object based were being asked to create something involving young people that would represent at least something of the time they had spent together. This challenge was ultimately met with solutions that were diverse, ingenious, unorthodox and provocative but not without negotiations along the way.

The enduring relevance of the *Futurology* project explores alternative models of collaborative working and shared practice, and proposes a role for art in supporting a sense of possibility within social and political thinking.

To their great credit, the openness of the project was embraced by all involved including the sponsors to whom we are extremely grateful. These included Walsall Council, Arts Council West Midlands, Black Country Consortium and Black Country Tourism whom I would like to thank on behalf of The New Art Gallery Walsall and Creative Partnerships.

We extend our warm thanks to the authors of the texts, newly commissioned for this publication, and the *Futurology* public speakers who have generously allowed us to include transcripts of their talks. We would also like to thank the artists: Barby Asante, Dave Beech, Nick Crowe and Ian Rawlinson, Simon Poulter and Becky Shaw. As well as artists Andy Hewitt and Mel Jordan for editing this publication.

Deborah Robinson
Senior Exhibitions Curator
The New Art Gallery Walsall

Opposite page:
**Futurology
Exhibition**, detail,
The New Art Gallery
Walsall, 2004

Introduction

This book documents and expands upon ideas that were initially explored in the project and exhibition, **Futurology: The Black Country 2024**, at The New Art Gallery Walsall in 2004 (30 July – 12 September). And it identifies and addresses key issues important for understanding the context and function of contemporary art practice today. Although this book is published some time after the *Futurology* exhibition, the issues raised through the project remain pertinent to the current discourse on the public funding of art.

Commissioned and funded principally by Creative Partnerships Black Country and The New Art Gallery Walsall, we developed the *Futurology* project as a means to explore the instrumentalization of art and culture. Our work for *Futurology* lies within the tradition of artists who investigate and discuss the role and function given to art practice. During the last decade culture-led regeneration has increasingly become the new paradigm for art funding and therefore needs to be critically interrogated. It is in this sense that *Futurology* can be understood as an artwork, a negotiated intervention in the tradition of an internal or institutional critique. It was our intention to produce a critical space for discussion regarding the social and economic conditions for art practice that might operate as a counterpublic sphere.

One of the key questions of the *Futurology* project concerned the role of the artist in social life; how to remain socially and politically active through art practice whilst avoiding the naïve

surrendering of the artist to the agenda of politicians, quangos and funders.

Creative Partnerships are instrumental in employing 'creative people' to work within their strategy to improve state schools. We wanted to understand what this meant; to ask how art could function via social policy and what could artists really bring to the Creative Partnerships project. At the same time The New Art Gallery Walsall was interested in supporting critical and social art practices. These types of practices more often reside in an education programme and could be seen as an omission by public institutions to acknowledge that artists choose to work outside the studio for conceptual, social and political reasons. Consequently the discursive and participatory nature of these practices becomes instrumentalized within the gallery education programme. The *Futurology* project brought process-based practices into the gallery. The display and presentation of the work within the gallery was to be considered within the context of contemporary art practices as opposed to being merely relegated to the gallery's education programme.

We used a utopian premise to enable the artists and young people to examine the current social, economic and political conditions in the Black Country in order to imagine their future. Six artists, a number of participants from Black Country schools and funding partners were invited to collaborate on the project. The artists and commissioners where encouraged to discuss and address a range of concerns including: citizenship, town planning and regeneration, social mobility, work, ownership, youth aspirations and education.

To introduce the project we held a two-day meeting at The New Art Gallery Walsall to present the project contexts to the artists. We invited a number of speakers to initiate discussions around the issues outlined in the project: academics discussed notions of utopia, the development of cultural economies and how young people use their bedrooms as both private and social spaces. Regeneration agency representatives introduced the artists to demographic information and a proposed new scheme for the area and the region, a town-planner from the borough council described future planning of the town and local teachers were invited to talk about their aspirations for their students. A discussion of the project contexts enabled the artists to gain information about the current conditions of the Black Country in relation to culture-led regeneration. This was not meant to be a convivial activity but was an attempt at open debate. Each artist then developed a new artwork in collaboration or with participation from a Black Country school.

This publication is organized into three sections; Artists, Writers and Speakers. The introductory essay, *A Transformative Art Gallery – Thoughts in Relation to Futurology* attempts to contextualize the *Futurology* project within culture-led regeneration, and considers autonomy and ideology of art and culture and the formation of counter public spheres within art practice.

In the Artists section, artist and writer Charlotte Smith interviews Becky Shaw to discuss her views on the development process of the *Futurology* project.

Barby Asante, Dave Beech, Nick Crowe & Ian Rawlinson, Simon Poulter and Becky Shaw describe and reflect upon the five commissions they developed for the project and exhibition. The artworks encompass and address various issues crucial to practice today; art's role in relation to education, social and cultural division, art and politics, participation, collaboration and authorship.

In the Writers section we have commissioned four new texts: Malcolm Miles explores instrumentatlization, culture-led regeneration and government policy, Ruth Robinson examines the politics of inclusion and arts role in civilizing 'the people', Mark Hutchinson develops his four stages of Public Art concluding that anti-art is the only way to make art and Esther Leslie, explores ideas of utopia; the future before us, behind us and the future now.

In the Speakers section are the transcripts from a series of public talks that were organized in the gallery space. The invited speakers discussed the following; collaboration beyond art practice (Rasheed Araeen), public art – from public spaces to public spheres (Malcolm Miles), the geography of gentrification (Tim Butler), the role of the creative city in the regeneration of a place (Charles Landry) and education's relationship to social change (Claire Fox).

Andy Hewitt and Mel Jordan

A Transformative Art Gallery - Thoughts in Relation to Futurology

Andy Hewitt and Mel Jordan

Introduction

Culture-led regeneration raises the question of art's autonomy by threatening it. This is in contrast to art's autonomy within the artistic autonomy of modernism that seems to call for isolation and lead to various forms of indifference and aestheticism. However, as Dave Beech argues, 'to rethink autonomy via Habermas' concept of systems and lifeworld is to ditch the old and still dominant idea that autonomy is a form of isolation and withdrawal from society'[1]. That's why for us, autonomy means self-determination. Autonomy is a social relation that cannot protect itself from social ills by withdrawing from the world. Autonomy requires a heightened awareness of the way society is present within art's traditions, values, institutions and a willingness to combat them. Withdrawal brings about only complicity and resignation.

Therefore, self-determination means resistance to steering media such as culture-led regeneration, and with this in mind, we aim to wrestle art from external agencies and ulterior motives. This involves public debates, setting limits and reversing the effect of capital and administration, and ultimately putting ourselves in the debate and attending to these issues. We believe that art maintains and gains autonomy by contesting and reconfiguring the social determinates of art. This was the premise from which we devised the *Futurology* project.

Culture-led regeneration does not function to revive democracy or to create counterpublic spheres. It does not encourage self-organization, the development of collective interests or the forms of collective agency that contest power. Art under these circumstances is without hope. Social transformation needs a transformative art and transformative institutions.

Cultural Conditions of Culture-led Regeneration

Like everyone else artists are part of the economic system of contemporary cultural production. We are interested in understanding these conditions so that as agents in culture, we reflect on how we might act and where we may intervene. Our primary interest in developing the *Futurology* project was to explore the function given to art within what has become known as culture-led regeneration. We see this as a specific example of art's self-reflective and critical relation to the economic conditions of contemporary cultural production. Culture-led regeneration highlights art's economic condition as extending beyond the art market, the commodity form and questions of public funding. Thus culture-led regeneration situates art within the economy at large, proposing a direct function of art. Questions of the various specific functions for art in society are central to our practice; we attempt to locate arts function in the social co-ordinates of capital and state, of patronage and artist, of artwork and audience.

Historically, cultural policy has provided a number of useful levers for the state, in other words, we have witnessed 'cultural policy as display', national aggrandizement and culture as a business proposition[2]. State funding and patronage of art and culture for political gain is not a new phenomena, but in the 1990s as the national economy became increasingly absorbed into a global free market economy, New Labour placed cultural policy at the heart of its political agenda. Culture-led regeneration has since become a key component by which liberal democratic governments within the economic and social systems of urban post-industrial contexts (and in some cases rural) – aim to counter the deleterious effects of shrinking former industries, in an era of rapid change and in light of advanced global capital.

Culture-led regeneration is a mechanism implemented by government to affect economic and social change. As patron for the arts, government influences the function for art and culture via conditions for state subsidy within cultural policy. Within the new cultural settlement, in which art is dominated by two massive emerging economic structures, namely culture-led regeneration and biennale style art fairs, art production has become a highly visible constituent of the enlarged culture industry of a global economy. Culture-led regeneration aims to bring about urban renewal, via economic diversification and enhancing the image of areas suffering decline, while claiming to solve social issues such as unemployment and crime.

In the last ten years we have seen a large increase in the number of agencies that commission an artist to work within various remits for regeneration, a move encouraged by the government. The Social Exclusion Unit was set up in 1997 by New Labour to make recommendations across all government departments. Since the 1999 Policy Action Team 10 report[3], Arts Council England and other cultural organizations in Britain have taken significant steps to widen access and participation in the arts. The 2001 green paper, *Culture and Creativity: The Next Ten Years* reaffirmed the government's commitment to widening access and increasing participation in the arts. The Urban White Paper (November 2000) set out an agenda for revitalizing urban communities, making it more accessible for British artists to become involved in public art. By including and emphasizing art in planning policy makers, architects, artists and communities are placed in direct association.

Government has prompted development agencies, quangos and charities to become the commissioners of art with various economic and social agendas. Artists are commissioned to deliver on specific aspects of a project, either visual or aesthetic works, or in some cases relational and communicative projects. Artists are brought in to fix a specific problem. Their task is to deliver the project outcomes like other professional contractors or members of the planning team. However, unlike conventional professionals the artist brings added value and good public relations to projects, attributes that some critics argue have a tendency to mask the negative aspects of development[4]. Due to the growing professionalization of cultural production artists have become a part of the administrative management of deprived areas.

Critics of culture-led regeneration point to such regeneration as not being any more effectual than other types of economic development. The main criticism being that artists involvement is sometimes symbolic and tends to occur in specific areas to maximize visual impact. Culture-led regeneration

has also been criticized for the limited distribution of the benefits it brings. It is sometimes aimed at cultural visitors to a city, and it can draw funding away from disadvantaged areas. Most importantly, the cultural development or gentrification of an area can force out low income residents[5].

The Social Function of Art

The justification for the funding of the arts is described in terms of social policy outcomes that aim to prevent society's social and cultural polarization and social disintegration in former working class communities of post-industrial areas. Policies of wider access and participation in the arts are said to function to improve a community, its health and criminal justice. According to the Arts Council England website the arts provide the, 'power to change people's lives and communities'[6].

Much of the rhetoric of art as a catalyst in urban economic regeneration stemmed from consultants such as cultural entrepreneur Charles Landry, an advocate of the social and economic benefits of art and culture in regeneration. In his book *The Creative City*[7], Landry regularly uses the word 'creativity' to describe economic processes within city planning. Regeneration, he claims aims to change the 'mindset' and 'behaviour' of residents, 'to improve their effectiveness in creating capital and growth in order to reduce what is seen as a dependency on state provision.'[8] Education initiatives and workshops aim to improve the citizen. In this way art commissioned and funded by the state becomes a vehicle for the government's campaign of public good and personal responsibility, at its heart an economic function to reduce the costs of state welfare provision.

Cultural betterment, as a form of social control of the working class, through the consumption of middle class culture, is reminiscent of the efforts of Victorian philanthropists to civilize the lower classes, as Tony Bennett has analyzed in his essay, *The Exhibitionary Complex*.[9] By making their collections available to an expanded public through visits to the newly built museums, cultural philanthropists sought to improve the manners, behaviour and aspirations of the lower classes, aiming to reduce crime and propagate a stronger work ethic in the process. Betterment in culture-led regeneration follows the Victorian model of self-improvement and modified behaviour, in the absence of tackling the structural causes of social division and inequality.

The architects of culture-led regeneration claim, that through contact with the arts, individuals in deprived areas are able to better themselves and their circumstances. And so education, via cultural activity functions to teach individuals new life skills and offers them higher aspirations. While there has been little evidence to suggest that art can make this happen, but it has been a remarkably effective argument to lever further funding for the arts from government.

In developing such cultural strategies government does not explicitly target social division and the gap between rich and poor. In the United Kingdom, the divide between rich and poor is now wider than it has been for the past forty years. It has been suggested that British society is moving toward the US social paradigm of 40:30:30 – meaning that the top 40% of society are secure, the middle 30% have insecure jobs and lifestyles and the bottom 30% are the controlled underclass[10]. In the managed economy of the Third Way Meritocracy, social mobility diminishes, while class structures ossify.

Culture becomes one of the few areas of government intervention, and in this way, as art critic and curator JJ Charlesworth says, New Labour have 'effectively transposed the responsibility for social development, amelioration and progress, however limited, away from broader interventions into social organization, and into the realm of culture'[11].

Two Crises: Art versus the Public

In order to understand culture-led regeneration as a cultural phenomenon we need to understand its place within post-modern culture and post-war politics. This means understanding two crises: the crisis of modern bourgeois art and the crisis of democracy.

The public art gallery in Western contemporary society has been experiencing a crisis of confidence – its function is under question. It's historic function as the epicentre of the formation of knowledge and taste for a bourgeois audience, as a bourgeois public sphere par excellence, is under attack. Third Way government politics wants such institutions to be accountable to the taxpayer, to provide a service, to become an instrument for the state. Within the dynamic of a global culture industry new forms of private and state co-operation have produced new cultural venues and events, including art biennales, in an alliance of instrumental economic and social functions. These public-private initiatives have aims that are consistent with the original function of the bourgeois public art gallery, namely that of controlling opinion formation.

The opening up of our public funded art institutions as spaces for discussion on the condition of the public sphere appears timely for two reasons. Firstly to counter the process of of increasing privatization. Secondly to attempt the further democratization of art against the traditional influence of autonomous isolation. Critic and curator Simon Shiekh has suggested a new function for art institutions, one that encourages dissonance. Sheikh calls for a need to 'unhinge stable categories of the public sphere'[12], he proposes that the art institution becomes a producer of instability, flux and negotiation, offering a conflictual rather than consensual notion of democracy. This might offer a new and much needed function for the public art gallery and provides an argument for its continued existence and funding.

Two Crises: The Debased Public Sphere

There has been a crisis in politics since the end of the cold war, visible in the loss of traditional forms of collectivity, the growing influence of the free market, and a sense of uncertainty in Western democracies. Western liberal democracies are stable yet are lacking a broader purpose or a cohesive social project. It is against this period of time that Third Way politics have emerged as a term to describe these new managed economies. With the movement of capital, shifts in industrial production, and the demise of class alliance via old employment structures, we have seen the atomization of social institutions and groups that had political memberships such as trade unions. In the absence of an active and participating citizenry, the state attempts to manage community relations; the deal for welfare payments and social rights are dependent upon accepting a contract of social responsibility regulated by agencies within culture-led regeneration.

There has been a colonization of culture by the state. Culture has become a new political sphere for acts of cultural exchange (for the state, for capital and those contesting them) in place of those lost systems of common experience and argument. In the absence of a coherent political culture the media and the cultural sphere have become more important as spaces for the articulation of the political imagination, so that in the arts – and often within art commissioned as part of culture-led regeneration – we see being played out representations of convivial democratic exchange and political agreement.

Using Jurgen Habermas' social theory of the bourgeois public sphere[13], we can call such a colonization of culture a form of debased public sphere. Habermas' ideal conception of the public sphere, often critiqued, was one where individuals would determine their actions without interference by either the state or the market through open debate and the formation of opinion. They would organize public opinion against the forces in power and create their own publicity in opposition to the publicity of the state or market. Culture-led regeneration and the art that it funds, is not designed to foster such democratic opinion formation. It is instead a strategic economic activity by the state in partnership with business. It aims to intervene within the social sphere, operating in the public realm to administer communities, via top down policies and to construct public opinion. With a general decline in participatory politics, the domination of culture via culture-led regeneration acts as a means to engender change but not openly in discussion as in a political sphere but by stealth and hegemonic means.

Habermas makes an important distinction between what he calls 'lifeworld' and 'the system' in society. The public sphere is a 'lifeworld' with communication as its medium, the 'lifeworld' is an unregulated sphere of sociality, where encounters with other social actors, provide shared meanings and where knowledge is created via critical reflection[14]. 'The system', on the other hand, refers to the opaque structures of the market economy and the state, with its mechanism and internal logic of money and power. Habermas says it is the 'steering media' that funnels people into patterns of instrumental behaviour. 'The system' is in the hands of experts and administrators and therefore operates away from public scrutiny and possible democratic control.

In Habermas' view, 'the system' has colonized the 'lifeworld' and 'brings in its wake a growing sense of meaninglessness and dwindling freedom'[15]. The steering media of money and power like those found in culture-led regeneration with its attendant quangos, bureaucrats, charities and the bourgeois institutions of art and culture distort intersubjective exchange. Instead they direct action and set values according to money and power without due discussion and debate. However, the 'lifeworld' has not been fully absorbed by 'the system', and therefore we as citizens, must do what we can to make our public institutions more democratic and transparent in order to prevent further encroachment of system imperatives on areas of the 'lifeworld'.

Opening up the institutions and systems of culture and culture-led regeneration to public scrutiny is therefore necessary in order to improve them. We can counter those instrumental imperatives that pressure our institutions and at the same time democratize their function. And where necessary form new institutions and close down those that function against democracy. Within the *Futurology* project we had two commissioners; a government agency with a function to improve state education systems by instrumentalizing 'creative' resources and an art institution that has a public remit for exhibition and education, but with an interest in maintaining the bourgeois function of the gallery. Both commissioners had different agendas but had been pushed together by the imperatives of the new cultural paradigm.

Between these two institutions, we formed our own temporary institution that we hoped would act as a platform for the necessary critique of these cultural conditions. We attempted to open up a space to question the system in which we all worked. *Futurology* formed a mini counterpublic sphere in which contributors could problematize these issues by discussing their interests and their differences.

Art's divisions

Art is a divided field. Within the politics of art, long-standing rival ideologies exist. The introduction of culture-led regeneration brings a new composition to the politics of art. Therefore, it is useful to characterize the opposing publics of art, we will call them: arts reformers, arts conservatives, and arts avant-garde.

i. Arts reformers

For us, arts reformers include those culture-led regeneration lobbyists and government agencies that give function to art within culture-led regeneration. The problem is, that in most cases, the result of the commissioning of art in culture-led regeneration, is a representation of the aims and priorities of culture-led regeneration – the authoritarian social policies of the state and economics of the market. The old Labour movement was suspicious of art and culture as being elitist, New Labour was instead eager to harness its cultural capital. Under New Labour a new generation of arts reformers took over Britain's art establishment, making demands for an inclusive agenda within the gallery sector, to increase access to art, often via an expansion of education activities alongside the main gallery programme. They believed that the opening up of culture to a wider audience, counters the elitist nature of art, and that art tied to an education agenda is egalitarian in nature, fitting a Third Way society. They represent a liberal tradition in the arts, their reformist desire is to help the working classes but mainly to improve them; arts reformers aim is to increase access to art, to democratize the existing system in order that its civilizing values are readily available and function for a wider user group. The art that is provided represents the values of the middle class for a working class audience.

ii. Arts conservatives

Arts conservatives form the old arts establishment and their ideas are based upon the aesthetic ideology that dominates art. Autonomy is a key issue here and central to aesthetic ideology. Autonomy as isolation, as practiced by art conservatives and the majority of arts institutions, stems from Kant's idea that you give yourself laws and determine your own limits. The autonomous individual that figure central to bourgeois universality is the model of freedom and self-regulation and is enshrined in Western art.

Terry Eagleton tells us that aesthetics is used to describe a universal, shared and harmonious whole or community, to counter the stark reality of 'the market place' and lack of 'ideological consensus' in 'actual social relations'.[16] The aesthetic ignores social division and capital; it functions within a narrow social context, operating autonomously in exclusive circuits, its politics defined by arts conservative institutions.

Arts conservatives then reject the state instrumentalization of art and arts institutions. For example, Andrew Brighton talks of an 'erosion of liberty', claiming the 'autonomy of domains of thought and action' contained in such bodies as the art gallery are 'a fundamental characteristic of a liberal society'[17]. Brighton suggests a reversal of access to culture, claiming that advocating public funding for the arts on the grounds that it benefits the working class is 'both effectual and dishonest'. Brighton's argument is that art is 'made by and for people who know or want to know about it'[18] and that this educated group is art's audience. His defence of the liberal status quo is that this group is without interest; they are custodians of culture, who are safeguarding the arts from any oppositional or political ideology. Brighton cheekily maintains that his new vision of an 'art for art sake' Britain would still be funded by taxing the working class.

iii. Arts avant-garde

There are competing and rival versions of autonomy; Habermas is concerned with Adorno's critique of instrumental reason in which Adorno does not challenge the isolationist autonomy of art. Habermas calls this 'deworlded' saying 'it is released from those relationships to the totality and those structures of intersubjectivity by which culture, society and personality are interwoven'.[19] Adorno's autonomy is as intolerant of the heteronomous world as Kant's. As Dave Beech points out, in Adorno's narrow and opaque social world, autonomous art takes a very special role within the history of human freedom; aesthetic autonomy, the absolute negation of instrumentality is the only possible response to the complete instrumentality of modernity.[20]

Habermas claims that Adorno has 'expanded instrumental reason into a category of the world-historical process of civilisation thereby over stretching his critique'[21] and that this exaggeration of instrumental reason leads to mindfulness, without agency or hope. It cannot be used to flatly describe all the methods by which we communicate and make social agreement in the 'lifeworld'.

Those artists who are working within the tradition of the avant-garde see culture-led regeneration as yet another manifestation, in the history of art, of the functions given to art, that form social division and maintain hegemonic culture; art contains art divisions when it crosses over to culture-led regeneration. For the avant-garde, there is a clear paradox within the social function given to art in culture-led regeneration by the state – the very tools that are being used to affect social policy are the ones by which societies social distinctions are made and status is conferred – the arts remain the ultimate product of social and cultural division.[22]

The avant-garde contest the art conservative and art reformer. The avant-garde have broken down conservative and instrumental forces in culture by the steady attrition of conservative values, and they have worked across culture to open up art to everyday life and to stretch the competencies of art. Contesting culture in this way, artists contribute to the critique of contemporary society and help shape our visions of a better future, even though the radical departures of the avant-garde are often absorbed back into commodity systems and capital.

Conclusion

The public art gallery is divided. It is divided by its two functions, either to support autonomy as a form of isolation in autonomous art, or to instrumentalize art to meet the demands of the state.

Arts institutions have a tendency to protect the art gallery from public politics and instead support a private politics – a long tradition of liberal art. Conceptions of the public are only evident as a form of administration of the public: what services can be offered?; How can people be educated?; And where can audience participation be included in the programme?

Two forms of opinion formation take place in the art gallery. Firstly, opinion formation as a bourgeois universal ideal, and secondly, as the construction of opinion formation – how can we get the public to think in the appropriate (educated, cultivated, bourgeois) way?

So there is fracture running through the art gallery along the lines of cultural division, and what is also fractured as a result is the public. The false universalism of the public gallery therefore promises exactly that which it is signally incapable of providing – a democratic public sphere and an un-debased art.

If the gallery were to become a space that was both detached from the idea of art as autonomy as a form of isolation, and from the administration of the state (and of capital), we might then begin to have a more public art gallery. Such a gallery would function for a broader public, for a range of collective and competing interests and therefore represent a broader conception of politics. With the function of the art gallery shaken up the public would get the art they deserve – an art neither geared towards the market or the state, but for the first time in history, a properly public art.

ENDNOTES

1. Beech D, 2007, 'Autonomy v Barbarism', Art Monthly, No. 309.

2. Williams R, 1985[1983], 'Towards 2000', London, Penguin.

3. DCMS, 1999, Policy Action Team 10: a report to the Social Exclusion Unit.

4. Miles M, 2005, 'Interruptions: Testing the Rhetoric of Culturally Led Urban Development', Urban Studies Volume 42, Numbers 5/6.

5. Ibid.

6. http://www.artscouncil.org.uk/.

7. Landry C, 2000, 'The Creative City, A Toolkit for Urban Innovators', Earthscan, London.

8. Ibid.

9. T. Bennett, 'The Exhibitionary Complex, New Formations: A Journal of Culture/Theory/Politics'. No.4, Spring 1998.

10. W, Hutton, 1995, 'The State We're In', Jonathan Cape.

11. Charlesworth J.J., 2002, 'Twin Towers: The Spectacular Disappearance of Art and Politics', ed. Beech D, 'Art, Politics & Resistance', Third Text, number 61 Volume 16.

12. Simon Sheikh, 2005, 'The Trouble with Institutions, or, Art and Its Publics', ed. by Montmann N, 'Art and its institutions, current conflicts, critique and collaborations', Black Dog Publishing. 2006.

13. Habermas J, 1962, 'The Structural Transformation of the Public Sphere – An Inquiry into a Category of Bourgeois Society', Cambridge, Mass., MIT Press 1989.

14. Habermas J, 1986, 'The Theory of Communicative Action. Reason and Rationalization of Society', Volume one. Polity.

15. Ibid.

16. Eagleton T, 1990, 'The Ideology of the Aesthetic', Oxford: Basil Blackwell.

17. Brighton A, 2006, 'Consumed by the political. In The Ruination of the Arts Council. Culture Vultures. Is UK art policy damaging the arts?', ed. Mirza M, Policy Exchange.

18. Ibid.

19. Habermas J, 1986, 'The Theory of Communicative Action. Reason and Rationalization of Society', Volume one. Polity.

20. Beech D, 2007, 'Autonomy v Barbarism', Art Monthly, No. 309.

21. Habermas J, 1986, 'The Theory of Communicative Action. Reason and Rationalization of Society', Volume one. Polity.

22. Bourdieu P, 1979, 'Distinction. A Social Critique of the Judgement of Taste'. Routledge, London.

Futurology Artists, L- R Simon Poulter, Nick
Crowe, Barby Asante, Dave Beech,
Ian Rawlinson, Becky Shaw, Andy Hewitt,
Mel Jordan. The New Art Gallery Walsall, 2004

Two-Day Event,
The New Art Gallery
Walsall, 2004

Interview
with artist
Becky Shaw
on Futurology

Charlotte Smith: As an artist involved in the Futurology project, can you describe the project? I am especially interested in how all the artists and partners worked together and what Hewitt and Jordan's role was and what you think the differences were between the Futurology project and other apparently similar projects? I am also interested in how Hewitt and Jordan managed the communication between the artists, The New Art Gallery Walsall and Creative Partnerships? I know they organized a two-day artists' event to introduce the artists to the contexts and partners in the project; maybe you could start by telling me about that.

Becky Shaw: Hewitt and Jordan wanted the means, partly, to introduce the artists to each other, but also, rather than us having to do all of the research, they wanted to set this thing up where the different types of contexts were exposed. They particularly wanted to ask, 'What was the Black Country?' – it's different for me because I've lived there, but most people may not even know the term. They also wanted to ask: 'Who are the young people?' 'What is the educational context?' 'What is the context of Creative Partnerships within the project?' 'How does the gallery fit in?' and 'What kind of context does culture-led regeneration have?' Hewitt and Jordan had had conversations with all of the artists about the project during the selection but this was the first time that they had brought us all together. This event happened in February 2004, the exhibition was in July 2004 so there were literally four months to develop a new work so it was quite tight.

CS: Did you see the two-day event as being integral to the project?

BS: Yes. When you are working on a new commission of any kind there is usually only one or two other artists within a project and the relationships between the artists can be non-existent. To have a gallery show as a context as well with six or seven artists brought together it could be even harder to build relationships. The two-day event launched the project as something quite innovative. I think because it happened at an art gallery it felt it was challenging public or educational sites and in return it challenged the gallery, as it gave the gallery the means to deal with these contexts. I think the other people at the event (other than the artists) felt it was novel and a good idea – I'm not sure they got as much out of it as we did.

CS: Who were the other attendees?

BS: All the gallery staff from The New Art Gallery Walsall, James Heartfield who was questioning the contemporary beliefs that lead regeneration, Sarah Middleton from the Black Country Consortium, who talked particularly about plans for the regeneration of the Black Country, there was Sophie Churchill from Re-Gen West Midlands, Esther Leslie from Birkbeck College, University of London talking about Utopianism, particularly in relation to architectural materials and power etc, Sylvia King from The Public, Matthew Biagetti from the planning department of Walsall Metropolitan Borough Council, Creative Partnerships of course, there was a young academic, Sian Lincoln talking about her research into teenager's relationships to their bedrooms. Hewitt and Jordan had employed some support staff too; Rebecca Owen who was Educational Manager and Michelle Cotton who supported the research for the project. Then there were also the teachers from the schools who were going to be involved.

CS: Had the participating schools been selected then?

BS: There was a group of schools that I assume Creative Partnerships had selected and thought it would be good to work with, but it wasn't cast in stone. We were asked to put forward a short proposal and Rebecca Owen very sensitively paired us up, taking into account our particular projects etc.

CS: How were the other parties involved in the two-day event, and how did they become instrumental in the rest of the process?

BS: I think bodies like the Black Country Consortium, Re-Gen and The Public etc were there to provide information and really had no purchase on the project. I think many of us wanted to go and work with them, I think it was a possibility because some of those people were really up for it, but the project was a partnership between Creative Partnerships and The New Art Gallery Walsall. Hewitt and Jordan tried to set up something that was very different to how Creative Partnerships generally work and that meant that we often fell through Creative Partnership's net. For example we were able to propose a project or an approach to a residency that was our response to the *Futurology* contexts, we were not necessarily responding to a brief from a school; the relationship was more equal, the school was made aware that as artists we held positions, and had aims and objectives related to our practice.

CS: The event gave the opportunity for the different contexts of the project and the different people involved to enter into a dialogue – do you think the event helped or hindered a dialogue?

BS: Basically, the speakers gave presentations then we asked lots of questions. I don't actually think within that two-day event there was really a dialogue between the artists and the other bodies involved. I think the artists were in dialogue with each other and we were asking the speakers questions and challenging what they said. Although I think the questions we asked were good questions. They all handled it very well actually; we became 'the bad ass gang' – a kind of team, all critical about the use of culture and regeneration. They were there to give us information about aspects of the project contexts, to expand upon our knowledge or instigate lines of enquiry. We were like a select committee – they arrived, spoke to us and then they went.

It was the end of the second day when the

teachers came when we all felt there was an issue with this, because we had been together for two days and were comfortable with each other, it was quite cold for them to enter the debate at this stage. We were all a bit tongue-tied and we had to explain to them who we were and what we did. They described what they wanted from us as artists and their expectations were quite tight. One teacher said he wanted a drum project – we had had two days together and had developed this joint ideology so we were all a bit 'I'm not doing that!' Having the teachers present at the end didn't work so well; I think it was a bit alienating for them.

CS: How did the different structures of the different organizations or institutions that presented at the event become evident? Did agendas become apparent during the event and did this have an effect on any of the artists' approach towards the project?

BS: Some of them were the antithesis of the artists; there was such a Blairite direction about the creative industries and wanting to address all of the problems of the West Midlands with a grandiose vision. I mean, artistic quality was never talked about and I think we all had a really clear, critical response to that. The people like Matthew Biagetti from the planning office spoke really beautifully and he didn't make any bones about how complex his role was. He talked about compromise and he talked about working within the different agendas and the really pragmatic contingencies of his job.
I realized that you can't always take sides and it's not all black and white. We were quite critical of the 'regeneration people' because some of what they said was ridiculous. They were talking about the Black Country and how Dudley was going to be for leisure and Walsall for education and Wolverhampton for something else and it was horrifying. I think I then realized how crude some of this stuff was. I think all of us were suspicious about Creative Partnerships. My gripe with Creative Partnerships is there are too many artists doing it as a day job and then they do their real work elsewhere and I think there was something very unusual about this approach: we were making a Creative Partnerships project because we all wanted to make work out of it and not treat it as a 'day job'.

One thing Hewitt and Jordan wanted to do was use the two-day event as a model and I haven't heard of anybody taking it up. I think it's amazing that they enabled us to do something that socially en-

gaged work is often criticized for not doing, which is to touch on things that are a bit beyond the actual context. That's what made it more than a school project because there were these other, bigger sets of ideas. I think other people should use it.

CS: Do you think that there is a conceptual framework that is embedded in the two-day event? The point of it seemed to be to open up a dialogue and bring the contexts together which perhaps became quite important to the project and shouldn't necessarily be seen as a bi-product.

BS: Yes. I think there was an intention right from the beginning and I think it stems from Hewitt and Jordan's work and practice. They had

Two-Day Event,
The New Art Gallery
Walsall, 2004

worked in contexts like Sheffield City Council planning department and they continually want to ask, 'can you get in a constrained space and investigate it?' I think Hewitt and Jordan tried to create a space and applied the same critical questions that artists use all the time. I think in a sense their intention was ideological rather than conceptual, there was an ideology there right from the beginning to respond to. In the beginning Hewitt and Jordan wanted to work with other agencies in order for us to look at the information and decide what we were going to do with it; to examine how these agencies are all currents or directives in society and to look at these at the same time as looking at a very particular situation. One thing we had to remind ourselves of is that although we didn't agree with the directives of some of the organizations or if we had problems with town planning etc it was because we thought it wasn't as imaginative as it

Two-Day Event,
The New Art Gallery
Walsall, 2004

should have been. We had to remind ourselves that they weren't the enemies and that artists working for these agencies weren't the enemy either.

CS: Do you think that those two-days shaped your input into the project and do you think the other artists would agree with you?

BS: Yes. I think Crowe and Rawlinson almost developed their project in response to the two-day event; they were really excited and interested by the ideas discussed. Poulter took information from the event too. I think Asante and I had a very different approach. I don't really work with information; I work with what it's like to go into a place. So in the first instance I had to put that information behind me. I wouldn't be able to make a piece of work with information unless I was to go and work in one of those people's offices and I knew I had to work in the school. And Asante had to go and be with young people too. I looked and looked and nothing happened and then I realized the problems in this school were what was actually stopping me. As soon as I realized how they were a microcosm for the whole climate that the two- day event had talked about I could then fit them back together and that was really important to me.

CS: Did the artists continue to have conversations together throughout the rest of the project?

BS: Not as much as we wanted. We did talk about that and I think Simon Poulter suggested that we make a work together and we were all in theory quite excited about that but when we realized there were five months, the school holidays were

coming, and actually that was an interesting thing because the exhibition had been booked for the summer, so there was lots of problems with timing. I don't know where these problems came from. I think it's purely to do with this bringing together of contexts and people that don't normally fit together very well. Because of this it was really a case of 'heads down'. We had another artists' meeting in April but this was more practical. There was collective emailing about things, about public information etc.

CS: The two-day event seems to have been the starting point for a curatorial concept developed by Hewitt and Jordan, and I wonder to what extent you agree how important the event was to how the project progressed?

BS: Well it depends what you mean by curating I suppose. All the curators I've worked with always start from scratch; whereas if I were a different kind of artist the curator would be choosing some work I had already made, so in some ways it was no different. It was incredibly open-ended because we really did not know what the work was going to be. The biggest curatorial decision was picking the artists and I know that took Hewitt and Jordan months of visits. And then, I suppose, the attempt to work in sites and then move into the gallery could be seen as unusual, although I think in some ways that's quite a traditional curatorial problem. I think they were less like curators and more facilitators in the process. There was no sense of it being mapped. We got to the point where some of the artists didn't appear to realize until quite late on that they had to work in schools, or the degree to which we had to be in school and the amount of days we had to do. Hewitt and Jordan wanted to give us time and space to think through things, without a particular emphasis on production.

CS: Do you think that something like this event could be perceived as almost another outcome of the project? Almost like Hewitt and Jordan's 'work'?

BS: I see the whole structure of the project and the communication as their work. The two-day event is and isn't their work. If you think of it crudely, it wasn't their work because it wasn't communicable to the public. I guess it would depend, on whether they chose to communicate it as such. To go back to Duchamp, whether they said it was 'art' or not.

CS: How do you feel that the role that they took then changed throughout the rest of the project?

BS: It was quite interesting because there was a degree to which Hewitt and Jordan soaked up the tensions and they protected us from the politics within the project. Although, I would have expected the gallery to have been much more involved in what the show looked like, I think the gallery saw it as Hewitt and Jordan's project and let them develop it and present it in relation to their enquiry and their proposal. The gallery were involved in practical questions like 'How big is your table going to be?' and 'What room are you going to go in?' I think Hewitt and Jordan were certainly the project leaders and the project shapers; they were particularly good at pulling out the verbal information and working out how to communicate the project.

CS: How do you think Hewitt and Jordan managed a project that didn't have a set of definitive outcomes or one final exhibition? I wondered how the project came back to the gallery space and how the different approaches of the artists translated to that environment.

BS: Well I think that because they are artists they were completely comfortable with it and that was one of the reasons why I wanted to be involved; I knew there would be this situation of trust. They knew that my process (of art making) was always open-ended. I think that they knew all the artist's work well. It was difficult for them and probably difficult for The New Art Gallery Walsall to envisage what we would end up with. It was deliberate that they said, no this project

is different; we're not going to have everything sorted. Each of the projects had a different degree of open-endedness like Crowe and Rawlinson, they had it worked out and had a proposal right from the beginning. Actually most of us didn't have a clue as to what we were going to do. Poulter didn't really know, he had some sites in mind and he's very versed in technology so it's quite likely he was doing something that used this. He actually made quite a tight gallery piece, which I don't think he normally does.

The works couldn't help but be representative of the process, for example, Crowe and Rawlinson represented their project with trees and it signified a process somewhere else. The exhibition needed the spectator to engage in it in a different way; as a viewer you were required to imagine and engage with activities that had gone on elsewhere. Asante worked with the young people in a really fluid process and then found the means to make a display in the gallery. I think I probably struggled the most. I wanted to do a live thing.

CS: So quite a lot of it then was to do with their relationship towards the artists?

BS: Yes, I think so. Which is what makes it quite a different project.

CS: I suppose everybody's work was always going to be quite documentary of a process, the process being 'the artwork', and I wondered whether that had been revealed in the two-day event or if it grew throughout the rest of the project.

BS: No it wasn't revealed, we didn't know. But again, I don't think that was an oversight; it was in the spirit of exploratory work. There was no sense of anyone saying 'that's not going to work' or 'that's not going in the exhibition', but I think that Hewitt and Jordan wanted to find something out which is quite unusual in art – they wanted to ask a question and they wanted to answer it, which is rather unfashionable. And this was at the same time as recognizing that art doesn't ask questions like that. In that sense they cared for what the whole project was for and wanted to do it because their aims weren't solely aesthetic, more social, which is really interesting.

Futurology Public Talks,
The New Art Gallery Walsall, 2004

Section 1
Artists

Barby Asante,
Comfort Zone,
detail, 2004

Comfort Zone
Barby Asante

Andy Hewitt & Mel Jordan:
The intention of the *Futurology*
project was to examine the
function of contemporary art
practice in relation to culture-led
regeneration. Currently, within
culture-led regeneration and
through organizations like Creative
Partnerships, art is being asked to
function as an educational process.
We are interested in exploring
the implications of the idea of the
artist-educator and hoped you would
comment on this.

In your project for *Futurology*,
Comfort Zone, you set up a process
in which the young people you
worked with could negotiate with
you and the rest of the group how
he or she spent their time during
the project. You requested to work
with a range of pupils from different

year groups, creating a new social
group that was different from the
usual year and form groups that
are devised in school for teaching
and learning. It seems to us that
you used your project as a space
in which the young people could
get to know each other and form
a new social group; the fact that
they are all participants in your
project creates a shared interest.
You filmed the group while they
talked, (having spent time getting
to know them and making them
feel comfortable with this process)
expressing their own opinions on
issues such as what sort of people
lived in certain houses, the history
of Walt Disney and why shopping
malls were not quite public spaces.
By playing this film footage back
to the group you were able to

encourage group members to
reflect upon what they believe in
and how they had come to hold a
particular opinion.

Returning to the function of
art, we were thinking that education
has long been considered a method
of tackling social exclusion, and we
wondered what you think about
the dilemma that might arise
from your desire to empower the
students through enabling them to
gain a better understanding of how
culture works and the social
control that we are all subjected to
through education?

Barby Asante: With the *Comfort
Zone* project, my intention was that
the voices and ideas that emerged
from the work were the voices of
the young people. This is not always

easy to do when working as an artist in a school environment and I was fortunate to have the support of a teacher who seemed to understand the project. He put together the group, negotiated the use of the school mini bus and he took the role of the driver. He took instructions from the young people as to where we were going; he enabled and allowed the relationship between the young people and myself to develop.

The project proposal required the young people to take me to places and spaces that they felt safe in and where they felt able to express themselves. Surprisingly one of those spaces was the school field where we spent the first sunny afternoon talking about the project and negotiating the places we would visit. We also visited the town centre, the library, the site of one of the young people's houses, a local leisure complex, a field and a youth club, which one of the group had to specially arrange access to, as the club was not usually open in the morning. Along the way we would talk casually and the young people would open up and talk about issues that concerned them. I introduced the use of the camera quite early on and allowed them each to take control of the camera at some point, which I think helped them to feel comfortable around it. When we went to the youth club, the young people insisted I played football with them, which I think also broke down the barrier between adult and young person.

Of course there were some parameters; we spent the morning and much of lunchtime out of school and returned in the afternoons, the young people had to wear uniform for all visits except on the last day of the project. This decision was negotiated between the young people and their teacher. There was a constant questioning from them as to why if they were not in school and not doing school activities, should they be wearing school uniform. Through the dialogic process I employed during the project the young people became

more and more vocal and seemed able to also challenge the school rules. I let them know I am an artist and I make it clear what I am doing. It fascinated them that the way I was working was not even close to what they were being taught about art at school, yet after answering a few questions and showing them some of the other work I'd been involved with they were happy and able to understand my way of working.

I always aim to hear the voices of the young people, within much of the work I create, my intention is to allow some sort of space for dialogue and so when working with young people, I want to create spaces where they feel safe to speak. This isn't something that I feel is often facilitated in school and the presumption is that if young people are given licence to speak they might be offensive. This is often because young people, especially those from working class families or particular cultural backgrounds have been considered to be the source of many social problems. Many young people do feel demonized by a society that doesn't acknowledge that they are growing up and this is a key time in their lives.

Integrity in working this way is something I often think about and returning to your question, I have been party to some of the debates around art education practice and social exclusion, but to be honest I pay them little mind, because I feel that often it is a way of talking about some of the problems that many young people face without actually getting to hear the opinions of the young people. My project for *Futurology* only lasted a week and although I invited all the young people to the gallery to help me set up the exhibition, what I thought would be a great way to close the project. Only one of them turned up. As with most projects like this I landed in their lives for a moment, did my thing and left. I'm not sure if this project had much or any impact on their lives, let alone tackle any thoughts or feelings they may have

had about feeling socially excluded. And who decides on who is socially excluded or what social exclusion is? If I am going to spend time with people for a week or even a couple of days I think it is important to reveal my position so the people do not feel used; I feel it is important that the people I work with feel that I am being genuine and that they understand my intentions. This is a very difficult situation to be in and can take some persuasion, but through each process I am improving the way I approach this.

One of the boys in my *Comfort Zone* group said that his mother and father had voted for the British National Party in the last election. It seemed to me that the other young people didn't hear him because they didn't respond. I point to this because the usual idea behind social exclusion seems to me to be centred on cultural identity, with the British white population being central and therefore the most included people within society. The increasing need by white working class people to express their needs have resulted in the shocking rise in votes for the BNP. There is no process put forward to have a dialogue about these issues, it is there and we are all supposed to think it's wrong and the assumption is the more we think it's wrong the more likely it is to go away. We often hear about the education system failing black boys, I would add to that that anybody who doesn't share the middle class aspirations of our current government would perhaps also find that the education system is failing them. The emphasis these days are on results. Results that provide fuel for the figures that this society is obsessed with. Results that say everything is working and going in the right direction but underneath the results, those figures demonstrate some very different thoughts and feelings about what society is and what is happening within it.

In your question you also mention that I enable the young people to

Clockwise from left: Barby Asante, Working with student group, 2004; Barby Asante, **Comfort Zone**, detail, 2004; Barby Asante, **Comfort Zone**, production, 2004

gain a better understanding of how culture works and the control we are all subjected to through education. I am not sure that I would necessarily agree with this, understanding culture is not really the thing I'm exploring, though this may have been something I have considered in other pieces of work. I would also question if you were referring to education in the school sense or as an overarching concept that connects to the idea of civilizing a society, because I personally see school as a small but significant part of this concept, with the media playing a major and continuous role in society's educational development. What I've found through working with young people, and it probably began with *Comfort Zone*, was that trying to share knowledge with them

about things such as voting how democracy might work, or anything vaguely political or historical just went completely over their head and didn't make sense to them. Perhaps this is because they see school as the place to learn and maybe they don't see these things as relating to them and their lives. The position I took was to invite them to consider themselves, their future, to question, and to enable them through their inquiry to answer some of these questions for themselves. It is not easy to track a thought, but what we do know is that a thought somehow creates more connections and my hope is that they will make the connections that will enable them to unpick some of the methods of control within our society.

Dave Beech, **Mapping the Future**, production, 2004

Mapping the Future
Dave Beech

Andy Hewitt & Mel Jordan: As you know our intention with the *Futurology* project was to examine the function of art in relation to culture-led regeneration; we were particularly interested in how artists deal with the negotiations and transactions that are intrinsic to working in a social and contextual framework.

In your practice you often employ a collective approach to the generation of an artwork; you devise projects in which the contribution made by others is given primacy in the work. As far as we can see, you always direct this transaction and you manage the participation of others in a particular way. For the *Futurology* project you responded directly to the idea that urban regeneration had a bearing on the future of the young people resident in the Black Country. For your work, *Mapping the Future*, you enabled the young people you worked with to believe that they do have the authority to speculate upon and create their own futures; it was with this knowledge that the young people led the content of the final work, we think this could be

considered a 'dialogical transaction'.

Critics of social art practices and this collective approach, deem it both 'reckless', in terms of the outcome of the aesthetic values of which an artist is normally expected to control, and at the same time 'exploitative' in terms of directing and engaging the participants; forcing them to create a work that the artist ultimately controls.

What do you think of these criticisms and how do you think they bear relevance to a number of key issues that contemporary art has a history of addressing; authorship, the relationship between artwork and spectator and also (which we know is one of your key principles) that artists contest culture?

Dave Beech: Responding to the title, *Futurology*, and my resistance to the preconceptions of the Creative Partnerships project, I had an early idea to set up a project in which I did not actually meet any school children. I didn't want to be an artist in a school, or a stand-in teacher, or worst of all, a 'creative'. I was more interested in the kids and their ideas of the future, so I hoped, at first,

MAPPING THE FUTURE
DAVE BEECH

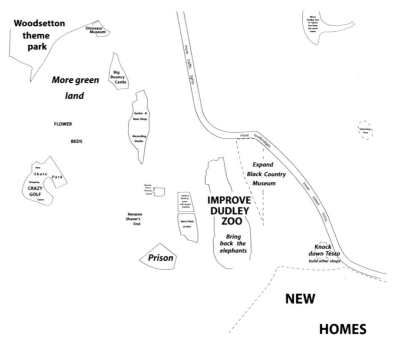

Dave Beech, **Mapping the Future**, drawing, 2004

to draw up a template for teaching in which anyone – teacher, artist, creative, parent – could draw visions of the future from groups of pupils. I ended up working directly with children from five schools because I decided – after a lot of soul searching – that I could enter the schools not as an artist or a creative or a teacher but simply as a citizen.

I began by leading the pupils in several discussions of the future, from the anticipation of likely futures to science fiction and hopes for the best possible world in which they can live as adults. We then turned to pages from the local A-Z and the children, working in small groups, adjusted them, writing notes over the top of sections and scribbling out features that they would like to see bulldozed. The result, when I combined all the maps from the different groups in the different schools, is a series of maps of the Black Country that is recognizable – it retains many key features – while being fantastically unlike any place on earth: a consumer's heaven and pleasure capital ('beach', 'fly-in cinema', 'arena', 'paintball', 'free drinks factory', 'biggest shopping centre in the world')

mixed with an authoritarian state ('military base with prisons', 'truancy patrol'), a nature reserve ('more green land', 'flower beds'), as well as basic living standards ('new homes'). These maps were painted directly on the walls of the gallery to the scale of the architecture, demonstrating the ephemerality of the desires and the epic framework of their dreams for the future.

Working collectively, collaboratively or socially – i.e. working with, for and through others – is a way of bringing ethics (care) and politics (dispute) into the fabric of the work rather than treating them as the work's content or effects. In a sense, working with others in this way simply brings the public of art into the experience of art at an earlier stage than would be typical for a more object based or studio-based artist. Not all artists who produce art in this way work dialogically, though. Some use people in the way that painters use paint and sculptors use materials: as stuff to be manipulated, transformed and manhandled. Others take their cues from the groups that they work with as if to protect the public from the artist's own ideas:

Clockwise from bottom left: Dave Beech, **Mapping the Future**, production, 2004; Dave Beech, Working with student group, 2004; Dave Beech, Working with student group, 2004

as mines of ideas like precious gems. Neither of these are dialogical in a full sense and for that reason they squander the social potential of the meeting between the artist and the group. I prefer something more engaging, discursive, argumentative and testing – a genuine exchange based on differences of opinion within a cooperative undertaking. The people that I work with don't agree with me when I work with them and we produce something that none of us would have produced alone. That is more than dialogical; it is collective.

The charge of aesthetic recklessness seems to be the polar opposite of the accusation of exploiting and control of the participants – one finding fault in a lack of control, the other in a surplus of control – but they stem from the same liberal root. Let me explain what I mean by this before going on to answer the question. Of course, I want to insist on, defend, nurture and celebrate individual freedom in my work and elsewhere, but it is important to recognize that individualism is an historical achievement – that is, individualism functions only within certain social formations and is not,

in fact, located within individuals themselves. Liberalism blinds itself to the social conditions of individualism and therefore neglects what makes individualism possible. This matches Volosinov's insistence that monologue is always dialogical – an insistence that contravenes the liberal humanist fantasy that dialogue is the merging of monologues. So, individualism needs to be championed only as part of a broader social framework. Individualism on its own – individualism misconstrued as based on the individual rather than producing the individual – is ideological. And it is the ideology of art's mainstream. This is one of the catechisms of art that my work sets out to dismantle.

Bourgeois aesthetic conventions uphold the same individualist principle as bourgeois ethics: that each individual ought to be free to do exactly what they want so long as it does not harm others. Accordingly, the artist is meant to be absolutely free (and therefore in total authorial control) of the work, while the viewer is equally free to interpret the work as they choose (even discarding the intentions of the artist). Roland Barthes' theory of the 'death of the author' simply

switches from one side of this failed dialogue when he condemns the traditional power of the author over the reader in order to liberate the reader to engage freely and idiosyncratically with the text. This conception of the aesthetic remains fixated by the liberal humanist individual, misconstruing dialogue as monologue. The charges of aesthetic recklessness and the exploitation of the public in socially engaged art is a failure to understand how the modernist fantasy of the aesthetic monologues of the artist and viewer is always already and necessarily grounded in the sort of cultural dialogue that socially engaged artists stress.

What liberal humanist individualism fails to recognize – ethically, politically and culturally – is our dependence on nature (air, food, etc) and our social mutual interdependence. What I aim for in my work is to relocate the individual within the entire field of dependencies, including the absolute necessity of others. Nobody acts alone, least of all, despite the legacy of Romanticism, the artist. My work seeks to remind us that we are all in this together, even when we are at loggerheads.

The Landowners
Nick Crowe &
Ian Rawlinson

From top to bottom: Nick Crowe and Ian Rawlinson, Student Group, 2004; Nick Crowe and Ian Rawlinson, **The Landowners**, detail, 2004; Nick Crowe and Ian Rawlinson, **The Landowners**, production, 2004

Andy Hewitt & Mel Jordan: As you know the intention of the *Futurology* project was to examine the functions given to art in the process of culture-led regeneration; we were particularly interested in how artists deal with the tension of working within this functional context whilst maintaining some space for comment and critique. It was our desire to look precisely at the demands made on the artist's autonomy and what that meant to the artist, artwork and audience.

For the *Futurology* project you responded by making a work that directly affected the future of the pupils you worked with. You spent your artist fee on purchasing a piece of land, which you then gifted to the students. For that group of young people you changed their status and de-mystified the notion of ownership and presented them with a new reason to remain together as a unit. In fact you transformed them into landowners, extending beyond the rhetoric of shares and stakeholder jargon into action and actual benefit.

As far as we can see the agency of this work, *The Landowners*, is located in the action and gesture that you made towards the young people. It is the tension between action and representation that we want to ask you about here.

In the project there was always an expectation that each artist would somehow develop a work in which a group of school children would participate. Such forms of exchange between artists and a non-art public can appear contrived, being merely symbolic of political or social change. But your work exists as an action, it is real; there is no doubt that the students are changed by their participation in the project. How did you deal with these issues when developing your project and do you think it is possible that the gallery can be an arena for social art practice?

Nick Crowe & Ian Rawlinson: When we began thinking through your invitation to contribute to *Futurology* we were informed by the demands made on art as a result of the policies that underpin both the gallery and organizations like Creative Partnerships. However, and perhaps not surprisingly, we had a certain resistance to producing work, which mutely fulfilled these agendas. Furthermore it was clear from the outset of the project that *Futurology* was not intended to serve the headline needs of Creative Partnerships, but rather to question and interrogate those needs.

On thinking about the work the critical decision we made as artists was to take the ideology of social regeneration at its word. We chose to respond to this ideology through a kind of deliberate literalism as a tactic for revealing the dubiousness of some of its claims. Thus the language of 'the stakeholder' and 'a sense of ownership' are, in our project, taken at face value and its application in the

Nick Crowe and Ian Rawlinson,
The Landowners, 2004

context of a group of school children is the concept that enables us to arrive at the work.

Whilst in a sense this is art holding up a mirror to bureaucracy we should not underestimate the extent to which we were motivated by the desire to do a project with the school children that has real world consequences. We wanted to do something that actually engaged with their lived experience and which had an effect on their sense of self. So this is really a double game we are playing. Mocking, through an over literal enactment, the rhetoric of social regeneration whilst at the same time using the opportunity to create a real shift in the participants' relationship to their social context. In trying to appraise what the piece was therefore one cannot fully separate one from the other.

Your question implies that *The Landowners* sought to privilege real experiences over symbolic ones. Certainly we wanted to affect something that would have real world implications and gifting land is about as real as it gets. Nevertheless this transaction is also bound up in a symbolic exchange, from the moment we enter an agreement to participate

in *Futurology*, to the moment we browse the property pages of Estate Agents lists, the coach trip with the students to view their acquisition, the certificates from the land registry etc. etc. In this sense the art status accorded to the act of gifting land is a conceptual requirement in so much as it reminds us that what has occurred is of symbolic rather than economic value. In making a gesture we are utilizing a symbolic language and so the action is necessarily bound up in its representation. Furthermore, the symbolic orders of the work cannot be disembedded from the material effect on the participants from Deaconsfield High School.

The act of gifting a portion of land to a group of school children has changed their economic status, but the extent to which the project can be said to have 'demystified the notion of ownership' is questionable. The implications of shared ownership, and indeed the specifics of land ownership as distinct from the ownership of a Gameboy or a bike, probably remain elusive. Briefly, we are suspicious of demystification as a role for art. On the contrary the work, rather than demystifying, might

more accurately be said to expose the participants to the mysteries of ownership. This concept may be more readily available to the group than would have otherwise been the case but this should not be confused with making the whole thing clear.

As children cannot be legally registered as landowners the land is held in trust by the artists on their behalf. The share certificates issued to the children denote ownership but also detail their asset's location and provide for ways for them to take control of their asset when they reach the age of legal majority. The project, therefore, has an effective lifespan well beyond the gallery presentation and indeed this publication. Our work created a property holding consortium and sometime after 2010 the 24 students of Deaconsfield High School have the legal right to organize for the transfer of the land registration. This is something of a time bomb, albeit in the form of 0.24 acres of Christmas Tree plantation. We can only speculate on a number of possible outcomes. Either way the gallery presentation of *The Landowners* forms a part of the chronology of the project rather than its culmination or focal point.

Glitch Space
Simon Poulter

Andy Hewitt & Mel Jordan: As you are aware the purpose of the *Futurology* project was to examine the functions given to art within the process of culture-led regeneration and how artists deal with the tension of working within this functional context and in what ways they might maintain some space for comment and critique.

Your practice has been concerned with collaboration and working in the public realm, and this was one of the reasons we asked you to be involved in the *Futurology* project. As part of the project remit there was an expectation that each artist would find their own way to work in a participatory, collective or collaborative way with a group of young people. Such forms of exchange between artists and a non-art public can appear contrived, being merely symbolic of political or social change and perhaps more so when presented within the privileged setting of an art gallery, this was a

concern we wanted to address.

For your project *Glitch Space (boy lost in.)* you did not want the transaction with the young people to be biased towards the powerful agenda of the artist, therefore you explored how you could affect a more equal exchange. In order to do this you began by thinking about participation and the development of an artwork as two discrete activities i.e. you proposed to carry out educational workshops providing technical skills and anticipated that the final work would be separate from this exchange and authored by you alone.

However, in the end you did in fact consider the two activities as one. You incorporated the drawings that the group made in your workshops into the final artwork.

This preoccupation with the transaction seems to us to be an important part of what you were addressing in the work, using this project as an opportunity to explore

the problematic of exchange when artists and participants work together. We wondered if you could talk about this and expand upon your approach to working in this way?

Simon Poulter: *Glitch Space (boy lost in)* is a ten-minute animation narrated as a children's story. The work follows a boy's journey through *Glitch Space* while providing a Meta commentary on regeneration in the UK under the Blair government. *Glitch Space* is a place where narrative is digitally cut up and reprocessed leaving evidence of the original plot while suggesting that stories have multiple entry and exit points – not unlike life.

After meeting with a number of representatives of regeneration organizations prior to starting the project, I noted that regeneration has its own internal language and a set of constructs that often come across as a 'sales pitch'. The descriptive narration of *Glitch Space* deliberately satirizes this.

Top: Student from Castle School Walsall, 2004. Image Roz Hall; Left: Simon Poulter, **Glitch Space**, film still, 2004

Simon Poulter, **Glitch Space**, film still, 2004

The story was created after carrying out a three-day workshop with a group of young people from Castle School in Walsall. I decided to devise the workshop element at The New Art Gallery Walsall as I thought the students would respond to time working at the art gallery – outside of the normal school environment.

The main character in the animation, Saul, was devised when working closely with one of the students. Although familiar with computers, the student had never used Photoshop before and so I scanned in a character he had drawn. I then observed that he enjoyed systematically colouring in the same image, so together we saved as many of these 'colouring-ins' as we could and it was these images that provided the many versions of Saul. Several of the students had excellent drawing skills and, in response to my request to produce drawings of the built environment, a large quantity of colourful images was produced. I then wrote a narrative and used the material made in the workshops to provide the imagery for the animation.

Originally I intended to separate out the workshop activities from the finished piece. However, I applied some pressure to myself in representing the efforts of the participants. Several of the boys involved were autistic and I saw an interesting connection and disconnection between autism and digital creativity. Digital equipment requires a systematized process in order to achieve results, whereas crayons and pieces of paper are more open to improvised working. In fact

one participant was clearly uneasy at the thought of using a computer and so a lot of what came about through the workshops was improvised. This improvised energy was adopted throughout the whole project, as a way of expressing autistic creativity.

As an artist I have had many experiences of developing 'socially engaged' projects. The *Futurology* project deliberately set out to examine this form of practice and the inversion of roles; the artists were encouraged to interrogate the agencies that were commissioning them.

With *Glitch Space* I was trying to avoid common production methodologies by deliberately leaving the ideas process very open. So in terms of the finished work it did not include a picture by everyone that had taken part, I took complete control over the story construction and the contributors only saw the work in its finished state; this is equivalent to apostasy in socially engaged practice. Nevertheless the visual feel of the end work was completely driven by the energy and excitement of working with the students from Castle School.

Some of the inspiration for the production process came from the artist Patrick Hughes who had recounted to me (as an art student) that storytellers were employed in Indian cinemas to assemble narratives based on unconnected pieces of film that had been spliced together. Although, I had some prior plans in terms of the project design, it felt like I was in the role of the editor in relation to the material that evolved from the workshops.

The meeting with representatives from various regeneration organizations at the start of the project set me off thinking about who and what these people represent. It is of note that I have pursued this element of critique in my subsequent work, although I acknowledge that it is difficult to broker a process where regeneration is both consultative and democratic and moves forward in an open and transparent way.

My experience of urban regeneration is that it is full of conflicting desires and agendas of unlinked agencies. 'The Temple of Culture' alluded to in the animation is 'The Public' building in West Bromwich and the 'Black Country Goddess' is Sylvia King. The Town Planner character is based on Tony Blair. In the animation I was trying to embody all of my experiences of the early part of the *Futurology* project; the one that stuck in my mind was Sylvia King's presentation, at one point she referred to a commission that her organization had successfully been involved in without realizing that she was standing right next to the artists who had made it – Hewitt and Jordan! The all-important 'vision' is fundamental to a successful urban regeneration project but perhaps it needs to be connected to the 'plot'.

The work I made examines the transactions between myself and the Castle School students, the workings of regeneration projects and the conflicts between activist art and capital projects. It is now archived at my web site: **http://www.viral.info/glitchspace.htm**

Becky Shaw, **Civics – The Science of Citizenship**, 2004

Civics: The Science of Citizenship
Becky Shaw

Andy Hewitt & Mel Jordan: As you are aware we wanted the *Futurology* project to examine the functions given to art in the process of culture-led regeneration; we were particularly interested in how artists deal with making work in this context; where art is being asked to deliver a specific function and carry out the aims of government social policy. One of the challenges of the project was to question how artists can avoid surrendering their agency to the agenda of politicians and funders but still develop work from within a social and political context.

When we agreed to develop a project for Creative Partnerships and The New Art Gallery Walsall one of our reservations was how we could ensure that we maintained some independence from the aims of the two organizations, in order that we could address the significant points of the *Futurology* project. As the project progressed we found ourselves operating more like an institution or an artist organization and we began to identify this activity as our contribution to the project.

It occurred to us that you would identify with our decision to operate in this way, as it is part of what you anticipate and address when you work within organizations and with groups. The method you have developed enables you to spend time with a subject or context in order to explore your understanding of it as well as its relationship to external conditions. It could be said that your work is less about a collaborative authorship; the people you work with are not necessarily invited to contribute to the work, but instead they are invited to help you understand the context and their own circumstances within it. You and your subject (whether its an informal group of people or an institution) collectively agree to share this knowledge with others through the development and display of an artwork, in the case of the *Futurology* project the artwork manifested as *Civics: The Science of Citizenship*.

Critics of social art practices comment upon the artist's loss of autonomy when artists agree to work

closely with an institution: it seems that there are suspicions about the artist being unable to maintain any independence from the agendas of the institutions with which they are working – asserting that the artwork delivers the aims of the institution rather than the aims of the artist. What do you think of these criticisms and how do you think about these problems in relation to your practice?

Becky Shaw: In early summer 2004 I attempted to spend some time with the art class at George Salter School. While teachers did their best to accommodate me it was clear that they were working under extremely difficult conditions. During each of the few workshops I was able to arrange a team of three boys without school uniform arrived and moved the furniture around us, sometimes literally moving the tables from under our elbows. The boys caused both a literal disruption of the space, and also a disruption in concentration as they winked at the girls and bantered with the boys. No information was forthcoming from staff about the strange conditions, but an artist on another Creative Partnership project told me that the school was having serious difficulties and had planned to move the subject areas around in an attempt to alter the student's behaviour.

I had been working with the students making collages exploring how the past of the space might interlock with a new future of Black

Country development, but it became apparent that the real conditions of the school were already making the pressures of development visible. As the boys moved Maths to French and French to Technology etc, so they mirrored Black Country development bodies' plans to spatially rearrange the area, making, for example, Wolverhampton the centre for education and Dudley for leisure and so on. The boys had just completed their GCSE's and were being paid a nominal amount to work as removal men. Their first job was paying them to dismantle the structure that had helped to build them and their expectations for the future.

I asked the removal boys if I could spend a day with them, implementing a kind of time-and -motion study of their work by photographing them every minute. The boys agreed and I amassed 341 slides of them meticulously packing and stacking boxes, and later, losing concentration and having a staple gun fight. The slides were then used as the structure of a lecture, exploring the microcosm of the school and the boys in relation to issues of citizenship, space, work, control and art. It was performed three times at The New Art Gallery Walsall. The removal boys were again paid to shift furniture, this time being hired to turn the gallery into a lecture room, and back again, for each lecture. The text and images form a publication, *Civics: The Science of Citizenship* the first edition of *The Journal of Occasional Trade.*

Becky Shaw, **Civics – The Science of Citizenship**, detail, 2004

CIVICS: THE SCIENCE OF CITIZENSHIP
BECKY SHAW

Becky Shaw, 2004

Becky Shaw, **Civics - The Science of Citizenship**, detail, 2004

My perspective on autonomy has changed as I've sought different ways to make work. In the early nineties I had a studio practice where I made sculpture. During this time I became uncomfortable with the isolation and repetitive tempo and frustrated by the lack of engagement I felt after making work. I began to involve others in making sculptural work, explaining this, to myself, as an anti-institutional position. I articulated my desire to collaborate as a stance against the singular artist, as a desire to have more relationship with society, as the pursuit of a discursive community to which I could belong, and, contrary to much of the contemporary argument against socially-engaged practices, as a pursuit for more free space than the studio could give.

After spending the following years making art within (usually) publicly funded commissions I became much more critical of the conditions of social practice, viewing, like the critics you mention above, art within commissions as inherently constrained. Or, to go further, that all art is limited by the wider institution of art and the conditions of seeking validation.

While validation mechanisms are undeniably part of art, recently I have begun to feel limited by my own

attention to them. I began to feel that the more I tried to make work that only answered the problems I found in institutions, the work became less imaginative and rich and, I feared, was not communicable outside of its context. Perhaps there was less for other people to engage with - a result that was opposite to my rationale for beginning this work in the first place. However, this problem did not arise from the inherent restrictions of a commission. Issues of autonomy are critically important, but they are not solely to do with for whom we make work, or where, or who pays and more to do with our preparedness to follow our individual intentions in the work. Being conscious of the conditions that limit work is important, but being able to push the work further than explaining them is crucial.

While *Civics* seeks to answer your *Futurology* invitation to critically explore how commissioners attempt to use art to ameliorate social ills, what excited me most was the space you made in which to find something out about the real play of relationships in the context of education. The 'removal boys' approach to their 'job' seemed to be articulating something about the nature of adolescence and the potential to maintain values or literally disman-

Becky Shaw, **Civics – The Science of Citizenship**, public lecture, 2004

A public lecture for all levels of ability. A broad syllabus including: Regeneration, Rights and Responsibilities, Stewardship, Creativity, Sustainability, Added-Value, Ethics, Artists, Zoning, Inclusion, Urban Renaissance, Management, Education, Consultation, Innovation, Community, Envisioning, Work Ethic, Entrepreneurialism, Participation and 343 minutes in one school.

Becky Shaw, **Civics – The Science of Citizenship**, text, 2004

tle them. This knife-edge between the dangers of conformity and the potential for change somehow mirrors how working in social contexts feels, and why they continue to maintain my curiosity and to develop ideas I haven't had before. In this sense, for me, social art practice is a means to find content rather than being the end in itself. The artist is not in the situation as a passive weather vane receiving information, but rather engaged in an active process of pushing what Allan Kaprow would describe as a 'social meniscus', or the dynamic between the individual and the social.

It seems that the arguments around social art practices and autonomy often mix up form and content. Critics see the form of social art practices as the problem, interpreting them as inherently 'un-free' and other forms of art, like painting, as being more 'free'. This implies that they are more or less free as a result of their physical form or even, as is usually the subtext, because of their tradition. In countering the criticisms sometimes levelled at artists for working with institutions, many critics and artists argue that all art is made within the institution of art anyway, as this is what defines what art is. While this is true, the conclusion of this thinking

can be a kind of over-emphasis on the negative, un-free weight of the social that results in a fatalistic acceptance of domination. There are two confusions wrapped up within this. Firstly the arguments pitch a weighty perception of the social where individuality is surrendered, against a narcissistic individualism. Both these positions ignore the fact that the individual is socially constituted and in a society you can't have one without the other. Individualism isn't a dirty word – individuals are the units that make history and that the social nurtures and allows, and vice versa. Secondly seeing everything as an institution runs the risk of missing an important difference, in that traditionally, institutions were defined as the mechanisms through which the state asserts its authority. In this context autonomy means more than individualism. Autonomy means freedom from the state, and so in this sense it is about us exercising our freedom from the state as a society. Seen this way, working together does not imply a loss of autonomy either.

There is a difference between working within social contexts and within the constraints of policy-led funding conditions. However, this doesn't mean that artists shouldn't do the latter, but that they make

deliberate choices to take on commissions knowing about the constraints. In the case of *Futurology*, Hewitt and Jordan consciously took on the restrictions so they could explore and not deliver them. In every commission, however constrained, there is the space for individual (or collective) ingenuity and original thinking and very often a pushing for space within the parameters of the conditions for which work is being produced. What seems to make the difference is whether work within a commission illuminates, communicates something new, or communicates in a meaningful way. The issue being, then, how good the work is. Some works in the social realm, like some paintings, are better than others. Contrary to what is seen as acceptable in liberal artistic circles, it is important to argue about quality because it enables artists to maintain autonomy. As we seek to understand what might constitute quality we are determining our own measures that are different to the ones of the state. By working like this we exercise a kind of autonomy – one that doesn't posit an individual in a vacuum but communicates the potential of the artist within the social.

Section 2
Writers

Downing the Master's Tools
Malcolm Miles

Introduction to an Introduction

In her address to the *Second Sex Conference*, New York, (29th September, 1979), Audre Lorde argued that, for 'those of us who have been forged in the crucibles of difference', survival was a matter of learning how to stand alone, and of making common cause with others identified as outsiders, to define a world in which all may flourish. Then:

It is learning how to take our differences and make them strengths. For the master's tools will never dismantle the master's house. They may allow us temporarily to beat him at his own game, but they will never enable us to bring about genuine change.[1]

These remarks raise issues of marginality and difference; what constitutes genuine change; the relation of means to ends; and the depth to which the master's codes are ingrained in the tactics of artists as well as the cultural policies of states.

Lorde's passion for social justice contrasts with the blandness of the concept of a creative city[2] as driving economic revival after de-industrialization. The ease with which the term post-industrial is applied to any city in which there is a new flagship cultural institution or cultural quarter belies tendencies to gentrification and a peripheralization of the poor, while multi-ethnicity is reduced to consumer choices. Charles Landry and Franco Bianchini claim that 'New ideas can be generated through cultural cross-overs'.[3] But Graeme Evans and Jo Foord are critical of the relevance of regeneration projects to diverse publics in East London[4]; George Yúdice, writing in New York, sees 'representations of and claims to cultural difference' as 'expedient insofar as they multiply commodities'.[5] For Tania Carson, 'the creation of cultural quarters is merely a kind of cultural branding'[6] and John Rennie Short and Yeong-Hyun Kim remark that images of social justice are rarely presented, while

The dominant images represent conflict-free cities,

where pluralism leads to a variety of ethnic restaurants rather than competition for scarce resources.[7]

For Landry and Bianchini 'Urban design is essentially about knitting together different parts of the city into a coherent artefact.'[8] And Happy Hours revitalize city centres.

Re-reading Lorde's remarks cuts through this crap, still (nearly thirty years on) I think they offer an appropriate way to introduce a context for *Futurology* for three reasons. Firstly, historically, the use of means that reproduce the power-relations which avant-gardes have sought to overthrow has undermined their project. This takes the form, often, of endowing the artist with privileged insight or power of interpretation for others. Secondly, while Lorde's emphasis on difference was ahead of its time in 1979 – before Iris Marion Young's argument against assimilation[9] – but is unexceptional in light of the prominence of concepts of difference in post-structuralist discourses, it touches obliquely on a self-marginalizing tendency, which is part of the modern artist's social contract.[10] If art is to contribute to critical visions and resistant cultural tactics, self-marginalization is as undermining as borrowing the master's tools (and may be one he has lent cynically). Thirdly, because these issues are not only historical but, I would argue, remain urgent for dissident artists and artists' groups today. A succession of departures from the gallery and art market in conceptual art, public art, and what is now called socially engaged art demonstrate a desire on the part of a significant number of artists to find other ways of working. There are new factors – the growth of collaborative practice and dialogic practice[11] and global networking parallel to that of campaigning groups – but still much to do intellectually and materially.

A reading of Lorde's remarks would be that, just as the master's tools will never dismantle his house, the dismantling of the tools is a beginning of building a house which is not the master's. In process, unforeseen relations to tools may emerge. One of the master's tools is to demarcate the tools and the house as separate entities. Effort is directed to the prospect of building another predetermined world while present arrangements of power remain unmitigated. To focus on ends in the form of an imagined utopia is, nevertheless, an attractive option or an escape from a political reality, which is irrational and violent. Yet ends are produced, not dreamt. The processes and relations of production determine them. That is, either, as Herbert Marcuse argued in his 1937 essay *The Affirmative Character of Culture*,[12] art displaces visions of a new society to an aesthetic realm which renders them ornamental; or, alternatively, art departs from the approved terms of its engagement and realizes the ends as the means.

To dream is a necessity because to describe an alternative society, and the alternative means integral to its realization is extraordinarily difficult. From my experience of it, *Futurology* is a contribution to this difficult work. Present structures inflect it, of course; but *Futurology* works in the cracks produced in their contradictions, an irritant which incrementally weakens those structures.

Instrumentalism - Culture as Toolbox

Lorde's remarks offer an apt critique of UK and USA cultural policy since the 1980s. From advocacy from an expanding network of arts professionals – and a liking for culture as lending a shine to the exercise of power, and a desperation as to how to address structural problems of urban deprivation and disintegration on the part of successive governments – the arts were increasingly seen as useful, not just a luxury. The aims of the Arts Council in its early years were to raise standards of production in the arts, and to widen access.[13] John Willett reads this as affirming 'the taste prevailing among dealers and critics and virtually the whole of the official art world'[14]. In the 1980s this became a doctrine of innovation and excellence, terms which could be defined as required but retained a neo-classical divide of the aesthetic from the useful – a separation based on class structure. In the 1980s, the arts were required to be managed (no longer administered) as businesses, subsumed to the creative and cultural industries. A proliferation of arts agencies and consultancies avowed the entrepreneurial line, and sought to increase the market for art by making new claims for its efficacy – seen by Sara Selwood[15] as undemonstrable.

References were made to the success of culture-led urban redevelopment elsewhere. It was frequently stated that the arts were central to national life because more people went to museums and galleries (which were free) than to football matches (which were not but could be viewed on television). The business model was instituted in the Thatcher years and is key to cultural policy under the Blair regime, for which the arts offer low-budget solutions for problems created by other areas of government policy. On the surface: the spectacle of Tate Modern; underneath, widening social divisions, alienation from representational politics. The underlying purpose of the arts is, as in Victorian times with the opening of public museums, the improvement of the poor and their assimilation into the ethos of the middle classes. Brandon Taylor writes of the founding of Tate on the site of a penitentiary as instilling pride in 'a nation that was now increasingly free of poverty, artistic illiteracy, and above all crime.'[16] Tate Modern is a New Labour success, after the debacle of the Millennium Dome – another definition of national identity, to which ordinary people were admitted for a fee after the first day – and the inept re-branding the UK as Cool Britannia.

For Esther Leslie, Tate epitomizes that re-branding by redefining the values of a public museum:

Tate Modern is in the vanguard of a reinvention of cultural spaces worldwide. Art galleries are overhauling themselves as 'for profit' spaces where the expertise of art workers is leased out to business and education. Tate is a brand that niche-markets art experience. Its galleries are showrooms this is still art and not just business. The commodity must not show too glossy a face. The reclamation of an industrial space lends the building a fashionably squatted aspect.[17]

International Modernism, shading into contemporary art, is subsumed in lifestyle consumption. Cultural policy is subsumed in a selective image of Britain, while claims are made for the arts as social therapy.

Modern art's history does not emphasize the therapeutic effect, however. It rests on the autonomy of aesthetic judgement derived from Kant and extended by critics such as Clement Greenberg and Michael Fried. Then there is the evidence, in the dysfunctional lives of artists such as Jackson Pollock and Willem de Kooning, that making art in the conditions of the post-war art market is not curative. Nonetheless, the problems the arts are claimed to solve are limitless:

No longer restricted to the sanctioned arena of

*culture, the arts would be literally suffused through-
out the civic structure, finding a home in a variety
of community service and economic development activities far afield from the traditional aesthetic functions of the arts.*[18]

This is from a report produced for the National
Endowment for the Arts (NEA), but a similar
approach colours Arts Council policies in the 1990s.
This is what I mean by instrumentalism – that, far
from residing in a hermetic aestheticism, the arts
are permeated by other areas of public policy as
a tool for solving problems, in effect for closing
down arguments. Instrumentalism underpins
the concept of a creative city, often in new forms
of partnership between the public and private
sectors, which produce a privatization of urban
spaces. Sharon Zukin argues that the cultural re-
coding of urban space follows the model of Disney:
where complex realities are replaced by glossy
simulations while tightly-structured depictions of
identity are implemented through spatial controls
in a new authoritarianism. This is attractive to city
managers:

*Take a common thread of belief, a passion that
people share and develop it into a visual image.
Market this image as the city's symbol. Pick an area
of the city that reflects the image. Then put the area
under private management.*[19]

The master, it seems, has painted his tools
in pretty colours. His toolbox contains flagship
cultural institutions, cultural quarters, the use of
redundant industrial buildings for the arts, and
zones of lifestyle consumption. One of his tools,
which he lends freely, is the notion that a toolbox is
the precondition for intervention.

An Aesthetic Turn in Cultural Policy?

Cultural instrumentalism has not relinquished
aesthetic autonomy but retained it in service of
business, limiting criticality but universalizing
cultural value. But there seems now a return to
a more overt aestheticism in cultural policy in
remarks by Tessa Jowell, Secretary of State for
Media, Culture and Sport, to the Institute of Public
Policy Research.[20] Jowell offers a justification for
arts funding based on the model of public service
broadcasting, that it ensures the production 'of
dazzling new work, of far-reaching innovation,
of new insights', yet increases in arts funding
depend on 'the contribution the arts could make
to other agendas'.[21] Work in non-gallery settings
enables arts professionals to speak in circles such
as health and urban regeneration, and the arts are

'integral to our personal and national life.'[22] There
is a question as to who is included, but Jowell has a
worry of her own. Claims for art as a social remedy
are not supported by the quantitative data required
by the Treasury. Her response is to fall back on an
argument that some qualities cannot be measured.
She looks to the arts as slaying the giant of 'poverty
of aspiration, or if you like, and as Nye Bevan put it,
poverty of imagination', while focusing on what the
arts 'can do in themselves'[23]. Jowell rehearses the
evaluation of arts subsidy in terms of lower crime
rates and truancy; yet worries 'that we talked about
these objectives so much that we actually rather
missed the point.'[24] The point is that the arts have
their own qualities, which cannot be assessed.

There are similarities with Greenberg's writing.
Jowell asserts that 'what the arts do that only the
arts do is most important. Out of that come other
benefits but the art comes first.'[25] Greenberg, in
1944, said

*Let painting confine itself to the disposition pure
and simple of color and line, and not intrigue us by
associations with things we can experience more
authentically elsewhere.*[26]

Is cultural policy a recapitulation of
Greenberg's reductionism? Is authenticity a new
cultural commodity? What I find most disturbing
is an informal attribution that Jowell sees artists as
endowed with a sixth sense – less Greenberg, more
Madame Blavatsky. Well, it's time to say no.

Downing the Master's Tools

In a previous publication, Hewitt and Jordan state
that they fail to agree. There is an implication that
not agreeing is a failure, a falling below the required
grade in civics. They write:

*Our practice is defined by our political and social
engagement; it is process-based and its outcomes a
result of the method and research carried out. We
work with sites of debates and usually in conjunction
with others. We intend to contest accepted
hierarchical structures as well as attempting to reveal
the ideological agendas that exist within art itself.*[27]

They contest the functionality of art, and the
operations of cultural-led urban redevelopment.
From this has come a series of four statements,
drafted with Dave Beech, (Hewitt, Jordan and
Beech are collectively known as Freee) on art's
economic, social, and aesthetic functions, and its
function in urban redevelopment. The first, which
arose from a project supported without intentional
irony by Public Art Forum, says: 'The economic
function of public art is to increase the value of
private property'.[28] It was displayed in Sheffield in

2004. The second, in Leeds in 2005 as part of the project Vitrine curated by Pippa Hale and Kerry Harker, says 'The social function of public art is to subject us to civic behaviour'; the third, that 'The aesthetic function of public art is to codify social distinctions as natural' – a banner for the Venice Biennale (La funzione estetica dell'arte pubblica é quella di rendere naturali distinzioni sociali). A fourth, on a billboard in Hackney commissioned by the curating partnership B+B (Sophie Hope and Sarah Carrington), stated 'The function of public art for regeneration is to sex up the control of the under-classes'. Better than sterilization I suppose.

In these works, and in *Futurology*, Hewitt and Jordan dwell on a creative tension between the criticality of aesthetic distance, and engagement in situations. They say 'we are acting as artists, it is our project'; and 'our engagement was one of contesting the accepted ways of working with the commissioners'.[29] The commissioners, Creative Partnerships Black Country, were unconcerned that their money would be used to critique their strategy for ending imaginative deficit in schools. As Jonathan Trayner writes, putting five artists into schools and showing the work in The New Art Gallery, Walsall 'sounds like the wet dream of the DCMS and the zombie nightmare of everyone else.'[30] Hewitt and Jordan's aim in *Futurology* was to renegotiate the expectations of the project's funding bodies and partners (from schools to the gallery), and hence the terms of its process. The aestheticism inherent in museums and galleries, and functionalism of Creative Partnerships, were mediated by their and the artists' insistence on a non-conditional inquiry, and a collaboration with students in participating schools which did not rest on the mythicized special status of the artist. I think this is utterly different from the role of lead artist developed in some public art projects, replicating the hierarchy of architect, planner, and dweller in urban design; and from that of artist in the design team, also a public art favourite. The artists here do not cross over to another discipline or profession; but neither do they rest on the 1960s notion of the incidental person. They are not incidental but engaged; they have agendas and tactics. The situation, above all, offers an investigation of how

tactics operate, how a situation can be encountered in a way which hands over authority (as in being an authority on a subject) to participants while knowledges of cultural provision, of the irreducible tension of art's aesthetic and social aspects, and of lateral communication, are respected. Hewitt and Jordan write that they sought to 'occupy the space of instrumentalization through Creative Partnerships and [the] New Art Gallery, Walsall.'[31] And that their aim was to question how art is used and how this is a problem for art. An important part of the method was discussion during a two-day event at The New Art Gallery, in February 2004, involving funders, artists, teachers, and social workers. I wonder why school students were not invited to speak as experts on the poverty of imagination in industrialized education, but they were integral to the project's development as soon as the artists arrived in schools. For example, Barby Asante was taken by young people to places they considered theirs, filming the journeys and playing back the footage. Asante 'asked to be led'[32] rather than arriving on the scene as an expert. In the gallery she made a wooden shed – 'a place to hang out. There are rules of entry and use; they might not even let us in and if they do, it is on their terms and our access could be limited'[33] – a social space of arbitration. This might be compared to Paolo Freire's[34] work in adult literacy in Brazil (1972), in which self-empowerment occurred when the material of the programme was the stories of participants.

In conclusion, there is both a radicalism and a willingness to work in untested ways in *Futurology*, a preparedness for what is not predicted, and cannot be except at the cost of liberation. There is an understanding that power is not donated, only de-centred or re-conceptualized (in the difference between the authority of insight and experience, and authoritarianism), and that whatever happens it is the method which constitutes the outcome. It is only a beginning, and one of several (thinking of the collaborative practices of Cornford and Cross, PLATFORM, and B+B, for examples); but it is a striking refusal of New Labour's prescription for a universal cultural happy hour.

ENDNOTES

1. Lorde A, [1979], 2004, 'The Master's Tools Will Never Dismantle the Master's House', in Rendell, Penner and Borden, eds. 2000, Gender Space Architecture: An Interdisciplinary Introduction, London, Routledge, pp.53-55

2. Arts Council, 1993, 'A Creative Future: National Arts & Media Strategy', London, Arts Council.

3. Landry C and Bianchini F, 1995, 'The Creative City', London, Demos

4. Evans G L and Foord J, 1999, 'Cultural policy and urban regeneration in East London: world city, whose city?', in Proceedings of the International Conference on Cultural Policy Research, Bergen, University of Bergen

5. Yúdice G, 2004, 'The expediency of Culture: Issues of culture in the global era', Durham (NC), Duke University Press.

6. Carson T, 2005, 'Cultural Ambiguity in an Urban Development Masterplan: Deception or Miscalculation?', in Miles and Hall, ed.s, 2005, Interventions, Bristol, Intellect Books 2005, p.15.

7. Short J R and Kim Y-H, 1998, 'Urban Crises/Urban Representations: Selling the City in Difficult Times', in Hall T and Hubbard P, ed.s, 1998, The Entrepreneurial City: Geographies of Politics, Regime and Representation, Chichester, Wiley, p.14.

8. Landry C and Bianchini F, 1995, p.28.

9. Young I M, 1990, 'Justice and the Politics of Difference', Princeton (NJ), Princeton University Press.

10. Kuspit D, 1993, 'The Cult of the Avant-Garde Artist', Cambridge, Cambridge University Press.

11. Kester G, 2005, 'Conversation Pieces: Community and Communication in Modern Art', Berkeley (CA), University of California Press

12. Marcuse H, 1968, 'Negations', Harmondsworth, Penguin pp.88-133

13. Willett J, 1967, 'Art in a City', London, Methuen, p.198.

14. Willett 1967; p.204

15. Selwood S, 1995, 'The Benefits of Public Art', London, Policy Studies Institute

16. Taylor B, 1993, 'From Penitentiary to 'Temple of Art': Early Metaphors of Improvement at the Millbank Tate', in Pointon M, ed., 1993, Art Apart: Art Institutions and Ideology Across England and North America, Manchester, Manchester University Press p.27

17. Leslie E, 2001, 'Tate Modern: A Year of Sweet Success', Radical Philosophy 109, p.3.

18. Larson, G O. 1997, 'Museums and Education', Washington (DC), Smithsonia Institution Press, Cited in Yúdice, 2004, p.11.

19. Zukin S, 1995, 'The Cultures of Cities', Oxford, Blackwell p.54.

20. Jowell T, 2005, Speaking at the Royal Opera House, London, 7th March, 2005

21. Jowell T, 2005, 'Why Should Government Support the Arts?', Engage, 17, pp.5-8 [address delivered in London, 7th March, 2005].

22. (Jowell T 2005: p.7)

23. ibid

24. (Jowell T 2005: p:6)

25. ibid

26. Greenberg C, 1986, 'Collected Essays and Criticism', ed. O'Brian J, University of Chicago Press, p.203.

27. Hewitt and Jordan, 2004, 'I Fail to Agree', Sheffield, Site Gallery, p.7.

28. Hewitt and Jordan, 2004, p.53.

29. Hewitt and Jordan (e-mail to author, 4th September, 2005).

30. Trayner J, (www.artistaid.com/criticalforum.asp).

31. Hewitt and Jordan (email to author, 4th September, 2005)

32. Futurology, 2004, 'Futurology: the Black Country 2024', gallery guide Hewitt and Jordan, The New Art Gallery Walsall

33. ibid.

34. Freire P, 1972, 'Pedagogy of the Oppressed', Harmondsworth, Penguin

The Exclusivity of Inclusion

Ruth Robinson

Social inclusion and other social and economic systems target the futures of the 'economically and socially challenged'; this term, along with 'under-privileged' and 'deprived', having been coined to emphasize poverty without the use of the word 'poor' or association with the redundant industrial working class. (In the definition of 'the poor' there would then be a requirement to define 'the rich'). In the attempt to induce the shared fantasy of social improvement – that is, not the improvement of independent living, but social reforms under the guise of inclusion for all – the 'excluded' are refined and re-presented within a vision of unattainable future. The relationship here between unrealistic and impractical utopian futures and the ethos of culture-led regeneration is clear (in contrast to the positive utopianism of hope), both reliant on a belief in the assimilation of the potentially volatile elements of society.

The 'poverty of aspiration' is an idea used by current government (first introduced by Tessa Jowell)[1] to describe a lack of ambition and achievement amongst the underclasses. This identifiable mood evolved from the industrial decline of the early-mid 1980s and was instigated by the actions of the Thatcher government. Service and leisure sectors were strategically partnered with business and marketability. These moves paved the way for the Creative and Cultural Industries and forced an emergence of the materialistic poor. The lack of manufacturing jobs and increased unemployment transformed the behaviour of the labouring class and gave rise to the acceptance of its redundancy and ultimately the denial of its existence. The development of a belief system fixed on excess and indulgence; individual desire as opposed to need had no place for organized labour. What unfolded was an underclass with little earned income and an overwhelming dependence on the state. This reliance and the enduring identity crisis of a working class without toil has resulted in a social and political apathy that is now generational. Presented with only fixed choices of 'future' disengagement is inevitable if the learning methods and themes covered are not valid to the lives of the participants. (However, the personalization of education and the use of 'educational innovators' may not be the solution to this. Personalizing may merely isolate children who are in need of a framework of social support in learning.) Participation itself is often interpreted and dictated as a level of control by artists and creative organizations and reliant on other individuals wanting to share or join in. The artist's role within this is not to act as a stand-in educator, but to provide alternative experiential and learning possibilities. It must be considered that without probing the governing systems of education, health and social sectors, unworkable standards and norms for the role of art in society will continue to be perpetuated.

The use of the arts within Social Inclusion Policy has become an evident part of local government strategy. Regeneration sectors in particular use public, participatory and community arts as a tool for public pacification and as a vehicle for their own agendas. This system has an influence on the publics' experience of art and the functionality of the artists involved. The artist's belief in the social power of art is contradicted by the requirement of art for social good. The negation of this involvement and the subsequent compromise of independent agendas and strategies in favour of appropriate well chosen art projects, results in assimilation of the radical promise of art, subduing the effectiveness of intervention at grass-roots level and replacing genuine active engagement with incidental participation.

The demands on art within social inclusion are to tackle social and economic inequalities that Government is inadequate of addressing with direct policy. For the artist working within the institutionally funded bracket, the pressure to deliver in a prescribed manner is more acute. Opting into the Creative Industries will find us all in competition for the attentions and monies of the same few providers. The Creative Industries are now so closely tied with regeneration and social inclusion that applications for funding must include a pledge to address the social ills of the diverse underclass. Projects used experimentally to gather data about specific communities and to subdue genuine public concern and unrest are blatant in their presentation. Reliance on such funding surrenders artists to the dependence of institutional agendas. Socially engaged practice, by its very disposition, demands resourcing from alternatives; implementing self-sufficient methods without fixation on the predictable sources of funding to direct all activities. Organizational funding is not fundamental to the production of critical art; our existence outside this system is.

The complexities of the relationships between art, community and gentrification are many. The use of the gallery to contextualize and present artwork is a tradition currently undergoing critical scrutiny. The context in which work is placed, or from which it develops, cannot be ignored within socially engaged art. Civic galleries are attempting to address the problems associated with supporting and displaying participatory artwork by forming associations with independent artists and government-led initiatives. In doing so this also widens their involvement with the politics of social inclusion. Creative Partnerships are one such initiative and galleries such as The New Art Gallery Walsall (as in *Futurology*) form relationships to explore new ways of involvement with local communities. Creative Partnerships provide school children across England with the opportunity to develop creativity in learning and to take part in 'cultural activities'. It aims to establish collaborative partnerships to enable the development of projects reflecting 'the interests, specialisms and shared vision'[2] of those involved, in the push to combine the fields of art and education. Educative programmes can be seen to take on a productive role by supporting practices that the traditional structure fails to support creating a platform for new ways of working.[3] However, here the participants are mainly directed through a specific pattern of learning that uses the traditional model of the gallery, and

of art, to prescribe results. A gallery finding space for the recognition of art created by and for the community is encouraging, but in curating these works, civic and flagship galleries are playing it safe. Traditional galleries are a restrictive source for local people in search of connection or inspiration. Collections of categorized works render it difficult to piece together a valid social history; contextualized for aesthetic qualities rather than apparent social content. The inclusion of working people is often avoided, unless to support romantic notions of labour. Aspiring to educate and refine the audience, this depiction reinforces rank.

The underlying purpose of the arts is, as in Victorian times with the opening of museums, improvement of the poor and their assimilation into the ethos of the middle class.[4]

Omission of a mongrel[5] (not multicultural) working class demonstrates a lack of awareness of surrounding communities. Focus on separate faiths supports the notion that contemporary culture is not a shared experience and that there is no overlap in our roots, customs or beliefs; unique characteristics are emphasized in order to feign equality. The decision to expand involvement and make a spectacle of the minorities of ethnicity, gender, sexuality and disability covers the general policy of 'cultural diversity' targeting identity politics and reinforcing boundaries and difference. The complexities of diversity can be considered within social practice without enforcing such prescribed stereotyped identities.[6] 'Multiculturalism', 'cultural fusion' and instigated 'cross-overs' are the consumer branding of diversity, whilst genuine flourishing diversity is swept under the carpet. In considering art as a tool of Social Inclusion Policy the ideology of 'multiculturalism' is used as a model for equality. Its preservation of separate cultures is problematic, as is the lack of agreement in its definition. Lord Parekh, Chair of *The Future of Multi-Ethnic Britain Report*[7] noted that the notion of different 'cultural communities' living self-contained ways of life has long been obsolete. The ideology of multiculturalism then, can be viewed as simplistic and unrealistically optimistic; causing division amongst people when there is need to unite in order to combat social injustice.[8] Strategic in the management of diversity, the multicultural policy supports the arts throughout the world.

The Black Country, the site of *Futurology*, is at the centre of major redevelopment, mirroring the fate of industrial towns throughout Britain. The appearance of daunting and inappropriate 'centres of culture' have claimed the spaces of ordinary public living. The emphasis on individualism causing decline in social bonding and shared group identity. Marginal places where custom remains indefinable and unpredictable have deteriorated in this climate and public perception of an ability to influence this system and the spaces they occupy is subdued. Independent exchange, discussion and debate are in suspension. The opportunity for projects to evolve from the critical dialogue between ordinary people sharing aspirations, concerns and more importantly the spaces they live in (having been confined by spatial controls and the privatization of urban public space) is squandered on implementing the educational role and affirming division amongst defined groups. The social perception of an individual is stereotyped in terms of group membership causing prejudice and supporting the formation and commodification of 'in' and 'out' groups.[9] This type of prescribed art intervention, without recognition of the existing connections and blurring of contrived borders in the public sphere aspires to include 'the excluded'. In re-defining cultural difference this has the potential for provoking social dis-order.[10] Within their artistic opportunity, the participants of socially inclusive art must be allowed to choose and implement a course of action that is most appropriate to their specific circumstance.

Since the Urban White Paper (2000) the Government's agenda for 'revitalizing' urban communities has encouraged and made it more accessible for British artists to become involved in 'art with people' via the promotion of 'culture-led regeneration'. The investigative report of the DCMS Policy Action Team (PAT 10)[11] greatly informed cultural strategy, having established fast-track thinking on social exclusion.[12] This led to the development of the National Strategy for Neighbourhood Renewal concentrating on the most 'deprived' areas of England. During 2003 Arts Council England commissioned a review of the progress of social inclusion within the arts since PAT10, particularly in regeneration programmes. It confirms that arts activity at community level has been acknowledged as: 'a primary means of reaching and engaging with people.'[13] The arts and education are placed within a context of improving 'quality of life for local people'.[14] That is: Urban Regeneration, Social Inclusion and Social Cohesion falsely regarded as tackling the improvement of health, job opportunities and reduction in crime. The emphasis here is on the holistic transformative power of the arts used to address specific social 'dysfunctions' creating phoney social benefits, art as social good without any genuine act of consideration or care.

As a strategy utilized in poorer areas this points to a reconditioning of the working class and the embracing of an all-consuming creative cultured citizen. The artist working within this context must be aware that conditions of said 'economically and socially challenged' are pre-judged by those who do not dwell in the margins and that their plans are not gleaned from actual involvement with people; the consultation process often omitting public opinion and including only the scrutiny of other interested organizations. There is a chasm between this hierarchy and the lives of ordinary people. These classifications have been conjured by those with a desire to exploit such environments and the presumption that we are disadvantaged or discontent in assumed states is mis-representational. This feigned concern, and provision of art as the resolve, does not directly address social and economic inequalities. It pacifies and subdues the voicing of genuine public concern. The extent of gentrification in post-industrial, urban areas promotes the culture of inclusion, but in truth expands exclusion and polarization.[15] Funders of participatory work within education, social and health sectors in particular, have grand intentions for the purpose and potential of participatory art. The missing link from their master plans is the consideration of who and what real publics are made up of. Artists must remember that they are not removed from this power relation and be aware that their experiences can be experimental, rather than designed for specific outcome. A reoccurring obstacle for artists in the public realm is their own inadequate sociability, apparent from their ability to successfully remove themselves from an identity within the given community and develop an external surrogate relationship. Here the artistic role, interfering with the role of citizen, removes the artist from any hope of objectivity and elevates superiority and the assumption of artist as expert.

The participatory art sector has evolved from artists working within communities as opposed to studio/gallery-based practice (as did community and site-specific art before it) and prides itself on its involvement with people and places, but since its recent absorption into the mainstream it is continually practised without contextualization of its activities or outcomes. The participatory arts sector is heavily supported by local government and is used in many socially inclusive settings. The practice of art workers in the community, voluntary and professional, went relatively unseen until governments recognized the potential of artist as facilitator within this relationship. Artists involved in prescribed interventions will often be utilized in holistic and therapeutic roles, as 'creative thinkers'; the artist's independence and alternative values annulled by the pre-meditated cure-all and commercial agendas of the leading organization. The assimilation of the critical outsider cancels any radical or alternative possibilities; the rebellious element of art here replaced with compliance. The banding and branding of practice is encouraged as a safeguard against disruptive elements. The encouragement and funding of collective projects is also on the increase in support of social inclusion; funding is provided on the proviso of highlighting minority concerns under controlled conditions. The true value of collective work is lost in this climate; debate and discussion swerved in the name of pseudo-consensus. The effectiveness of the social practice of art is in it's unpredictability and autonomy, not in dealing with people and social space as a separate entity, but exploring its connections and separations with surrounding institutions and the sites for negotiation in and between. The demand on the artistic role to encompass government policy imposes a set agenda onto artistic practice. The contradictions, problems and issues that exist within a given context cannot be discussed unless a range of approaches exist; critical practice relies on an awareness of higher agendas and their influence. The challenging of established structures is necessary in order to reveal the complex relationships between public, artist and institution.

The necessary multiplicity of socially engaged practice is often an enemy to itself. It cannot be categorized as easily as more traditional modes of practice and this can complicate any academic understanding of it. It is therefore disregarded in the realm of high art (unless re-presented in a subjective or abstract manner). The problematics of this art world view and the actuality of social intervention are many. The art system itself has become the obstacle that trips us up and prevents us from action. Inefficiency to tackle and deconstruct the terminology of cultural policy, and the language of art, hinders functionality of practice and complicates basic acts of human interaction. The widespread activity of simulated mutual participation results in 'de-politicisation of both subject and artist'[16] and the outcome merely passive engagement, which alone is no evidence of a project's success.[17] The idle 'creative'

participating through leadership and direction only; the 'non-creative' guided into the passive role for self-improvement, education, and refinement. Within the interpretation of art directed by Social Inclusion Policy we are confronted with restrictions on the possibilities of what art can be.

Socially engaged practice can grapple to deal with the compromise of its function. For some social practitioners the work involves instigation; prompting others to attend to the issues around them. This may be demonstrated in conscious alternative forms of engagement, occupation and in resistance to existing structures and agendas. Struggle, breakdown and contradiction encountered in the criticism of organizational structure may become the strength of the work in the exposing of difficulties and the denial of inflated idealism. Artistic practice and its relationship to social change (not therapy) has the ability to unite or separate contradictory social realms, opening up terms of engagement. Resistance does not mean ignorance and exists not only as a defiance of opposing systems, but in questioning what artists might do. Experimental engagements may reveal underlying relations and produce new perceptions, developing practice that questions structures (physical, social, intellectual and otherwise) and operating in the gap between art and elsewhere – the starting point. These spontaneous and unexpected outcomes should be viewed as attainment and not as failure. Engaging artists for critical thinking within given contexts and allowing artists to make proposals rather than being briefed by the institution[18] will lead to ongoing development of the artistic role. There must be further resolve of the traditional artistic temperament in order to forward critical practice, which relies on challenging established notions of 'art' and 'culture'. Art is only capable of effect when the role is transformed and practice altered according to necessity and specificity of the space in which we find ourselves:

The first condition of art's independence is not art's isolation but its contestation of the cultural field, either by setting up alternative spaces or by occupying existing spaces differently.[19]

Convincing galleries to engage with art practices that usually operate outside the gallery space and encouraging them to question their role and position in relationship to contemporary art practice is key to change, but the soft option of partnering government-based programmes will not result in long-term radical change in gallery and curatorial practice or permit sincere relationships with a working class public. The links made between arts, health, education and voluntary sectors are an optimistic aspect of this circumstance and are proven to lead to constructive action in communities. The problem arises not in the 'opportunity', but in the idealistic management of projects and those stifling volition and freedom of speech by tiptoeing around government policy and political correctness. Functioning art used beyond the traditional format is deemed out of control outside of these boundaries and lacks backing. While art professionals remain inept in applying their own practice and voicing opinion, these opportunities will continue to be impotent, adding to the ambiguity of artistic practice and leaving process and outcome open to institutionalized manipulation.

De-industrialization has seen the establishment of Creative Quarters where industrial zones have been reinvented as swanky commodities in the name of the Creative and Cultural industries (that incidentally, include the endorsement of lap dancing clubs and casinos as part of their vision). Flagship buildings and cultural institutions have advanced gentrification and marginalized the poor while cultural policy indicates that 'culture' improves life, transforms social relations and shapes the future. Futurology (the forecasting of future events from present trends) involves not only statistics, but also speculation, influence and construction from those making the prediction. These pre-conditions limit the potential of future;

imaginations constricted by circumstance, environment and the infringements made on our shared and intimate spaces and customary behaviours. This generalized concept of future is reliant on rank in society, the predictions of the few restricting the lives of many. Probability is limited by the assumptions of identity and class stereotyping enforced by inclusion. The support of marginality (as in non-conformity and not in limitation) is not about 'social inclusion', but the acceptance of diversity in its most raw indefinable state.

An ongoing critique must be built into artistic practice if there is any hope of liberating its independence within the current social, political and economic climate. Art remains a domain where difference and diversity are only accepted on the terms of the elite. The potential of art in society is futile if the philistine, as an individual or collectively, is not allowed to address self-proposed critical issues within creative situations. Publics have a right to deviation, anonymity and the refusal of arts imposition of class values; artists have the right to independence from the systems that enforce such impositions.

The confrontation of arts functionality, autonomy and freedom within society is an obligatory duty to anyone wearing the badge of artist. Might we allow ourselves to consider what art and public and institution can be and what effect this will have not only on futures, but on the here and now?

ENDNOTES

1 Jowell T, 12 April 2005, 'Tackling Poverty of Aspiration Through Rebuilding the Public Realm', Toynbee Hall, East London.

2 Creative Partnerships, 2003, 'About Creative Partnerships' ,(www.creative-partnerships.com).

3 Carrington S, 2004, 'Thoughts on Politicised Art in a De-Politicised Society', Engage Review-15.

4 Miles M, 2005, 'Downing The Master's Tools', *Futurology* by email from editors.

5 'Mongrel Nation', 2003, Discovery Channel.

6 Carrington S, 2004, 'Thoughts on Politicised Art in a De-Politicised Society', Engage Review-15.

7 Parekh B, 2000, 'The Future of Multi-Ethnic Britain', The Runnymede Trust.

8 Barry Brian, 2000, 'Culture and Equality: An Egalitarian Critique of Multiculturalism', Cambridge: Polity Press.

9 Flanagan C, 2000, 'AS Psychology', London: Letts.

10 Ryan K, 2006, 'Arts & Social Inclusion-Special Feature.', Charnwood Arts, Mailout Magazine for Participatory Arts, (www.e-mailout.org).

11 Department of Culture, Media and Sport, 1999, 'Policy Action Team 10'.

12 McEvoy A, 2006, 'Arts & Social Inclusion-Special Feature.', Charnwood Arts, Mailout Magazine for Participatory Arts, (www.e-mailout.org).

13 Mailout Magazine for Participatory Arts, 2003, (www.e-mailout.org).

14 Ibid

15 Butler T, 'The Geography of Gentrification.' Futurology Public Talks.

16 Carrington S, 2004, 'Thoughts on Politicised Art in a De-Politicised Society', Engage Review-15.

17 Ibid

18 Hewitt and Jordan, '*Futurology*: The Black Country 2024', 2005.

19 Beech D, 2006, 'Institutionalisation for All', Art Monthly, Issues:294

The Obscene Secret of Art
Mark Hutchinson

It is all very well for commentators to enjoin artists to understand their own struggle within the ideological and productive apparatuses, but without an explicit attempt to grasp the materials (including the conceptual materials) with which a technical transformation may be at least dimly thought, we are left with no more than conviction and sentiment. [1]

For any artist who suspects that the routine and dominant terms of contemporary art perpetuate closures and silences in the practices and interpretation of art, it is going to be a necessary and urgent task to analyze the structures that govern meaning. However, to become aware of the ways in which meaning is constructed and perpetuated in art and to become articulate about one's own position in relation to these structures is not enough. The point is not only to understand the absences, divisions and silences in the ways in which art functions but also to have some idea of how change might occur. An analysis and critique of what is wrong within contemporary art only goes so far; art must address the potential transformation of art.

These demands are nothing new. The historical avant-garde, in various forms and at various times, struggled against the dominance of established institutions in art, with their concomitant discourses, conventions and so on. The avant-garde sought not only to understand and contest its own position within art but also to transform the social relations of art within which it was constituted. Refusals to conform in practice to accepted methodologies and technologies for art making were allied to demands for the merging of art and everyday life. Nowadays, these two projects of the avant-garde are routinely caricatured and separated as, on the one hand, a

simplistic and nihilistic rebelliousness within art and, on the other, a naïve utopian longing outside the proper sphere of art altogether. In contrast to such dismissive accounts, it needs to be maintained that the radicality of the avant-garde was precisely in the insistence of the necessary conjunction of the two projects: the struggle to negate the absences perpetuated by the then current institutions of art together with the transformation of the social relations of art. Indeed, these could be seen not as two distinct projects but as two aspects of the same project. Anti-art practices of destruction, negation, refusal, confrontation and the like were not signs of nihilistic revolt: rather, these things were aimed (on the whole) precisely at undermining specific, constraining, orthodoxies within art. And these constraining orthodoxies were taken to be the specific expression within art of the general divisions of a divided society.

The idea of the readymade is a prime example of the negating practice of the avant-garde: the absenting of absences. Contemporaneous accounts of artistic subjectivity held the artist to be an intuitive and expressive vessel: an account which absences a good deal of the artist's self, including, for example, intelligence and criticality. These absences not only despoil those things they leave out; they lead to a limited and false view of what they purport to value: intuition and expression, for example. The readymade does not add on positive characteristics to the intuitive and expressive individual but absents the absences of that model. In so doing, the readymade demands a transformation, not adaptation, in the ways in which we can think about and make art. This radicality in the idea of the readymade is routinely passed over. The traditions of art which the readymade aimed to negate, judge it to be merely a provocative and illicit move: the readymade is cast as an inversion, which implicity confirms established divisions and distinctions. The readymade is seen as a temporary exception to which side of the division is valued. Such a reading is only made with a good deal of inattention.

For example, Tristan Tzara's infamous recipe for a poem is routinely taken to be a first order account of his practice: a nihilistic embracing of chance. The text runs as follows:

Take a newspaper.
Take some scissors.
Choose from this paper an article of the length you want to make your poem.
Cut out the article.
Next carefully cut out each of the words that makes up this article and put them all in a bag.
Shake gently.
Next take out each cutting one after the other.
Copy conscientiously in the order in which they left the bag.

It is at this point that most accounts leave off. But it finishes:

The poem will resemble you.
And there you are – an infinitely original author of charming sensibility, even though unappreciated by the vulgar herd. [2]

These last lines make it clear that this is not to be read as a first order account. Indeed, the irony of this writing is a precise negation of the habitual and entrenched contemporaneous modes of attention to poetry. In the face of an interpretation that is going to take whatever words a poet presents as a sign of individual sensitivity and expression, one might as well draw random words out of a bag. What is being negated from within the then prevalent cultural orthodoxy, is the negation of the poet as a self-conscious and critical being. This negation of a negation (in Tzara's work) is the attempt to transform not the structure and form of the words that a poet writes but rather what it is that a poet is (and is not). Nowadays, the readymade has been thoroughly absorbed into the positive lexicon of art. To describe the readymade in positive terms (as an innovative methodology, for example, or the assertion of the power of the artist) is to obscure the radicality in negating negations.

For the historical avant-garde, the divisions within art were continuous with the divisions elsewhere in society. The merging of art and everyday life was not about overcoming a putative division between art and everything else but about seeing the divisions within art as being the same as those in everyday life: divisions predicated upon, and reproducing, absences, lacks, ills, aporias, negations and so on. It was necessary to impugn the idea of art as something special and separate from everything else as a prerequisite for transforming the divisions and absences internal to art.

Transformation is neither an end, nor a good, in itself. Terry Eagleton reminds us that: 'No way of life in history has been more in love with transgression and transformation, more enamoured of the hybrid and pluralistic, than capitalism.'[3] Capitalism is both thoroughly egalitarian and instrumental in the way it makes everything subservient to the need to make a profit. It is the transforming practices of capitalism that themselves need to be transformed. The point is that capitalist transformation propagates division and absence in bringing everything under the spell of the commodity: of universalizing exchange value. Radical transformation, in contrast, is the absenting of absences. Absences (such as those of freedom, equality and mutual self-determination) are real determinate factors in hindering the flourishing of all. It is these negations that need to be negated.

Without the radical idea of transformation we are left with the liberal idea of corruption and change. The liberal supports individual freedom without seeing the need for radical social transformation: without seeing the freedom of all as a condition of the freedom of each. This view leads to a doubling of reality. For the liberal, the misworkings of the present system can only be blamed on human failings: a lack of organization or will; the wrong person in charge; the contingencies of evil. Thus, behind the reality that can be readily perceived – the global scale of suffering and poverty caused by the workings of capital – there is postulated another agent or agency responsible for the system going wrong. The concentration on isolated individuals and events deflects attention from the need of a critique of capitalism itself. Against the liberal, the Marxist must insist that poverty is intrinsic and inevitable to the workings of capitalism itself.

A corollary of this liberal thinking is what Slavoj Zizek calls interpassivity[4] : this is change in order that things stay exactly as they are. Zizek gives the example of humanitarian aid to the Third World. Whilst absolutely necessary in alleviating the immediate pain of others, such good deeds do nothing to alleviate the cause of the suffering: the cause is, in the last instance, the necessities of capitalism itself. Indeed, the provision of aid is necessary for the continuation of capitalist business as usual, which sees capital flowing from the poorest countries in the world into the richest, with crippling results. At a personal level, the liberal can invest time and money in good causes or doing good deeds: these actions both assuage guilt and at the same time prevent his or her privileged position from being jeopardized: a position dependent on the current relations of capitalism. It is telling that the liberal inevitably invests political action as being elsewhere: at a remove from his or her own places of work and living.

If it is thus vital for artists both to contest the meanings and interpretations of what it is that they do as well as to do things that might resist comfortable and contented interpretation, this is not all. To avoid interpassivity, artists must be engaged with their immediate conditions. Transformation must be critically self-aware: agency is the unity of theory and practice in practice [5]. However, it is neither easy nor straightforward to see how this might be done. For conceptual art of the late 1960s and early 1970s, the very inclusion of self-reflexive, critical theory into practice was a political act against the modernist hegemony of sensuous particularity. Conceptual art smashed to bits the modernist idea of the artist as an emotive, universal-expressing subject. Radicality lay in the process of groups of artists talking about philosophy, language and art, not necessarily in the particular words said. It could be remarked that this does not sound like a very robust form of resistance – but what is it about resistance that might make us expect that it should be robust? Robust or not, this was not just a question of interpretation or what artists could say: it was to change what it was that artists could do.

The political gains of conceptualism have long since been recuperated. If the so-called 'conceptual artist' is the mainstay of contemporary art, this is in an impoverished and tamed manner. The idea of the articulate artist can come to mean a kind of entrepreneur of meanings and techniques: the artist as someone who pitches ideas to curators, critics and the like. It is now expected that the artist has a lot to say about what it is that he or she does. However, the content of what is said is largely irrelevant in relation to the structural necessity that something is said. What is said is treated merely as a kind of circumstantial evidence in the pursuit of meaning. Art is now full of theoretical talk. The dominant ideological discourses of the interpretation of art encompass and embrace such talk: an artist's theoretical talk goes to promote his or her art over and above what the particular content of that theory might be. The discourses of those responsible for the reception and distribution of art can accommodate contradictions and critique. Talk is a necessary accessory for art, where what is promoted as art is ideas. The dilemma for any artist wishing to articulate discontent with the current constitution of art and its discourses is that the words of the artist, however provocative,

irreverent or oppositional, are liable to be taken as confirmation of the power of art as it is. Words are not enough.

For the conceptual artist of the late 1960s, the battle to gain a voice was a radical move against the then current cultural division of labour, which rendered the artist mute. For the radical wing of conceptual art, becoming articulate was not about the promotion of ideas but part of the interrogation of the ontological status of the art object and the processes through which art came to acquire meaning. The pursuit of such questions was in itself a transformation of what it was that an artist did or might do. In the current, competitive, de-materialized environment of art as an economy of ideas, radical transformation must be not only about what artists say and think but about what it is that they might do.

Ideas are the latest form that the products of art have taken. Ideas can be just as much products as objects, videos and performances. Only a severely curtailed ontology would take art's products to be physical entities. Art is not products and their meanings, of whatever kind. Any adequate ontology of art must include the processes of the production of art and the social relations which maintain it.

Thinking of art in terms of the work and agency might offer a way to situate the artist in current social relations, whilst holding out some kind of promise of the transformation of those relationships. Work is, perhaps, one thing that contemporary capitalism cannot easily colonize or turn into consumption. Work, as a fundamental category of capitalism, is elided in its accounts of itself. Zizek notes how organized labour is only ever depicted in mainstream cinema as criminal activity, which must be destroyed: think of the master-criminal's industrious lair in any number of James Bond films, for example.[6] To think of art in terms of the work of the artist (and its possible transformation) might be one way to avoid both the contemporary dominance of ideas supported by objects and also the modernist paradigm of objects supported by ideas.

To talk of work is not necessarily to rehash ideas of the dignity of labour nor other romantic misrepresentations of oppressive toil. For Marx, work is the transformation of natural things by human agency: it is the fundamental category in the production and reproduction of society. Against the alienated work of capitalist necessity it is possible to put forward a Marxist and utopian potential for work to be unalienated, collaborated and self-determined activity. This is an argument against the division of labour. The problem nowadays is not only the division but the denial of labour.

In a recent essay on the colonization of utopia, Steve Edwards ends up with the speculation that art could stand as a utopian model for work. The task is to rethink work on the basis of the combination of the revolutionary tradition with the innovations of the avant-garde. According to Edwards, this is what William Morris did, although the extent to which he could re-imagine work was limited by his fixation on craft labour, with its conception of individually produced artefacts. In contrast, Edwards concludes:

The model of twentieth-century art provides a different conception on which to re-engage work – one that still combines the mental and manual, and which sees work as a project of self making – in that it also allows us to image such a vision combined with technology and technical specialism, capable of grasping contradiction and the energies of metropolitan life: film, video art or photography, not the handicrafts, provide our models.[7]

Edwards insists on the idea of work as the necessary core of revolutionary utopian thought. It is precisely work that contemporary capitalism does not and can not colonize and transform into a consumable commodity. Indeed, work, in the West, is something denied and hidden by both the ideology and structure of contemporary capitalism. According to Zizek:

What characterises "late capitalism" is the split between the production of cultural experiences as such and its (partially invisible) material base, between the Spectacle (of theatrical experience) and its secret staging mechanisms; far from disappearing, material production is still here, transfunctionalised into the supporting mechanism for the stage production. In today's ideological perception, work itself (manual labour as opposed to the "symbolic" activity of cultural production), not sex, appears as the site of obscene indecency to be concealed from the public eye.[8]

This insistence on work is an attempt to hold out against the colonization of utopia by contemporary, consumer capitalism. The usual terms of utopian thought are abundance, sexual freedom and idleness. Capitalism has colonized all three. These utopian themes, in their capitalist guises, can be clearly seen in contemporary art practice. Appropriating plentiful consumer goods; exploring and exploiting slacker themes; and a wholehearted embrace of sexual transgression are all familiar enough.

In the West, capitalism has colonized the idea of abundance through its ability to deliver vast quantities of consumer goods. It is fundamental that these goods and their consumption are divided off both from the conditions of production of the goods and the conditions of work under which the consumer earned the money to pay for the goods. Continual and excessive consumption is normalized and internalized. It is this picture of the abundance of goods in the West that global capital uses to 'encourage' free market economies and deregulation in the Third World. Of course, what this means in practice is both the removal of barriers to capital being taken out of poor countries by global corporations and the creation of an 'ideal' workforce: one free from such things as unions, health and safety laws and employment laws. And the fulfilment of the promise of a consumerist lifestyle to Third World workers is endlessly deferred.

A corollary of all these consumable goods is the leisure time to purchase and enjoy them. This time of consumption equates to the utopian ideal of idleness. Idleness comes to mean the act of being consumed within the process of consumption, rather than a break from the oppression of meaningless toil.

Sexual freedom is also colonized by contemporary capitalism. What were once transgressions of perceived norms of sexual behaviour are now routinely discussed and promoted as potential cultural experiences. Last year Time Out recommended its readers try dogging (strangers gathering to watch other strangers having sex in public places) as something to try as a casual New Year treat. Sexual experience and identity become consumable events. Excess and indulgence are normalized by contemporary capitalism: the contemporary Western subject is saturated by the super-ego injunction 'Enjoy!' Consumption is radically broken off from both it conditions of production and its consequences.

For Edwards, the transformation of work remains one area of revolutionary utopian thought that has not been colonized by capitalism and for good Marxist reasons. Despite continually reinventing itself, capitalism fundamentally still relies on the extraction of surplus value from labour. And unlike abundance, idleness and sexual transgression, which are terms of consumption, work is agency.

Following Morris, Edwards looks to art to provide a model of utopian work. I want to argue that this relationship cuts both ways. Social and cultural divisions run equally and continuously through both the worlds of work and art, not between them. It is equally pertinent to look to work to provide a model for art in this precise sense: as a way to understand and position the artist within the relations of production.

Walter Benjamin theorized the idea of the author as a producer as a way of grounding the meaning of the author's activity within its conditions of production. For Benjamin there was no point in analyzing the author's practice in terms of sovereignty over the meaning of objects; a critique of the author's practice should look at the position of the author as a producer and not at the objects that he or she made. Thus:

The dialectical approach to this question [of form and content] has absolutely no use for such rigid, isolated things as work, novel, book. It has to insert them into the living social contexts.[9]

Benjamin is concerned to shift attention away from the question of the attitude a work displays towards the relations of production of its time, towards the more radical question of what is its position within those relations of production. For Benjamin, this is to be concerned directly with what he calls the literary technique of works. And this, in turn, is to situate the writer as a producer who struggles and intervenes within his or her conditions of work. In contrast, the writer as author, who contents him or herself with jurisdiction over meaning, can never contest the mechanisms which generate and fix the possibilities and limitations of meaning.

Art & Language revisited the question of author and producer. They were concerned with the ways in which the artist qua producer is misrepresented in the discourses of the artist qua author.

To say that art is produced is not to reduce it to something entirely determined by the economic, nor to a mere expression of the economic. Furthermore, we assert its relative autonomy. Indeed, "basic" to certain formations will be certain practices. These will involve beliefs and so forth. And these in turn will involve representation of other practices and forms and so forth. We are not concerned to be seen to theorise the absolute priority of the economic. We are concerned to point out that the world of art produces contradictions (that is, misrepresentation of it basic structures), and that these are necessary for those basic structures, and furthermore that given the relativity of relative autonomy these may themselves be misrepresentation, or entail misrepresentations of structures basic to capitalism etc. These misrepresentations involve contradictions of a special sort. And they are to be understood causally.[10]

So, the discourses of art, which habitually perpetuate the meanings of the author and the author as location of meaning, form a closed circle of interpretation. There is, of course, plenty of contestation and diversity of meaning here. But the terms of a discourse which focuses on works and meaning render certain questions and attitudes unthinkable. It is only by refiguring the artist as a producer that the terms of art discourse can be made corrigible. This must be a necessary element in any transformation of art.

Contemporary art would seem to offer many possible models of work. That is to say, at first glance, contemporary art seems to be characterized by an abundance of different methods and technologies for making art. It is a truism to reiterate that nowadays virtually anything can be appropriated for the purposes of making art. It was with conceptual art that ideas of the 'dematerialization of art' began to appear. In contrast to those conceptual artists who were engaged in a critique of the structures that generated and fixed meaning for modernist art, some took, for example, the sudden preponderance of words to mean that words were a new material out of which to fashion art. The shift to ideas could not be contained as a critical, second order practice. Instead, ideas became the new, dominant currency of art discourse and authorial practice.

This dominance of the idea of ideas and the subservience of material production in art, fits in snugly with the general, dominant forms of contemporary capitalism. For contemporary art, work is just as much something to be denied and hidden away as it is for contemporary capitalism generally. Many of the ideas adopted and explored by contemporary art and their concomitant technological novelties, are trivial and distracting. As such, they conform to the logic of promotion of other consumer goods. Ideas compete against each other for attention and recognition.

When The Sun newspaper adopted a philistine sneer at the destruction of art in the Momart fire, it did so in terms of work. It paid a seamstress to recreate Tracy Emin's tent. This, it claimed, was done in less than a day. The sneer was at the difference in the value of the tent in the art market and the value of the labour of the seamstress it took to reproduce it. In fact, The Sun's implicit argument is that the tent is not really art at all because the labour that went into making it can so easily be reproduced. For The Sun, art is the name of a special and unreproducible kind of labour. The art world defence of Emin was that the work that had gone into making the art was not what mattered: it was irrelevant to meaning. What mattered, as far as those putting forward this argument were concerned, was the idea. These opposing views seem irreconcilable. But what both sides tacitly agreed upon, was that meaning should reside in the art object: for The Sun the art object is valuable as the accumulation of a special kind of labour; for Emin's supporters the art object is valuable as the embodiment of an idea. For both sides the art object is made meaningful through the exceptional character of the artist qua author: meaning is imparted through a special kind of making in one case and a special kind of thinking, in the other. Neither side can situate the artist in a position to work within and upon the relations of production of art.

Opening up the possibilities of work for the artist qua producer is a way to start, dimly perhaps, thinking about the possibility of the transformation of art. It is, amongst other things, a way of situating the work of the artist in relations to the work of others: as embedded in social relations. The making of art, as with everything else, is at base a collaborative and dialogical affair; a fact which is obscured and mystified by the ideological idea of the isolated artist working independently of others. The idea of independence is radically double edged here. On the one hand, the putative autonomy of the artist (and the freedom of the market) enables the artist to resist both the division of mental and manual labour and to have self-determination over what it is that he or she does. On the other hand, this autonomy cuts off the artist from other producers: separation is a condition of dependence, subtended to the market and the mechanisms for the reception and distribution of art. This contradictory pair of independence and dependence are not easily reconciled by, for example, treating independence as a condition of the artist as author and dependence as a condition of the artist as producer. It seems more productive to think of this contradiction as being an expression of a more general contradiction in the social constitution of art or culture as such.

Working in a critical and self-aware relationship to others is no guarantee of anything, of course. It is certainly not a way to escape from contradictions. However, it is in relation to others that we might conceive of an artist's actions as embedded in social relations and practices. That is, there are different ways in which we might conceive of the artist's work, when it is not seen as part of a private or self-contained practice.

The following are some ways in which an artist's actions or work might be conceived. This list is not intended to be exhaustive. It's schema does, however, follow a Bhaskarian dialectic.[1]

(i) A first possibility is for the artist to do just what he or she wants to do, without any concern for, or ostensive influence by, what goes on around him or her. Ideas of what the artist does, of work, can be unaffected by, or actively resistant to, the location in which the work is done. In this case, the artist carries on regardless of context, perpetuating an established working method. This situation can be characterized by the non-unity of the artist's work and the location of that work. The artist is merely displaced. And that displacement goes to reiterate or emphasize the separation of art from everything else.

(ii) Secondly, the artist can allow what he or she does to be determined by the environment in which it is done. In contrast to (i) above, the work of the artist can be directly tailored to the location or circumstances in, or for, which the artist is working. This entails the recognition of the absences and neglects in the idea that the artist's work is self-determined and unaffected by its context and other determinants. It is the negation of the indifference to difference. Here we have a self-awareness of the artist's work as work within social relationships: that the artist's work exists in the same world as everything else. Work becomes reflexive to its particular circumstances. In practice, this means, to some degree, working to the needs and demands of others; indeed, it could mean adopting the ideas and practices of work of others.

(iii) Thirdly, the artist can work with a critical and self-reflexive understanding of the environment in which that work is done. If (ii) implies a recognition of difference, then it is possible to go further and conceive of the artist's work as part of a collaborative, reciprocal relationship. Rather than working as a response to, or in relation to, given circumstances, this means to conceive of the artist's work and its circumstances as a totality. This is to say, it is possible to conceive of work not as something prescribed by circumstances but forged out of self-conscious and self-reflexive awareness of circumstances. This is to recognize that circumstances are not fixed or objective: the context of work is always the work of others. Thus, to have a self-reflexive awareness of circumstance is to be committed to interaction with others, as equal subjects. This is to see work as dialogical.

(iv) Fourthly, the artist's work can transform what it is that the artist's work is. This is to conceive of the artist's work as the practice of agency: as self-transformation. This is more than changing the relationships between the artist's work and the work of others. It is to change, and be changed by, the process of work. Such work might not be recognizable as artist's work nor, indeed, as work as such. Radical agency will also transform the conditions of recognition.

It remains to be seen what the implication of analyzing types of work, as in (i) - (iv) above, or other ways, might be. To follow the progression from (i) to (iv) is to imagine stages in the removal or absenting of constraints, absences, ills, prohibitions and so on, upon the practice of art. And the practices of art, as I have argued, can usefully be thought of in terms of work rather than objects, as part of an attempt to illuminate even the dimmest prospect of emancipatory potential.

It has long since been possible to produce any number of ideas, actions, events and objects as art. It seems possible to do absolutely anything under the guise of art and for absolutely anything to be considered an appropriate working method for the artist. This diversity may be, in some ways, exemplary of the possibilities for art practice: of arbitrary limits and closures in the discourses and practices of art having been transgressed. The problem seems to be, not so much any inhibition on things to do, but rather a question of choosing something to do out of almost infinite possibility. The idea of the readymade started out as a Dada negation of the negations of a dominant and hegemonic idea of art. The readymade was important for what it wasn't: it actively avoided being seen as a product of skill, sensitivity, taste, or interest. The fate of the readymade is instructive. That is to say, the readymade cut against the idea of the artwork as an accumulation of a kind of enchanted, individual labour. It is now a normative tactic in contemporary art for appropriating some kind of interest or meaning. It is a way for artists to make choices, to act as consumers. As a way of making art, it conforms to contemporary capitalism's model of consumption. In such circumstances, what the idea of transformation might help reiterate is that art is made under and out of material conditions. Cultural acts are never performed unattached but within hegemonic ideological co-ordinates.

There is a stark choice, here, for artist and commentators. Either art is seen to exist in the same world as everything else, and to be subject to the same social processes, mechanisms and determinants as everything else, or not. Art & Language sidled up to this by toying with the question of how much Degas paid his models.

Asking how Degas' work was produced entails asking how the co-producer of his work exists or existed. If someone interprets Degas, then they are going to have to be seen as part of the same world as that in which he paid his models. If you can't understand that world, then neither can you understand how someone interprets Degas' work. You will still merely be present at the congregational constitution of 'Art'.[12]

The diverse, 'de-materialized' and revolutionizing practices of contemporary art perfectly fit the logic of contemporary capitalism and the global market. It is not just that conceptual practice has become hegemonic: within contemporary capitalism it is the commodity which supports the image and no longer the other way round. Conceptual artists are not the only ones who are adept at de-materialization: the largest corporations in the world today have no workforce and own no factories nor warehouses. Outsourcing production leaves these corporations

free to concentrate on what really matters: promoting and selling ideas. The product is merely a necessary adjunct to these ideas. For consumption in the West, goods are not there so much to fulfil needs as to define lifestyle choices. It is within such a world that so-called conceptual art practice has come to have the hegemonic position it does. The question remains of what might be the limits (or how limits might be conceived) of the hegemonic ideological tolerance of art practice in its reception and interpretation. As Zizek says of contemporary capitalism, perhaps the question is: 'how are we to revolutionise an order whose very principle is constant self-revolutionising?'[13] Cannot the same question be asked in the local and particular case of art?

Art needs the New, it is constantly revolutionizing, to keep itself going. New art with new styles, techniques, ideas and media competes for attention or recognition. But here is the problem. Having the need to be attended to, to be recognized, is to appeal to a subject in the position to do the attending. Within psychoanalytic terms, this is the 'subject supposed to know.' With psychoanalytic practice, the analyst is the subject supposed to know. The treatment of a patient ends, not when the investment of the analysand in the analyst has been rewarded by the imparting of knowledge but, on the contrary, when the patient accepts that there is no subject who knows and that there will be no reward of knowledge. The analysand disabuses him-or-herself of an investment in a Master-figure that guarantees meaning. The scandal of psychoanalysis is that there is no compensation for the investments of the patient, merely a disillusionment with the process of investment. It is in disinvestment that freedom lies.

The idea of art occupies the place of a Master-figure: art can be a site of investment and not just for artists. However, to be an artist, to make art, is always to risk being attached to the idea of art: to seek recognition and compensation from a pervasive and universal 'Art'. Art can be one form of the Lacanian Big Other. This is to allow the idea of 'Art' to act as a guarantor of meaning and purpose for artists.

The genuine, radical act must do without guarantees; it must transform its own conditions of possibility. This is to go into the unknown without the prospect of recognition, reward nor compensation. This is why anti-art is such a powerful and pervasive idea: not as a negation of the protocols and procedures of proper art but precisely as the attempt to manage without them at all. Anti-art is not against art; it is the attempt to manage without art: to manage without any guarantee at all. This is the truly revolutionary act: to transform oneself and one's situation without a belief in a reimbursement by some guarantor of meaning (the Lacanian Big Other, whether History, Art, God or whatever). For the authentic act there can be no responsibility, accountability or so on. If work is the obscene secret of art, that which is currently hidden and disdained, then this is not something in which the artist can take refuge. The task of the artist is to make do without making investments. To act is to manage with nothing.

ENDNOTES

1. Art & Language, 1984, 'Author and Producer Revisited', reprinted in Modernism, Criticism, Realism, ed Charles Harrison and Fred Orton, Harper and Row, London, p. 253.

2. Tristan T, 1992, 'To Make a Dadaist Poem', Seven Dada Manifestos and Lampisteries, Calder Publications Limited, London pp. 39.

3. Eagleton T, 2003/2004 'After Theory', Penguin, London, p. 119.

4. Zizek S, 2002, 2004, 'Revolution at the Gates', Verso, London p.170

5. A formula of the philosopher Roy Bhaskar: see, Dialectic: the Pulse of Freedom, Verso, London, 1993.

6. Zizek S, 2004, 'Organs Without Bodies: On Deleuze and Consequences', Routledge, London, p. 213.

7. Edwards S, 2004, 'The Colonisation of Utopia', catalogue essay William Morris curated by David Mabb, Whitworth Gallery, Manchester, p39.

8. Zizek S, 2002, 2004, Revolution at the Gates, Verso, London p.289

9. Benjamin W, 1999, 'The Author as Producer', Selected Writings, Volume 2, Belknap Press, London, p. 769.

10. Art & Language, 1984, 'Author and Producer Revisited', reprinted in Modernism, Criticism, Realism, ed Charles Harrison and Fred Orton, Harper and Row, London, p. 256.

11. For a more detailed account of the application of Bhaskar's dialectic to art, see my, 'Four Stages of Public Art', Third Text, Vol. 16, Issue 4, 2002. For the genuine article, see, Roy Bhaskar, Dialectic: the Pulse of Freedom, Verso, London, 1993.

12. Art & Language, 1984, 'Author and Producer Revisited', reprinted in Modernism, Criticism, Realism, ed Charles Harrison and Fred Orton, Harper and Row, London, p. 259.

13. Zizek S, 2004 'Organs Without Bodies: On Deleuze and Consequences', Routledge, London, p. 213.

Fanning the Spark of Hope: On Futurology

Esther Leslie

The Future Before Us (History's Continuum): on Utopias

The future is a place we have yet to get to. The future is in advance of us. The future is somewhere or somewhen to which we progress. Our technologies will transport us there. That is the usual image. Utopias are conceived in order to imagine future worlds for us. Utopia is a place or, more strictly a non-place, one not yet established on earth. Utopia's time is the future. Utopias imagine future worlds, projecting into the aftertime the outlines of a perfected society. The utopias that approached concrete form in the nineteenth century, such as Robert Owen's or Charles Fourier's, just like the utopias of the twentieth century grounded themselves in real technological developments. Many utopias only come into being once technological preconditions are already in place, or almost in place. Such utopias echo Marx's idea: that humanity only sets itself such tasks as it is able already to achieve. For example, utopian socialist Charles Fourier devised a great translucent palace called a phalanstery as part of his utopian vision called *Harmony*. Fourier worked out a scheme of natural association, where gratification of individual desires and passions would serve the general good.[1] The scheme was based on an elaborate theory of human motivation described by Fourier as the 'geometrical calculus of passionate attraction', and which he claimed was in complete accord with the Newtonian principle of gravitational attraction. For the layout of his utopia Fourier adopted the then current arcades building style, imagining crystal palaces of iron and glass. In the next century too, Le Corbusier and Bruno Taut and Paul Scheerbart wanted to resurrect the utopian house of transparent surfaces and transparent relationships, in a self-aware, modern rejection of the brickwork and clutter of the Victorian epoch and in line with the contemporary possibilities of glass, steel and concrete. Glass, a transparent material, is the material to banish social and architectural confusion. Le Corbusier voices a typically modernist slogan in the 1920s – when he notes that for the current age the watchword is not entanglement but transparency.[2] Le Corbusier was responding to the fact that certain technological possibilities in building make possible new modes of habitation, that is to say, new modes of living, or relating public and private space. Without a closed-off private realm all life is exposed to the glare of public judgement. Under such an exposure a new public morality is incubated. Some embraced this, convinced that the existence of private space allows for corruption and that privacy's abolition expunges it. However, from another perspective, in a see-through world of buildings, the onus might be to appear constantly socially useful. In either case, technological possibilities allow for a remoulding of social relations, in a quest to better them, and here this is traced right into the most intimate of zones.

Typically Adorno voiced contrary objections to the utopian association between technological possibility and new modes of living. In *Minima Moralia: Reflections From a Damaged Life*, an entry titled *Sur l'eau* (1945) he argues that this conventional notion of utopia does not start out from human need but rather from the needs of production, turned into an end in itself. Adorno's specific target of attack is the socialist utopias of the nineteenth century, where life is posited as rich and bustling, on the basis of technological expansion and its colonization of the lifeworld. In such a utopia the collective undergoes a 'blind fury of activity':

The conception of unfettered activity, of uninterrupted procreation, of chubby insatiability, of freedom as frantic bustle, feeds on the bourgeois conception of nature that has always served solely to proclaim social violence as unchangeable, as a piece of healthy eternity.[3]

Such a vision of utopia, based upon ceaseless production and human activity, is an analogue to the bourgeois *idée fixe* that maintains humans are like, and will always be like, animals, acting unreflectively and out of blind necessity, not rationally and consciously adaptive. Adorno's broader point is that utopias imagine the future, but they are rooted in the present, even when they seek their inspiration in the past. Utopias can never escape their own present moment of writing. In some way or another the currently achieved state of technological development frames the utopia. Further development along the same lines – that is a quantitative rather than qualitative change – is envisaged. The equation runs: progress is the future is utopia.

In his usual contrary fashion, Adorno, of course, turns all this upside-down. He wishes to imagine a future utopia as emancipated from present mores. His utopia is one that does not conceive the forces of production as the sum total of human endeavour. Perhaps, he muses, humans will grow tired of the idea of development and expansion and collectively decide to leave all sorts of possibilities unexplored, 'instead of storming under a confused compulsion to the conquest of strange stars'. Once deprivation is no longer an issue, it will become clear how all the propositions designed to eliminate want only increase it on a larger scale for many. What is then utopia for Adorno? It is, instead, a sliver of experience, a moment of rest and contemplation. *Rien faire comme une bête,* lying on water and looking peacefully at the sky, 'being, nothing else, without any further definition and fulfilment'. This is fulfilled utopia standing in the place of process, act and satisfaction. Fulfilled utopia is a luxurious indolence, an everlasting peace.

Such a glimpse of utopia occurs only within a rare experience that is not social, but primitive. Not for Adorno, Ernst Bloch's anticipatory consciousness, where traces, spoors are found in the present, in a 'landscape of hope', which inspires images of a better future. No role either for that highly socialized thing called art in imagining utopia in any concrete sense. For Adorno art cannot and must not picture perfect futures. Art is set under that Jewish Bilderverbot, the ban on images of the future. A better world cannot be given concrete form now, for us, in art, because all that ever comes to light are the schemes and patterns of the present, generated by the paltry environment of our impoverished imaginations.

The future, that is, the happy future, can never be represented, because of our entrapment in current concerns. Instead the outlines of our cages should be drawn and redrawn, in an effort to expose the contours that we inhabit and that therefore frame the edges of our world, which remains invisible to us. The art of the future, a more progressive time to come, remains under this edict likewise:

Even in a legendary, qualitatively better society of the future, art cannot afford to disavow the remembrance of accumulated agony. To do so would mean abrogating art's form.[4]

Art under this sentence refuses to provide ameliorating solutions, but rather it exposes the contradictions and woundings, the 'primary alienation', the split in species being occasioned by the division of labour, which accompanies the unequal division of cultural access and benefit. Culture is slashed by, negatively formed by or located in relation to social division, social determination. Utopia is always qualified by a dark term in Adorno's writing: negative utopia, impotent utopia, failed utopia. It can never be thought without its opposite. And yet art does not simply repeat the contours of oppressive society. In Adorno's schema, it bears a special role.

It is not the office of art to spotlight alternatives, but to resist by its form alone the course of the world, which permanently puts a pistol to men's heads.[5]

It is art alone that might, because of its precarious and anomalous situation within commodity society, bear a relation to utopia. If art does ever signal utopia, then it does so only perversely. Art can utter the unutterable, which is utopia, through the medium of the complete negativity of the world.[6] Art holds a place for utopia, though it cannot represent it, instead figuring this future time negatively.

We may not know what the human is or what the correct shape of human things is, but what it is not and what form of human things is wrong, that we do know, and only in this specific and concrete knowledge is something else, something positive, open to us.[7]

Enmeshed in present concerns art, as much as any future scheme of happiness, can only regurgitate the present in its efforts to distance itself from it. This is visible in future thinking's frequent recourse to maps, the layout of land, to architecture, to issues concerning property, around which it can only ever circulate. Utopia is a rare no-place for which maps already exist.

The Future Behind Us (Debris Piling Skyward): On Cultural Policy

In contemporary cultural policy the association of art and utopia - or more specifically art and the better life – is frequently made. Such an association might be derived from weak echoes of the avant garde position of better-world-boosters such as Malevich, Tatlin, Rodchenko, Popova, Rozanova, Matiushin and El Lissitzky, who conceived their art in terms of blueprints for the future. This means less that art represents tangible images of the future but rather that it institutes modes of non-commodified production or test-runs transformed social relations whereby art segues into life. In the case of the Soviet artists there was some justification, for they operated in times of transformation, not least times of transformation for art, which emerged from the galleries and museums, dropped its preoccupation with individualistic artists, instead organizing itself into agit-prop groupings, grasping towards new technological forms of expression, and rushing forward to meet its audience on newly defined terms.

Contemporary cultural policy attempts likewise to shape the future. Cultural policy, scrabbling for justification and cash in gloomy days, when social policy amounts to surveillance, punishment and privatization, moulds art policy into a plus, the only plus, an ameliorative measure recruited to lighten blighted lives and neutralize zones of anti-social behaviour in the city. Art is charged with the task of letting the people expand their horizons, love their community and improve it and, thereby, their own lives. In neo-liberal times, cultural policy works with the model of cultural industries. The term cultural industries (or creative, sunrise or 'future oriented' industries) comes from the jargon of contemporary 'development' initiatives, which argue that culture be instrumentalized to promote 'satisfactory intellectual, emotional, moral and spiritual existence', and 'allows groups, communities and nations to define their futures in an integrated manner'.[8] The cultural industries include publishing, music, audio-visual technology, electronics, video games, the Internet and spectacular events, globally organized industries that possess 'a determining role for the future in terms of freedom of expression, cultural diversity and economic development'.[9] But art too is subsumed as a branch of the cultural industries. Adorno's horror, the 'culture industry'[10], in his day associated with highly capitalized media forms such as film and radio, becomes, as 'creative/ cultural industries', more broadly any type of creative endeavour, now measured according to its value-added economic outputs, direct or otherwise, even as it claims to be about a measurable productivity in the spiritual realm of values. As UNESCO put it:

Cultural industries add value to contents and generate values for individuals and societies.' The 'intangible' contents of the cultural industries are

property, in the normal sense, for they 'are typically protected by copyright'.[11]

Do-goody forces may wring their hands in worry that these industries will be dominated by a few large culture providers, but the development of capitalist logic shows again and again that conglomeration is the very movement of its industry, and use of the term 'industry' signals acceptance of capitalism's logic. But because these industries are the vector of jobs – service jobs, good jobs, bad jobs – and wealth for someone, there is no other option. Culture is the ultimate in busy productivity. All this could be no further removed from the sphere of future-dreaming as indolence, as the blank space that marks a better life as either unimagined (under the compulsion of Bilderverbot) or, in itself, the space and the no-place or some-place in which nothing happens at all.

The Future Now (Danger Flashes, Sparks Of Hope): On Futurology

Art might be instrumentalized by policy makers now, but this is not to suggest that once upon a time it was a zone of undirected, fulfilling experience. And yet that observation does not mean that one cannot dream about its possibility, as Adorno did when he wrote:

One of the crucial antinomies of art today is that it wants to be and must be squarely Utopian, as social reality increasingly impedes Utopia, while at the same time it should not be Utopian so as not to be found guilty of administering comfort and illusion. [12]

The curators of *Futurology* set up an experiment, operating within the context of culture as given. In this respect, the project shares something with the 'sociological experiment' undertaken by Brecht in 1931, when, dismayed by G.W. Papst's film of *The Threepenny Opera*, he sued Nero Films for breach of contract and theft of intellectual property, knowing full well that capitalism's sympathy for tangible property owners meant he would lose.[13] *Futurology* operates in the choppy waters of cultural policy, community funding and the push for art as a plus – where, for example, the critical avant-garde flushing of art out from the inaccessible galleries of privilege is translated into 'empowerment' in a gesture of compulsory anti-elitism. *Futurology*'s theme is that of imagined futures, which dovetails perfectly with the rhetoric and practice of regeneration. Here the most hopeful imaginations of the young, with the quantatively most future before them, are marshalled in order to nourish the greater project of Black Country transformation, which means of course the transformation of these very children compelled to fantasize their own better future. And yet that is what they do not, or cannot, do. Steered by the enabling hands of specifically-selected artists, the experiment reveals the vanity of this concept: thematically, the past forces itself forward in the guise of the present. There are maps of future towns that mirror the post-industrial service economy organized around the commodified leisure (a zone of low-paid work for the many) promoted by urban planners. There are share certificates for land, raising the question of the future as a time for investment and return on private property, only if things, that is, social relations, continue as they are, only more so. There is a private space – a den – with rules of entry and usage, an analogue of the privatization and policing of space, as much as it participates in the 'empowerment' of a certain section of the populace. There are the school-leavers snared in an economic relationship to the place where they used to learn, flexibilizing themselves and their environment, abandoning mental endeavour for physical labour as they re-arrange a space in an effort to improve other pupils' future experience without substantially increasing resources. From one angle, then, there is the reinforcement of categories of the now, which extend hopelessly into the future. From another, of course, something else is at work or at play, because theme is not everything. Modes of production present another facet. Here collaboration and exchange between 'official' artists and school pupils have been a constituent of the work – whether it has been meshed into the textures of a video, or is apparent only as the work of discussion prior to the settling on objects, or is captured in the glitches and contradictions caught on tape. If utopia is adumbrated negatively, what comes to light is the present horror marking the site of a potential liberation, which might be gestured, in the specific mode of art's making.

Through art's specific materiality, understood in its broadest senses as its substance, its material presence in the world, its 'madeness', a social and formal analysis of art might be made. What type of labour art constitutes is a fascinating question, and cannot be disconnected from the category of alienation. That art exists – or culture more broadly – as a specialized activity practiced by the few means that it can become an alibi for the mass's non-cultural life. In this sense, art is a justification for exploitation and oppression. Marx notes that human activity constitutes social reality through praxis; and truth is gained through process, the process of self-development; or, as Marx more famously put it, the rounded individual of mature communism is a hunter in the morning, an angler in the afternoon, and a critical critic at night – without being defined socially as either a hunter, an angler or a critic. Lest for the Adornians all this talk of praxis and process seems too busy, perhaps one of those roles might be, as Fourier would have insisted, bed-tester or boatman. It is an unfreedom characteristic of class society that some people are charged with the task of being an artist, and bear that social role, while others are excluded from it. Conversely, marred by commodification, artistic practice today is a deformation of the sensuous unfolding of the self that indicates real human community. The reification of human activity into the separate realms of work and play, of aesthetics and politics is injurious and must be overcome. All culture might be assessed according to how it imagines all lives to be liveable. But only imagines, perhaps setting out only the barest, merest outlines, while it does not prescribe or illustrate. Intrinsic to this imagining is a social component: that the fantastic future is collectively conceived prior to being collectively realized. In capitalist times of output, throughput, outcomes, product, such process is hard to discern and difficult to document. Collaboration, social labour, is that which is so often not shown. Therein lies our future promise.

ENDNOTES

1. Fourier wanted to realize his plans, but the one experiment during his lifetime in 1833 produced a travesty of his ideas and Fourierist communities in the New World of American in 1840's fell victim to state repression, internal schisms over doctrine and financial insecurities.

2. See Benjamin W, 1999, 'Arcades Project', Harvard University Press, Cambridge MA, p419.

3. Adorno T, 1978, 'Minima Moralia: Reflections From Damaged Life', Verso, London, p516

4. Adorno T, 1984, 'Aesthetic Theory', Routledge & Kegan Paul, London, p446

5. Adorno T, 1977, 'Commitment Aesthetics and Politics', ed. by Ronald Taylor NLB, London, p180

6. Adorno T, 1984, 'Aesthetic Theory', Routledge & Kegan Paul, London, p48

7. Adorno T, [1953], 1986, 'Individual and Organisation', Gesammelte Schriften vol. VIII, Suhrkamp, Frankfurt/Main, p456

8. See UNESCO website, www.unesco.org.uk/

9. See UNESCO website, www.unesco.org.uk/

10. Adorno T, Horkheimer M, [1947], 1989, 'The Culture Industry: Enlightenment as Mass Deception', Dialectic of Enlightment Verso, London, pp120-167

11. See UNESCO website, www.unesco.org.uk/

Section 3
Speakers

Beyond Collaboration
Rasheed Araeen

Transcript of a talk and paper
given by Rasheed Araeen with
questions from John Roberts

Contributors

Rasheed Araeen (RA)
John Roberts (JR)
Mel Jordan (MJ)
Andy Hewitt (AH)
Becky Shaw (BS)

JR: I'm just going to offer a few introductory remarks before Rasheed gives his paper. One of the reasons, Rasheed has agreed to talk with me this afternoon, was that I have recently been collaborating with Rasheed on a special issue of Third Text, on the very subject of collaboration. So this is something that has been the subject of our joint thinking, over the last couple of years. Having said that, I'll let Rasheed start.

RA: Thank you John. Well the title of my paper is *Beyond Collaboration*. Maybe I should give a brief introduction to the paper before I go ahead. You can ask me if there are any problems in not understanding what I'm saying, or if there are contradictions or unresolved things in the paper, we can discuss them later on. 'Recently a friend of mine asked me, and I quote, 'Why would we need the intellectual creativity of artists to conceive and manage dam building projects?'

He was of course responding to my proposition of Nominalism, in which I had suggested the building of a dam in Baluchistan (which is in Pakistan) as a work of art. What is implicit in this question are two things: - If dam-building is something which was already there as a recognized activity of a civil engineer, and dams are always built to store and conserve water, why is it necessary for an artist to suggest dam-building and what is new about it? Although this is an extremely pertinent question, as it goes to the heart of the matter, it somehow betrays a lack of historical knowledge and makes us re-engage in what was already somewhat settled quite a while ago. If we look at the whole thing historically, from Duchamp's ready-mades to 1960s conceptualists' land art, it becomes clear that what lay behind artists' attempt to enter into the territories of others was to confront what separated and isolated their work from the work of everyday life. A mere depiction of everyday life in their work would not help much. It would still maintain the separation, as the depicted life would become an aestheticized object. It was necessary for the artist to enter into everyday life itself and demolish the very process that created aesthetic and non-aesthetic categories.

The issue is therefore not about dam building, but about art. How far art can go to intervene with existing things, and in the process redefine its own role in the productivity of everyday life. It was to push the role of art to function as an agent of material change in society that led me to the idea of the dam. And this reference to them is what I wrote under the title of Nominalism.

This idea has resulted not only from my specific experience of land in Baluchistan and its specific social condition, but, more importantly, from my preoccupation with the question of art. The situation that I initially faced was not how to make the arid land productive, but how to express this experience through a work of art that is historically significant, but which also intervenes in the object of this experience and transforms it into a socially meaningful process beyond it merely becoming an art object open to commodification and reification.

What I am trying to do here is to stress

the primacy of art. It is art that takes the form of a dam, or for that matter, any other form from everyday life, and in the process, by becoming part of life re-defines its role not only as a sensuous object but also a transformer of society. The result may or may not be recognizable as a work of art; in fact it is important that what is conceived, as art remains an everyday object or phenomenon in order to function as part of life.

Collaboration is fundamental to this role of art. Depending on the nature of the project, it must include people from all walks of life and all professions, forming a collective so that art is no longer an individual activity or an expression of individualism. However, it should not just be a collaboration for the sake of collaboration, but must lead to a model that serves an organizing function and confronts the values based on individual ownership of property. It must go beyond a mere collaboration between artists and involve not only professional individuals from different disciplines but also a non-specialist labour force. It must, in the end, produce a process that remains attached to its being an idea of art but it must also go beyond. In other words, it must lead a double life: on the one hand, it is conceptual artwork but, on the other, its material form must become independent of whether it is a work of art or not. Only when it can escape from being merely an art concept or form, can it avoid its reification, and only then can it continue to maintain its transformative function within the productive force of the everyday life.

Although what I propose as a collaborative practice, results in a material form – it may be a farm, I mean, it will be an agricultural farm, a factory, a supermarket, a transport system, etc – collectively run, and owned by the workers themselves – I continue to call it a conceptual artwork. Why? Because it is not possible to get rid of art as a special category, or completely dissolve it in other things so long as there exists capitalism and its division of labour. Art will remain art and things will remain things, and art will return to its traditional roots and its social function again, becoming trapped within its own institutional framework. In

other words, arts' function as a liberating force is dependent, not only on it becoming something other than art, but its own liberation as a material practice from its containment within the art institution.

Historically, to put in simple terms, collaborative art practice emerged when it was realized that art was being made only for a few people whose interests and privilege were detrimental to the interest of the whole society; and the main cause of this was the isolation and the alienation of the individual artist from the masses and their aspirations and the struggle for a better society. What was then needed was to get rid of the individual practice, offering not only a critique of art privileged and legitimized by the bourgeoisie but also producing art for the interest of people. This shift towards a collaborative practice has recently taken up new dynamics with the emergence of new ideas and political

theory as a resistance to the globalization of capitalist economy and the collapse of the autonomy of the enlightened bourgeois art institution and its total dissolution in the globalized art market forces. But in most cases, this shift has occurred only partially and has failed to go beyond what I would describe as a discourse of difference and reactivity. Being trapped in bourgeois altruism, it has somewhat failed to create a radical alternative that would not only offer a revolutionary model for the re-organization of society but also make artists relinquish their individual social positions and privileges in favour of a collective empowerment of people.

In my critique of altruism, as part of my initial formulation of Nominalism, I have given the impression that I exclude the role of altruism altogether from the collaborative art practice that is meant to empower others. Altruism does help the needy others, particularly in times of their extreme distress, such as in famine, violent conflict or wars, but it does not usually empower them so that they could avoid this distress occurring in the future. This does not mean that altruism can be dismissed altogether from human relationships. In fact, altruism can act as a stepping-stone towards the empowerment of the deprived or oppressed. Let me take an example from art to show what I mean by this. This example illustrates a failure of collaborative work, although its claim was to intervene in people's lives and cause its transformation, it even failed to enter it. Its potential to enter everyday work was there,

but was not realized. Had there been an altruism that transferred the arts' material resources to the people to carry on the work, the works' ultimate result would have been different.

I refer here to the last work of Joseph Beuys, his proposition for the planting of 7000 trees in Kassel in 1982. The importance of this work lies in it being a collaborative work, and it physically exists in the public space. Its aim was, in Beuys own words, 'to make a symbolic start for regenerating the life of human kind, and to prepare a positive future.' Although for Beuys this project was meant to be a symbolic start, its real ambition was to

go beyond it and become part of people's life – their everyday work. In Beuys' own words – and I quote – 'We shall never stop planting.' But despite good intentions and laudable ambition, why did the whole thing fail? Why did it remain trapped in its initial idea and fail to go beyond it and become an actual phenomenon of tree planting worldwide as Beuys himself wanted? The first problem here is of perception. How do we see the role of art – particularly when it is a collaborative practice that enters the public domain for the interest of the public? Should art merely be a prescription for the public to follow? If it is a question of tree planting, the public doesn't need Beuys to tell them to do so. In fact, millions of trees have since been planted worldwide by people themselves and without Beuys' symbolic start. But the point is not about tree planting, it is about art. How could it go beyond a symbolic gesture and become part of the material reality of the world?

Joseph Beuys was one of the most celebrated artists of his time, and he had enormous resources – both intellectual and material. By the time he created the work of tree planting, the art institutional power had turned him into a modern shaman. And thus, anything he touched became art. His tree planting was a work of a shaman. Others could enter his space and collaborate with him, but only as a function of his power, the power, which was bestowed upon him by the art institution. And therefore, although Beuys' work of planting trees could not be materialized without the participation of non-art collaborators, it was assumed that this collaboration had to be contained within the art institutional framework in order to maintain its status as a work of art. It could not thus go out and enter the domain of public where it could be transformed into an actual tree-plating exercise. It may be said that Beuys had no choice, it was essential for him to maintain the status of his art as art. But I want to argue differently.

Beuys' basic failure lies in his inability to think beyond the art institutional constraints. He could not think that if he wanted his work to become part of people's life it was necessary for his work to exist

at two levels: both as what is legitimized by the bourgeois art institution but also as non-art within the collective domain of people's daily life. It was only then, tree planting as art could have become an art movement with the participation of people all over the world.

What was in fact required, moreover, was Joseph Beuys' altruism. He had enough resources to set up an organization to support and finance actual tree planting by people themselves. But, if he had transferred his project from the confines of the art institutional space to the domain of the public, and handed it over to the people with the material resources, required to fulfil his ambition, would this have diminished the status of his work as art? I don't think so. On the contrary this would have given an added dimension to his work as art, and also given some power to those without whose participation Beuys' ambition for a social intervention has remained unfulfilled.

I am of course not suggesting that this would have created a revolutionary praxis, or led to a destabilization of the system and created conditions for a revolution. Art alone cannot do such things, but it can set up organizational structures – both symbolic and material – that can empower people without whose revolutionary struggle nothing can change. The mass of landless farmers and jobless workers alone cannot produce a revolutionary situation either, particularly when they can no longer be organized together as part of national struggles. Hungry bellies cannot stand up and fight this system. They must have some resources to provide them with basic needs of life before they can organize themselves as a resistance to the system.

What I am talking about here is not about the revolutionary struggle, but a transitory stage between the bourgeois consciousness and revolutionary consciousness. This stage provides us with means to intervene both in the bourgeois consciousness and a stepping-stone into the world of people's struggle against it. If bourgeois altruism can facilitate this double life of art, so be it. But we should not allow altruism to determine and dominate life.

The point of all of this is that it is not enough to shift art from an individual practice to a collaborative work. History tells us that even collaborative groups or collectives often become self-serving organizations or closed shops, producing art objects, which end up in the art market or museums. The example here is of the artists' village in the Netherlands called Atelier van Lieshout.

Even those collaborative works that claim today to provide a radical alternative to the capitalist, market-orientated art, often end up as alternative art forms or processes within the control of those who initiate and produce these works. They seldom escape from this control and become part of people's own resources. Many collaborative groups or collectives now work directly with people to help them with their needs. But when this collaboration with people ends, the whole thing begins to collapse. Not because people don't have an ability to carry on with the work, but without the continuous availability of resources, the work cannot proceed further. Instead it becomes consolidated in favour of the artists' collectives, which promote themselves exclusively on the basis of the groups' own identities. In other words, despite their engagement with people they continue to act as something separate and superior. We can see these collectives showing their work in international biennales and their work discussed in art journals, but outside of the art world, they have little impact.

The picture I have painted here is of a general situation. There are of course exceptions, but it is important that distinction is made between the collaborative work as a closed shop and that which allows people to take over the work, with all its resources and ownership, and turn it into a continuing process as part of people's own struggle for self-empowerment, as well as a tool of resistance against the system. Collaboration for the sake of collaboration is little different from the art -for -arts sake's syndrome.

Recent ideas of collaboration do represent a radical shift in our thinking about art, its presence and its role in the world. But, despite this shift, is this not a paradox that there is no network, or an emergence of movement that can bring together various groups or collectives together not only to exchange ideas but to work together, and in parallel with people's world-wide struggle for economic resources, equality and justice? Without such a network or movement, this shift has little significance.

JR: OK Thank you, Rasheed. What I'm going to do is respond to Rasheed's paper with some questions and then open it up to the audience.

What was crucial to avant-garde thinking in that period was the idea that the artist might be able to work freely with certain engineers, scientists, workers and other social technicians in order to transform not only what art might be, but also the very nature of social reality. And more than that also transform the nature of what it was to be an artist and to be a non-artist. So could you explain a little bit about how your work coincides with that?

RA: I don't know exactly. Maybe there isn't a major difference between that model and what I'm proposing but there is a historical difference. You see that model was conceived within the framework and situation, which was already transformed into a revolutionary situation. They were in the midst of revolution. But we don't have that situation now. We are living in a situation, which is not easily definable. I propose that it should be seen as a transitory state, because a struggle has not ended. We might have said that recently, but we have not given up the struggle. The arrangements needed for the revolution are there. We have to reorganize differently. So, within that context, I'm proposing a model, which is a model based on altruism.

JR: Could you elaborate a bit more on what you mean by your model as having an organizing function because at the end of your paper you talked about collaboration in specifically democratic, or potentially democratic terms, that is, for you, a democratic model of collaboration has a necessity to involve, should we say, non-artists, the public, in its elaboration and development. So could you talk a little bit more about that, and how that might operate now in these conditions that you've just mentioned?

RA: Well, no, as there is no single answer to that question. It depends upon what the situation is. Is it a struggle of the working class or of the technologically advanced countries? Is it the struggle of the landless peasants in Asia or Africa? You see, it is very difficult to say – the basic tenet of my model is that, and it is only what I presume at this moment, and it doesn't have to be that way. I presume that some initiative has to come from somewhere. I'm proposing that this initiative can come out of the imaginative power of the artist. And then this can be taken to the worker, to the peasant, to the agricultural workers, and give them a role in developing that model, and will very much depend on their dialogue, on their discussion, but basically it should be based on the collective ownership of whatever you want to achieve. But here again, there is a problem. Even if you reach in the end, the farm or factory, which is owned by collective labour workers or peasants, it can still become a closed shop. If you look at what happened in vast countries, there was a very strong movement for the collective human but today it has degenerated into another capitalist, corporate organization. So, we have to develop models, not one model, and we have to link those models. We now have the technology through which all those models can be linked together with some kind of revolutionary consciousness.

JR: Do you think that the category of the artist then, is a redundant category? In your talk, you talked a little bit about Joseph Beuys and of course, Beuys' most famous formulation was that everyone is an artist, would you concur with that?

RA: No. It was an anti-slogan. What he was saying was this: 'Everybody is an artist but I'm the genius!'

MJ: Yeah, everyone can be an artist but I'm the best artist!

JR: Yes so some artists are more 'artist' than others. You were very disparaging about Joseph Beuys, for good reasons, but of course there are other socially participatory models of collaboration than Beuys. I know that you have been quite interested in the writings of Boris Arvatov.

Who was, to put a label on it, a soviet productivist theorist, and an artist, thinker, during the early years of the Russian Revolution. He argued for a model of the artist as someone who could work on many fronts simultaneously, and through that process simultaneously dissolve him or herself, into everyday social practice.

RA: Yes. I agree with that. But he didn't have a perception of the kind of non-art position, which emerged out of those days, as a critical practice – because there wasn't any need for the idea of the collective within the revolution. What he needed to do was improve conditions, it was like no art and class movement existed, you know. Basically, he wanted to improve the condition of the industrial worker. And he wanted to start to breed the industrial work at the level of artwork.

JR: That's right, in the end, in his model of collaboration between artist and non-artist it became subordinate to the demands of heavy industry. And improved design and so forth and clearly we are in a very different historical moment.

RA: The other point, the question of the artist taking a different role; in my model art is also taking a different role. When the art is living in the institution, it is one role, when the art is living with the people, involved with the people, and producing art rather than developing something then that relationship is different. There may come a time, you know, the whole relationship becomes dissolved together, I don't know when and how, probably between a revolutionary situation.

JR: I'm becoming aware of time; we'll open up the discussion to the floor, would anybody like to ask a question?

BS: I was thinking about your quote – an art process or artwork to lead a double life – the best example of this I could think of and the one that always gave me the most problem was from Alan Kaprow's book, *The Blurring of Art and Life*. Alan Kaprow uses an example of his friend who was really sick of being an artist, I think he was actually quite a well known artist, he got really fed up of it and he decided he was going to be a candidate in a local election

in the States; he runs for candidate and he gets elected, and he has an amazing term where he makes a massive amount of difference in his locality. At the end of it, another friend, who happens to be Paul McCarthy, says "So you'll have to call that art now, because that was your artwork". And the man didn't actually enter into it as artwork he just wanted to run for election, but then it becomes articulated as art. For me this made it fantastic because it's not a work that I ever heard of again apart from in this one book but it did, for one minute hold that double life of both being actual change and an artwork. And my problem with this model is that I just don't understand how it won't become assimilated and just become the same as everything else. How do you stop it from becoming assimilated into the art market as an artwork and then losing its tension?

RA: Of course it will be assimilated if it enters the institution, but, if there is a material production of that idea, it can exist in the institution independently whatever happens to the idea. That's what I mean by a double life. It's not new. Take the famous painting, the Mona Lisa – there are a thousand million prints around the world – they have no value as the work of art but they have a value as a commodity, as a product, as an image. People look at it and enjoy it. They like to hang it on the wall. But the actual artwork is in the museum, so the artwork has a double-life. So even in those cases you know it can be art and non-art, although people take it as art. Because there now exists awareness in society, that even when they buy a print, you buy it on the basis of it being art – but its very material existence is very different from what is inside the museum, within the institution. With regard to what I said about Joseph Beuys, if he had allowed and supported people to plant tress all over the world, he had the resources, the money left after his death was sixteen million dollars. Now if that had happened, tree-planting would have taken place in the name of Joseph Beuys it would have not affected the original idea of tree planting – it would still be regarded as an artwork, it would be talked about in art history books. At the same time it would have had

a connection with the actual tree planting all over the world. That's what I mean, artwork existing at two ends.

MJ: I wanted to ask something, about collaboration in art, and I might be being really literal about this but it seems like we are sort of calling for a collectiveness in the name of art. Can you comment on this please?

JR: This is a question to do with philosophy and aesthetics. What kinds of things come into play when you are engaged in making art, either by yourself or with others? What are those things? Are they usually things that connect to playfulness? To non-functional or non-instrumental ways of doing things? Different kinds of, forms of attention that you would take etc.

RA: As a whole, you mean? You mean in an organizational structure?

MJ: Yes, I was just interested in, how art could bring a sort of democracy to these collective situations that we were talking about, of ownership of land or of a dam etc. I was just wondering how art could help establish these sorts of collectives.

RA: Let's be clear, if we take the debate on an instrumental level. If we are only thinking of building a dam, for the benefit of people, the community which is benefiting from the dam, should organize itself as a collective based on classic ownership of the whole thing. This can be achieved without the artist, no, you don't need them.

What I'm saying is, aren't we constructing the role of the artist to conceive the thing because, they are within the grasp of the artist because artists can think in a non-instrumental way, in terms of pure idea. And then it can take water. It's very difficult for an Indian; of course I'm not saying there are no socially conscious Indians. But I want to bring the whole debate into art, what is after all the purpose of art now? If its purpose is only to document life; how we live, their films, their photography, they are very damn useful. They are so useful. Even to allow people who want Sunday painting, they are useful; they are part of people's lives, because they enjoy making paintings on Sunday. It is part of their creativity, that's my thoughts on art and the world. I'm talking about art as a historically developed idea. That idea has reached the point where it is needed to be integrated into life and become part of a whole and that is one of the things I'm suggesting we can do this way. I don't know if that has answered your question.

JR: Walter Benjamin, the German writer talked about this problem in terms of the possible development of art as social technique, or what he called in German 'technick', that is 'technick' for him wasn't simply technology plus technique, rather it was the very transformation of the world of appearances of essential appearance through art. Would you agree with that? In contrast to that, what we have at the moment is simply technologies and art or the occasional meeting at institutions like this I suppose, bar the technology. We don't actually have art and technology as 'technick', as a social force, something that is actually embedded in everyday life.

RA: I don't know if you are talking in terms of its ultimate achievement or in the process of reaching that achievement.

JR: Well I'm just trying to get a handle on what it is you actually hope for from your model of collaboration. I've just brought up this question of technology, because we haven't so far mentioned the place of technology within your arguments – how might we get to this place you are talking about?

RA: I haven't put it in this paper, I haven't proposed any model. What I have done in this paper is to explore how collaborative art practices can go beyond collaboration, unfortunately that point, how we develop collaboration, hasn't fully developed. I have to think in global terms, how can we create links and create movement. I was only thinking of the models which were already available to me like the Russian model, what Joseph Beuys did, what the land artists around America tried to do, all those things, so I based my argument on that and I have suggested what Joseph Beuys did – he could have gone beyond. And it could have become a process. It

could have become a model. Wherever art leaves its institution, not denying its existence without, but extending itself into public domain and becoming non-art. But the link is there between non-art and art. The people themselves can also recognize it as art as they develop their awareness. I don't exclude that so this is the model, a hypothetical model. If you are asking me how I am going to achieve my own model, that's a different question, I don't think I'm discussing that here.

JR: OK, let me put a philosophical conundrum to you then, if what's important about your model or non-model is the disillusion of art into non-art, but at the same time we need to hold on to this category of art, how do we recognize art when it's non-art?

RA: It would be recognized because disillusion is always recognized. How do we recognize art now? How do we recognize art? I did my minimalist sculpture in 1965. It was the first minimalist sculpture done in Britain; it should have gone into history books, why didn't it go into history books? Because it's not dependent on people. It's dependent on the kind of work, which could only be recognized by the institution, through institution mediation. Because they did not offer institution mediation – it's not a work of art. After I showed in the Hayward Gallery it was thrown on the junkyard. Do you know that? Would they have thrown Henry Moore's work on the junkyard? Or Anthony Caro's work on the junkyard? They said they had no place to keep it. So how do we recognize a work of art, John you can tell us?

JR: Well, artworks are recognized as artworks when they are nominated as artworks.

RA: Exactly.

JR: By the institutions of art. If they are not recognized by the institutions of art then they don't get nominated as art. It's as simple as that.

MJ: And maybe Beuys' work could have that double life because it was Beuys.

RA: It was already nominated as a work of art. And if it had gone into the public domain it would have not lost the understanding of it as art. But if he was not an artist and if you'd gone into the public saying let us plant trees that would, of course be a good thing, but that would have nothing to do with art. You can call it a paradox. It is a philosophical question. I don't know if you believe it is resolvable. There are contradictions with which we have to put up with, to carry on the work itself I think it's in the process of the work itself those contradictions might be resolved as the conscience develops, as the people themselves take hold of things themselves and begin to transform.

JR: Any more questions?

BS: I've been trying to read some Adorno and I've read the introduction and not got particularly far, and there is a bit where the editor says that Adorno was very uncomfortable with how knowledge and subjects are compartmentalized, sociology, philosophy and art etc. And very simply, he talked about how one of the problems with life is that what's seen as manual labour, is separated from mass production and art. It seems that in a very simple way this kind of model you are talking about is a big effort of bringing all those things together, and so, when you said just then about the material of the bridge being important I suddenly thought, the fact that it is this big material object is really important, because you are squeezing the intellectual and manual labour together.

RA: Yes that would be possible only when the material thing is there and in the possession of people. On the other hand, what land artists have been doing is taking life processes and documenting them, and then taking those photographic documents into the museum. And once the photograph had come into the museum, what they had documented was life as it is, as if there was no intervention within it. It was a pure operation of the life processes. What I'm saying is I want to reverse these processes. I'm really critical of Joseph Beuys, that particular work. But I also admire that work because it has potential. We can use that model to critique it and push it further, that's why I keep on using it. There were only three trees planted. One was in New York, one was in Sydney and one was in Oslo. So it remained as an artwork.

JR: Shall we close there? Well, thanks to everybody for coming.

AH: Yeah, and before we all scatter can I just say, thanks to Rasheed and John for their contributions.

Public Art and Citizenship: From Public Spaces to Public Spheres[1]
Malcolm Miles

Introduction

My topic is public art and citizenship. I approach it with a number of questions in mind: about public art, which became a specialist area of art practice and management from the late 1960s; and about citizenship, today increasingly drawn into a rhetoric of normative behaviour; and about where (literally and figuratively) public art and citizenship are located. One question is whether public art commissioned in urban redevelopment constitutes a new generation of public monuments, no longer to lend the legitimacy of history to a regime, but now to lend an equivalent status to the power of capital. Another question, given that monumental spaces are generally designed to constrain rather than liberate the citizen, is whether public space is an appropriate site for intervention on the part of those who challenge the current state of power. If not, a third question must be what else is viable, which may be the most interesting. But there are questions too, about citizenship. An obvious one is what it means and whether anything of the aspiration to be free, which can be read into the appearance

of a modern subjectivity in Europe in the sixteenth and seventeenth centuries, can be reclaimed. But at the same time, there is a need to ask how this aspiration, which shaped and depended on the idea of a unitary human subject, might be transposed into post-modernity. That is, to read it as a subjectivity now experienced as endlessly contingent, while encroached on by a globalized network of capital itself fashioned by globalized media, leisure, and entertainment industries, in which the art world is at least in part subsumed. And while I note the claims made in sociology and cultural studies for consumption as a means to identity (or subject) formation, I am unsure that consumers really play the market's games on *their* terms rather than *its* terms - buying, as it were, the dreams the manufacturers make available.[2]

So, while I want to reclaim citizenship from consumerism, my enquiry begins unevenly since I have no equivalent wish to reclaim public art. Much of it seems either an effort to lend urban redevelopment a mask of cultural value, or reproduces the post-war Arts Council notion that there is a public good in widening access to the kind of culture favoured by its staff; or is merely inept.

Transcript of a talk and paper given by Malcolm Miles with questions from Becky Shaw

Contributors
Malcolm Miles (MM)
Andy Hewitt (AH)
Mel Jordan (MJ)
Members of the Audience
(MA1, MA2, MA3)
Becky Shaw (BS)

There are, of course, exceptions. But the kind of intervention I find most interesting today does not situate itself exclusively in public spaces but moves between a range of sites inside and outside the gallery, and deals with issues for both broad and art world constituencies. There is an enjoyable irony in Hewitt and Jordan's *The Economic Function*, in Sheffield in 2004, when a piece of public art commissioned by a national public art network states that, 'the economic function of public art is to increase the value of private property.'

It probably no longer matters whether such a work is called public art, or art. It operates in a terrain in which the boundaries between art, design, and media have been deconstructed and which is now informed by factors such as activism and environmentalism the content of political campaigns that may begin around a single issue but soon move into global networks of resistance. Oliver Ressler, for instance, states that,

I call myself an artist rather than an activist, because I see myself more as an artist who realizes some of his work in relation to activism than an activist with a background as an artist.[3]

In contrast, the term public art implies attachment to a monumental tradition aspiring to permanence and clear-cut boundaries. I would argue this is no less the case for, say, 1970s painted and rusted steel sculptures as for naturalism; and that the removal of the plinth does not indicate a newly democratic art form. The question, after all, is more who determines who or what shall be represented than the mode in which it is done. Advocacy for public art, however, has achieved a professionalization of the practice and in particular of its management, with increased budget levels for international-status artists, while localized connections to the environmental, social, and cultural needs of specific publics are overlooked.

But my aim is not to paint a picture of unrelieved gloom. Alternatives exist to remind us that just as we are conditioned by our circumstances so we can intervene in the conditions which condition us: imaginatively to move them, if modestly, in new directions.

I begin with three contexts for a debate on public art and citizenship: that of globalization; that of public art as an adjunct of the art world; and that of modernity and its characteristic construction of a subject. I question the privileging of public spaces in urban design, and as sites for public art, to suggest there is a difference between these physical and geographical sites of a public realm and a more ambivalent, perhaps less visible, public sphere of social interaction. I then refer to some current practices (among many others) which, to me, suggest alternative means of operating in contemporary urban societies and which are less insertions in monumental spaces and more interventions in a public sphere.

Globalization

The New Urban (referring to slide) is a world of globalized consumption encountered in malls from Baltimore to Barcelona and in waterfront developments in which the literal signs of affluence – the familiar global brands of fast food, fizzy drinks and entertainment – appear in the global 'American' language. This realm includes new flagship cultural institutions too, such as Tate Modern in London and the international outlets of the Guggenheim brand of contemporary (late modern) art, as in Bilbao. The publics for these sites may arrive by air via the 'non-places', as Augé calls them (1997), of airport departure lounges. Or they may be from the host city. In Barcelona the planning authority sees malls as places in which young people can meet, not only for consumption. For Zygmunt Bauman (1998), such sites cater for a new global class of consumers. They are differentiated in their mobility from a more abject class of economic migrants and asylum seekers for whom crossing national (or other) borders is made increasingly difficult in a world which is increasingly dis-ordered under the banner of a new world order. He writes:

Thrown into a vast open sea with no navigation charts and all the marker buoys sunk and barely visible, we have only two choices left: we may rejoice in the breath-taking vistas of new discoveries – or we may tremble out of fear of drowning. One opinion not really realistic is to claim sanctuary in a safe harbour.[4]

The last remark cancels the aesthetic dimension. I am not sure trembling is an option either, in that it probably leads fairly quickly to drowning or being sucked under by the after-tow of the sinking hull of modernity. But if only complicity remains, with neither swimming away allowed nor anywhere to swim to, there are complexities. There may even be a creative tension between consumption and a latent utopianism. The latter is rendered uncanny in the mall, likened to the ersatz world of Disneyland, but does not entirely depart the affluent city. And while Bauman argues: 'it is often said that the consumer market seduces its customers. But in order to do so it needs customers who want to be seduced', understanding that compulsion may be more interesting than bemoaning its effects. Bauman notes it's masking as consumer choice, and adds, 'The consumer is a person on the move and bound to remain so';[5] but this does not explain why seduction is possible.

The goods and services on offer in affluent consumption have little use value and are more often signs of status. Thorstein Veblen noted this (1899) in his theory of conspicuous consumption, though now the status-giving objects are more ephemeral, in many cases not objects at all, but say, being a habitué of a particular art gallery or bar. Conrad Lodziak provides what seems a viable explanation, drawing on a traditional sociology of class. He asserts that 'for at least three-quarters of the populations of the so-called affluent societies the manipulation of this need [to survive] by the social system imposes on them a pattern of consumption relevant to survival';[6] and continues that such consumption appears to those implicated to be compulsory. This he explains through the theory of alienation: 'the alienation of labour ensures that most people do not possess the resources that enable them to produce for their own needs'.[7]

Another viewpoint might read the array of visual spectacles in the mall as an extension of the arrays of goods from all around the world first glimpsed in the arcades of Paris from the 1830s to the 1860s – a visual display which is a key component of modernity, set in an architecture engineered of cast iron and glass. For Walter Benjamin these displays were not only objects of a fetishistic gaze (on which Georg Simmel had previously written) but invoked a latent utopianism – cornucopia as sign for a Land of Cockaigne – which he saw as potentially awakening other forms of utopian imagination in the apprehending subject. This is linked to, but the inverse of alienation, a reaction in terms of an intuition that there is a world (usually situated in an as yet unrealized future), which is indisputably better than that of present conditions. Just as the Nazis saw the advantage in stealing, so to say, the clothes of the left when they appropriated their tactics such as the torchlight procession, so the market knows that this imaginative utopianism can be appropriated for consumption – and must remain unsatisfied to produce future consumption. It is like foreplay without intercourse, or, as Adorno says in another context, requires the diner to be satisfied with the menu in the absence of the meal. This does not mean the imagined more just and more joyful world is invalidated.

Consumption, however, can be all consuming. It strengthens the tendency to new social formation observed by Louis Wirth as specific to urban (or metropolitan) societies. Seeing urban dwellers as unable to exert control over their environments and no longer parties to traditional structures of support such as the geographically specific social group or family, he says:

While on the one hand the traditional ties of human association are weakened, urban existence involves a much greater degree of interdependence and a more complicated, fragile, and volatile form of mutual inter-relations over many phases of which the individual as such can exert scarcely any control.[8]

This is remarkably post-modern for 1938, when it was first published; and reads the modern unitary subject as defunct.

Consumption, though, increases the degree of non-control, moulding diverse demands, which arise from what Lodziak might see as the needs of survival into a unified request for membership of

consumerism. Sharon Zukin writes:

Styles that develop on the streets are cycled through mass media where, divorced from their social context, they become images of cool. On urban billboards advertising designer perfumes or jeans, they are recycled to the streets, where they become a provocation, breeding imitation and even violence. The cacophony of demands for justice is translated into a coherent demand for jeans.[9]

If Zukin is right, then globalized consumerism marks an end to the project of liberty and equality, which can be seen as phase two of modernity after the inception of the subject. Whether such concepts are sustainable or inherently flawed – sinking with the ship of liberal humanism – is too large a question for this paper. But – as a bar in Manchester's Castlefield district proclaims – Revolution in funny letters is a sign for designer drinking (referring to slide). Down the canal is another called Choice. So there you have it (or go without).

The issue here is the effect an emphasis on consumption has on the discussion of the public realm. Increasingly, urban redevelopment is thought by the public and private sector alike to be effectively driven either by flagship cultural institutions, such as MACBA in Barcelona (referring to slide), or by blue-chip property schemes likely to be sites for public art and to include some open space. The uses of such spaces, and the users, tend to be unidentified – the generalized inhabitants of a permanently piazza-sitting society who neither go to work nor go to the toilet, nor exist. Public space, it seems, has become yet another badge of affluence like public art before it. This is not to say that citizens cannot re-appropriate the spaces provided, as some do, but it is to say that discussion has moved towards a narrow concern for public space, rather than for the multi-use and transitional spaces in which everyday urban living takes place.

To assume that public debate occurs in public spaces trades on a mythicization of the public square, or in north America the commons, as where people of different genders, races, ages, and classes mixed and formed opinions as to the common good. My guess is that, from classical Athens to Boston in the late eighteenth century,

these sites were not open but gendered and racialized.

Where then, does public life take place? Elizabeth Wilson writes of Vienna before 1918:

Public social life was important in Vienna. The Corso section of the Ring saw the daily promenade of Viennese society, and the Viennese cafés were centres of intellectual discussion.[10]

If the café was important then (though exclusively for men), in Armenia pre-1989 it was in the kitchen that: 'underground discussions were going on and alternative thought was formed'.[11] To privilege public space in urban design denies this mutability. Public space is not, in any case, a site of democracy but of power: it is in public plazas that processions and executions are held and since the mid-nineteenth century, that public monuments co-opt history to the regime. This is not to say it does not matter when public space is privatized but that there is a need to identify what can be replaced or redeemed, or cannot. The non-planned is improvised and does not translate into design. Yet it is public spaces which have been colonized by art since the late 1960s. Claims are made for place identity, local distinctiveness and a contribution to economic growth, while it may be more accurate to say that commissioning a sculpture by Oldenburg and van Bruggen in Middlesborough, say, was an attempt to put that city on a footing with Barcelona, which also has one. This is not the aim stated by public authorities who more often repeat the undemonstrable claims to various kinds of efficacy made in public art's advocacy. Birmingham sees its record of commissioning public art and its new public squares, instead, as an aspect of its claim to be a city of culture (but was not successful in its bid to be nominated a European Capital of Culture for 2008, which went to Liverpool, home of a branch of Tate). Meanwhile commerce knows that opinions are formed not in the plaza but in spaces of communication like the mobile phone – or the Orange Bus (referring to slide).

Art worlds

A genealogy of public art might trace two contrasting roots in the late 1960s:

a move out of the gallery by artists seeking to defy the commodification and institutionalization of mainstream art; and efforts by disenfranchised groups to gain visibility and to broadcast their political positions at street level, as in wall paintings. These never coincided. They have different histories, the former in an aesthetic tradition and the latter more in community mobilization. A further rift occurred when practitioners of both public and community-based or street-level arts tended not be employed in art school teaching posts which connected those who were so employed not only to a regular salary but also to the semi-formal networks of opportunity which feed the consensus of taste.

Yet the history of public art, differentiated from street-level art, can be read, as within that of mainstream art when the mainstream itself is constructed as a sequence of departures. Each departure then becomes the next link in the mainstream in a trajectory, which shifts from politicized progressiveness in the 1850s to stylistic revolution in the 1950s, given its most reductive form by Clement Greenberg. So, from Romanticism to Realism and through the various secessions of the 1890s, art became a graduated withdrawal. While, obviously, a product of the conditions of its production, art from the 1880s onwards ceased to attempt to change those conditions and turned instead – perhaps as reaction to the defeat of radical art in the Paris Commune in 1871 – towards an aestheticism seen as self-contained, a world in which yearnings could be expressed and even satisfied, but which was ever beyond the materialities and actualities of social formation. In one way artists sought to gain control over their activities by organizing independent exhibitions; but in another they saw in solitude and that transcendent aesthetic the regressive omnipotence that is allowed in a world of make-believe. Now, art's refusals of the art object – from 1960s happenings and 1970s conceptualism to live art – are subsumed by a market trading on reputations instead of objects.

For Martha Rosler, art is part of the global entertainment industry:

The anti-institutional revolt was unsuccessful, and the art world has now completed something of a paradigm shift. *The mass culture machine and its engines of celebrity have long redefined the other structures of cultural meaning, so that patterns of behaviour and estimations of worth in the art world are more and more similar to those in the entertainment industry.*[12]

Bringing the story more up to date, Esther Leslie's description of Tate Modern is apposite:

Tate Modern is a brand that niche-markets art experience. Its galleries are showrooms. However, this is still art and not just business. The commodity must not show too glossy a face. The reclamation of an industrial space that provides the shell for the Tate Modern lends the building a fashionably squatted aspect, like Berlin water towers or crumbling arcades that serve as edgy art galleries or music venues for a while. After religion and industry, the next great force is art. Its powers were to be harnessed to a bit of urban regeneration.[13]

Meanwhile other voices leave traces in incidental spaces, though it is not always clear what they mean.

Paradoxically, it is now as likely that critical voices will be encountered in the gallery as in public art. Commissioning processes tend to restrict freedom of political expression, substituting for it the transcendent aesthetic of modernism or a trivializing embellishment – today's answer to Victorian beautification, in both cases for which recipients are intended to be grateful – while in the work of some gallery artists an awkwardness appears, which breaks the routine and interrupts the narratives by which the dominant society maintains itself.

There are also moves to a newly critical tendency in curating, helpfully refusing to accept labels such as 'socially engaged art' as meaning as much as they say. For example, Claire Doherty writes on the danger of compromise in *New Institutionalism* (which attempts reform from within the art institution):

If the conventional gallery or museum is becoming a social space rather than a showroom, do we run the risk of creating a new set of conventions - the convention of role-play or prescribed participation - in a wider socio-political context of impotent democracy?

Furthermore, as art institutions adapt to include peripatetic and participatory practices in their programmes, declaring certain exhibitions or projects to be 'socially engaged', there may be little or no understanding of how to support the visitors' negotiation of a social space within the gallery.[14]

The practices, which Doherty criticizes, run parallel to expediency in cultural policy as art is increasingly seen not only as granting place-identity but also now as solving problems such as social exclusion. For me the difficulty is not just that the claims, like those of public art advocacy in the 1980s, are spurious and indemonstrable, but that the idea of a solution itself takes attention away from problems and means and directs it towards ends. In this context I believe in a world without end.

There are other tactics, other less ham-fisted forms of immersion in the world. Slovenian artist Marjetica Potrc, for example, works with gallery technical teams (who make decisions such as colour) to re-create the shanties and sheds of informal settlements and urban improvement schemes in non-affluent cities. Displaced to gallery spaces these become reminders that the majority world is very different from that of the world in which the term Art has currency. The structures are re-presented non-judgementally, disconnected from the scenarios and survival tactics of their inhabitants, to mirror back the estrangement of the gallery. They remind us, too, that those who make them in their original sites have an ingenuity of survival, which neither needs nor requests help from the agencies of our affluent society.

In another project, Potrc has used images of urban animal sightings – bears by the pool, a coyote in the elevator – grabbed from the internet and exhibited with them the (real but empty) canister of a pepper-spray manufactured to deter urban bears. She writes, under the heading *The Pursuit of Happiness*:

...animal sightings prove that city space is constantly negotiated. Furthermore, they draw attention to the creativity of border spaces in general.[15]

I read someplace that by 2100 national

states will have yielded to city states. If you can imagine that, it becomes clear that the idea of border space will change too. It will become a close proximity experience, all due to survival instincts, and of course, the selfish pursuit of happiness.

I wonder what kind of consumption will characterize this society of near-in borders and permanent negotiation.

Other cases of gallery (and digital) work which does not use public spaces to articulate its critique include John Goto's series of digital images, *Capital Arcades*, which take their compositions from the European tradition and re-populate them with contemporary shoppers; and Mierle Laderman Ukeles' work while artist in residence at the Wadworth Athenaeum, Hartford, Connecticut – a traditional museum. In *Cleaning the Mummy Case* Ukeles declared a glass case containing an Egyptian mummy as art – the case not the mummy. This might seem an arty gesture, but the significance is in that while cleaners are allowed to touch and clean cases, only curators can touch (and presumably also clean) objects classified as art. This gesture interrupted institutional routine and upset a hierarchy. The curators' patience was tried beyond endurance when Ukeles, on her last day at the museum, took possession of the keys to randomly lock and unlock doors, including those of the curatorial offices. This is not just funny; it impacts power. And it begins to touch on the construction of an autonomous subject, or a subjectivity, which assumes the autonomy of its actions, its self-determination of the plot of the drama in which it acts.

Subjects

This context will be briefly outlined, but it seems to me necessary as part of an understanding of the assumptions which shape both modern art's claim to aesthetic autonomy and the privileging of public space in urban design today. It is a lingering presence of liberal humanism in a deconstructed world, yet for me has elements – in particular rationality – which I cannot relinquish. This subject, too, seems to exhibit an ambivalent desire for permanence and, at the same time, a recognition of temporality (and consequent mortality). It is a subject which tries to script its life, perhaps to ornament it, but leaves the world crying "I have not finished!"[16]Its inception can be seen with a particular clarity in the history of English drama – when the domination of players in medieval drama by representations of vices, virtues, angels, and devils who contest for their souls, gives way to a plot in which the actors assume agency. Later, the proscenium arch and introduction of scenery add to the illusion of a theatre of characters.

Catherine Belsey situates the modern subject of liberal humanism at the point at which, with the English Revolution, the bourgeois class assume power of determination over the shape of English society:

The implication of the argument from staging is that the unified subject of liberal humanism is a product of the second half of the seventeenth century, an affect of the revolution. Liberal humanism, locating agency and meaning in the unified human subject, becomes an orthodoxy at the moment when the bourgeoisie is installed as the ruling class.[17]

Belsey goes on to point out that signs of this shift begin in the early 1640s, or earlier in Shakespeare and Marvell; and that the inalienable possession of the subject is interiority.

There, however, is a source of contradiction between the unity of the subject possessing interiority and the voices, which express it. In Hamlet, whose soliloquies are the exact vehicle of interiority, is madness, inertia, and dis-accord.

Belsey cites Francis Barker (1984) to affect that Hamlet establishes an authentic inner reality in duality with a thereby inauthentic exterior world, while the quest for Hamlet's subjectivity is 'endless, because the object of it is not there'.[19] Citing Barker that Hamlet's interiority is gestural, she continues:

It is as if the hero is traversed by the voices of a succession of morality fragments, wrath and reason, patience and resolution. In none of them is it possible to locate the true, the essential Hamlet.[20]

This is interesting not least because it has taken academics until recently – from the intervention of feminism in the 1970s –

to abandon, as some have, the objectivity of the third person voice in their professional writing, to replace it with that of the subjective first person. But Belsey brings the argument into the twentieth century in a discussion of dramatic suicide:

In the absolute act of suicide the subject itself is momentarily absolute. As an individual action, therefore, suicide is a threat to the control of the state. The democratic liberal-humanist state, claiming to represent the legitimate community, cannot afford to recognize an act of autonomy which it does not itself authorize. But the free west has now found a new way to put an end to finitude while simultaneously holding the subject in place within the community as the state defines it. The nuclear apocalypse, closing off in the moment of its fulfilment the desire to be absolute, is liberal humanism's diamond of unnamable desire.[21]

I remember the Aldermarston marches against nuclear weapons and thus find the passage strangely dated now. Yet it illuminates the reproduction of the terms of tyranny in the philosophy of the state which theorizes its rejection (as in the abolition of absolutism in the execution of its personification in a king in London in 1649) and replacement by a rationality which is both liberating from the vicissitudes of mysterious and remote Fate and – in its development in the histories of modernity – an assumption of power-over rather than the more radical power-to of self-empowerment. Of course, I cling to that disenchanted world as where an ending of unfreedom is negotiable and where a more direct democracy can test the limits of representation.[22]

Spaces and spheres

The spectre that haunts subjectivity is, apart from the hollow inside, its temporality. I think the public monument might be as much, in a way, a defence against this – for a society which accepts representation as its political structure, so that personal desire is subsumed in national policy just as personal grief is subsumed in national rites of mourning in the ceremonies performed at war memorials on certain anniversaries – as a device for the legitimation of regimes. The latter remains the case, as demonstrated in countless monuments

across Europe and North America. These utilize history, perhaps a quite remote history of which conveniently little is known so that almost any imprint can be put upon it, to lend a regime the inevitability of slabs of time too vast and heavy to be overturned. So, in the monument contrived for the millennium of Hungarian monarchy in Budapest, within the pre-1914 Austro-Hungarian Empire, Emperor Franz Joseph stands beside King Steven to span – as if seamlessly – a thousand years of history of which he, Franz Joseph, is the culmination. But it is also permanence as a condition of society, distinct from and above the lives of individuals, which is represented.

Augé writes:

The monument is an attempt at the tangible expression of permanence or, at the very least, duration. Gods need shrines, as sovereigns need thrones and palaces, to place them above temporal contingencies. They thus enable people to think in terms of continuity through the generations. The social space bristles with monuments which may not be directly functional but give every individual the justified feeling that, for the most part, they pre-existed him [sic] and will survive him. Strangely, it is a set of breaks and discontinuities in space that expresses continuity in time.[23]

Perhaps one reason for the general acceptance of elevation, as in the plinth and in the decision to view some individuals as models for society or as celebrities, is the need – as a survival tactic – to find continuity. The collective subject is then a mass of fragments, only the mythicized embodiment of power, the unified subject, the king of the castle.

To return to public space: this too, gives form to a myth of continuity. It represents the notion of a free and democratic society, which in effect is not free but subjected to the tyranny of representation. Yet when public space is privatized it is not surprising – from the above discussion – that efforts are made to preserve it. The difficulty is that preservation – I use a term suggesting heritage culture on purpose – may rely on a nostalgic concept of the city, one which differs in its unitary representation from the non-coherence and contingency of the cities in which, now, a majority of the planet's human inhabitants live. Those cities fall too easily into an otherness if compared to the idealized notion of 'the city'. This leads to an urban dystopianism which justifies increased security measures on the part of the state – or today of capital as it assumes the functions of the representative state as quickly as it encroaches on public spaces.

Zukin writes of the development of Business Improvement Districts (BIDs) in New York, and of the enclosure of open spaces as commercial spaces such as Sony Plaza, noting that advocacy for BIDs represents them as 'an attempt to reclaim public space from the sense of menace that drives shoppers, and eventually store owners and citizens, to the suburbs',[24] and that the only opposition to Sony Plaza was from the Coalition for the Homeless:

'Public space that is no longer controlled by public agencies must inspire a liminal public culture open to all but governed by the private sector.'[25] She adds that an abstract aesthetic of development avoids conflicts of representation and that culture 'functions as a mechanism of stratification' separated from the everyday actualities of occupancy when developers select a 'nostalgically remembered city' akin to Disney World. If this seems a model specific to North America, it is about, as I write, to be piloted in the outer London borough of Kingston-on-Thames.

Objection to the privatization of public space on grounds of access and social equity does not validate the premium placed on what are often pseudo-public spaces in urban redevelopment. The models appropriated tend to be those of an idealized past such as Sienna and Florence. What emerges is a sentimental mythicization of the city, as offered by Herbert Girardet in *The Gaia Atlas of Cities*:

It is a great art to make a city convivial, as the best examples we have inherited show us. Cities, such as Florence, Salzburg and Prague, seem to have been purpose-built for lively interchanges between people. Narrow, human-scale streets contrast with well-appointed public buildings and wide, open gathering spaces. They are products of good planning but also of organic growth; they are functional but remain on a human scale; they are centres of economic activity

but also of social and cultural energy.[26]

This aligns public space with the notion of liveability advanced in the US as new urbanism. Journalist Bettina Drew writes of the Disney township of Celebration, Florida:

Like American small towns before World War II, Celebration has tree-lined streets and houses with front porches; parks, a school, and a downtown shopping district are all within walking distance. The homes, linked to the school and businesses by a fiber-optic network, are a blend of traditional American styles; and there are townhouses and apartments, as well as a golf course, swimming pool, tennis courts, and a health care center devoted to wellness.[27]

All of which is fine for those prepared to sign up to the regime of the Disney Company: curtains must be white or beige, only certain kinds of shrub are allowed and garage sales are permitted only once a year per household. But the white picket fences and colonial facades denote an exclusivity while the nostalgia which informs the new urbanism (aligned to neo-liberalism) denotes a return to a past which was not as simple as imagined.

The human scale streets of medieval and Renaissance cities were as often sites of gratuitous violence as of harmony: Richard Sennet draws attention to the high instance of crimes against the person in fifteenth-century Paris,[28] and Edward Soja writes:

The New Urbanism is essentially a contemporary historicist transmogrification of the New Town Ideal, packaged with nostalgic references to the small towns-cum-urban villages of early America [sic] and poured into the Outer and Inner Cities of today.[29]

He adds that it draws on notions of 'peopled public spaces and pedestrian life' from Jane Jacobs' impression of Greenwich Village and on the 'soft environmental socialism' of the New Towns Movement as well as on the idea of 'defensible space' from Oscar Newman.[30] Permeating new urbanism, I would add, is fear of crime, disorder, difference, and of others seen as carriers of these contagions. Sennett's account of white suburbanites' fear of outsiders, in *The Uses of Disorder*, remains useful:

Individuals have achieved a coherent sense of themselves precisely by avoiding painful experiences, disordered confrontations and experiments, in their own identity formation. Having so little tolerance for disorder in their own lives the eruption of social tension becomes a situation in which the ultimate methods of aggression seem to become not only justified, but life-preserving.[31]

Abuse may proliferate in the domestic interior but on the manicured lawn all is harmony. Like all utopias this is a brittle dream unable to incorporate change or to accept the maturity that arises, for Sennett, through experience of the conflicts of value, culture, and identity which difference produces. The armed response signs on suburban Los Angeles lawns of which Mike Davis writes (1990) are extensions of this fear of difference, as is the construction of a myth of an underclass (like the 'mob' of the nineteenth century) and the similarly marginalizing demonization of asylum seekers.

I wonder to what extent the design and beautification of urban public spaces today reflects a view of the city akin to such fantasies. In contrast, drawing on Hannah Arendt and Iris Marion Young, an idea of a public sphere rests less on the spaces of public monuments than on the transitional, multi-use, and in some ways self-regulated spaces of the street, the home, and the media of communication. The Internet and the mobile phone are now as public a means of social interaction as the market street and town square, for societies which have widespread access to them. A public sphere emerges, too, in occupations of spaces for purposes other than those for which they are designed but for which, by unspoken consensus, they are appropriate – as when skateboarders take over the dead spaces of commercial buildings. In *The Death and Life of Great American Cities*, Jacobs writes that 'The casual public sidewalk life of cities ties directly into other types of public life', and that 'Formal public organizations in cities require an informal public life underlying them, mediating between them and the privacy of people of the city'.[32] She asserts that 'a city cannot be a work of art' and that if art and life are integral, they remain different: 'Confusion between them is, in part, why efforts at city design are so disappointing'.[33] I would argue that confusion, too, between representation and democracy is why the design of society, so to speak, is so disappointing.

Arendt uses the term natality: a growth of individuals in society to a mature self through the perceptions of others gained amidst others. For Arendt, denial of being-in-public is painful and a precondition for persecution. Kimberly Curtis, in a critique of Arendt's political philosophy, writes of natality as:

An ontology of display suggesting that reality in an appearing world is something born out of a highly charged mutual sensuous provocation between actors and spectators that is essentially aesthetic in nature.[34]

Natality is like a second, conscious birth equated with freedom and reality in a post-metaphysical world. Curtis adds that:

Our capacity to sense the real depends on a mutual provocation between appearing beings. Our ability to actualize the plurality of the human condition [and] to give experience some permanence by establishing a minimal sense of a common world rely on the vitality of this mutual aesthetic provocation.[35]

A denial of appearance is 'the insult of oblivion'.[36] Arendt's argument is compatible, if in a modern rather than post-modern frame, with Iris Marion Young's idea of deliberative democracy:

Participants in the democratic process offer proposals for how best to solve problems or meet legitimate needs and they present arguments through which they aim to persuade others. Democratic process is primarily a discussion of problems, conflicts, and claims of need or interest. Through dialogue others test and challenge these proposals and arguments.[37]

Through dialogue, as well, it is possible to address the limitations of a modern subjectivity. Belsey writes that the subject in liberal humanism claims unity as a self-governing author of her or his moral, electoral and consuming acts but that this was denied to women:

A discursive instability in the texts about women has the effect of withholding from women readers any single position which they can identify as theirs.[38]

Looking to academic discussions in the early 1990s, Leonie Sandercock alludes to voices from the borderlands:

The voices of the multicultural city, of those who have been marginalized, displaced, oppressed or dominated. The subjective voices of experience, insisting on the relevance of that experience to the task of making theory.[39]

That insistence is a reclamation, in a viable form, of the modern subject, not exactly now autonomous yet not given over to heteronomy – rule by others – either, any more than regressed to domination by kings and emperors, or corporate chief executives, or rule by fate. Art cannot achieve this but it can begin to open understandings of the conditions in which a voice is consciously constructed, to intervene in the conditions of its formation, and re-formation.[40]

Interruptions

If art has a critical role in urban spaces, then, it contributes to a contestation of meanings in a realm traditionally given over to monuments of national identity. A case of this is the work of Krzysztof Wodiczko in projections of images onto public monuments. Using images of homeless people, or weapons of mass destruction, Wodiczko draws attention to the ideological content and intrinsic violence of the public realm. On a work in Trafalgar Square, London in 1988 he says:

The aim is not to 'bring life to' or 'enliven' the memorial nor to support the happy, uncritical bureaucratic 'socialisation' of the site, but to reveal and expose the contemporary deadly life of the memorial.[41]

Similarly, Henri Lefebvre writes:

Any space that is organized around the monument is colonized and oppressed. The great monuments have been raised to glorify conquerors and the powerful.

adding another aspect:

Although the monument is always laden with symbols, it presents them to social awareness just when those symbolized, already outdated, are beginning to lose their meaning, such as the symbols of revolution on the Napoleonic Arc de Triomphe.[42]

Perhaps, then, a requirement for intervention is to facilitate such awareness as pertains to the present with a directness that avoids symbolism. This is quite difficult because all language tends to abstraction, including the visual and textual. There is no such thing as a representation of a raw reality, only its mediation as the cooked, whether aestheticized, moralized, or politicized. The codes, however, like the forms, can be worked on and played with. The codes themselves may be an appropriate site for intervention, for a renegotiation of the categories through which we classify and make sense of what (and whom) we encounter in the world.

A case of this might be *porque e existe o ser em vez do nada?* by José Maças de Carvalho in the project *Capital do nada* in Marvila, a social housing district of Lisbon in 2001 (referring to slide). The artist made his first visits to Marvila a year before the production of the work's final image of Débora (leader of the African association) sited on the side of the six-storey block in which she lives. In all, the images of twelve participants were published as posters on bus shelters, in magazines, as postcards, and on advertising sites in public places around Lisbon. Participants were provided with mobile phones and dedicated numbers for the duration of the project, the numbers published beneath their portraits. When called, they described leisure and work activities, from Mario's graffiti to Beto's music, Maria's assistance to the Friar of the local church and Sr. Casimiro's quoits. The project publication states:

Equidistant from art and photography, this project consisted of a relatively long and phased process which offered visibility to those the artist defined as the 'heroes' of Marvila. Since the images were scattered around the country and city of Lisbon, many people called the heroes asking for information about them, the district and the event.[43]

At first glance, the project is about visibility. It lends the visibility of public exhibition to the images and names of participants – co-producers – while those involved are not categorized as members

of a minority but are demonstrably a multi-ethnic majority in their own environment. Perhaps the project is about visibility but not visuality, creating signs for lives shaped by a terrain triangulated by media imagery, communication, and activity, which entail voluntarism or self-organization more than affluent consumption. The locations of the work in magazines and bus shelters put it in the world in which the subjects spend time, yet I would hesitate to call this public space. It seems more a liminal zone collapsing the binary division of public-private, as public spaces are occupied for personal ends and the mobile phone translates outside into the inside of a conversation.

My last case is the work of PLATFORM, artists' group in London. PLATFORM remain artists, in their view, not activists, though some of their closest contacts are in campaigning organizations and one member of the group left to join Reclaim the Streets. In the past they have distributed spoof newspapers to commuters to draw attention to the operations of the globalized oil industry and worked with students at a London college to design and manufacture a solar-powered vehicle for street video projection. One of their current activities is a series of guided walks through the centre of London, pointing out the nuances and contradictions of an imperial and financial history in the city's built environment (referring to slide). A number of artists, including Janet Cardiff and Tim Brennan, use walking as a medium for art, and introduce a consciously subjective voice in resistance to the objectivity of the conventional narrator, or problematize narration, but for PLATFORM the aim is to reveal the city's ideological foundation not to muse upon its imaginative recesses.

I have a question, however, as to the instrumentality of such work (not this one in particular).

I would argue that a viable role for artists is to expose contradictions or to indicate the non-sustainability of the project of capital; but I must be wary of saying that artists occupy a privileged position or have special insights into alienation or immiseration, to take two classic conditions of capitalism, or into environmental injustices which tend for the most part to impact on members of the majority (non-affluent) world – who have their own voices. I am not saying at all that PLATFORM claim such privilege – their reading of Paolo Freire (1972) alerts them to the issue – only that the difficulty faces any artist seeking to bring about change by the vehicle of art. This is apart from any question of ends dominating means. For many artists working with socio-economic issues, the process carries the desired qualities of the project rather than being a way towards, or representation of, an eventual aim, which it expediently assists in attaining. To put it simply: the means are the ends. It is the immanent not the imminent, the pervading present not the soon-to-come: abolition of rent in the landlord's lifetime.

But the specialist education of artists, and the institutionalized validation of their work as constituting art, tends to enforce a modern sense of agency which is above that of the supposedly voiceless for whom the privileged, illuminated or enlightened, voice speaks. John Roberts summarizes the difficulty in a response to the Whitechapel exhibition *Protest & Survive*:

The 'bringing-truth-out-there-into-the-gallery' approach to politics in art is, of course, a conventional social-democratic model of ideological appellation. The 'social content' of art is appealed to on the basis of its capacity to 'raise consciousness'.

[But] political art (as understood on the social-democratic model) assumes that those whom the work is destined for (the fantasized working class) need art in as much as they need ideas in order to understand capitalism and class society. There is never a moment's recognition that people are already engaged in practices in the world which are critical and transformative.[44]

For Lefebvre, it is such moments that fracture routine, which constitute an immanent rather than an imminent revolution:

Those instants we would each, according to our own personal criteria, categorise as 'authentic' moments that break through the dulling monotony of the 'taken for granted' moments outflank the pretensions of wordy theories, rules and laws, and challenge the limits of everyday living 'revelatory of the totality of possibilities contained in daily existence [they] would pass instantaneously into oblivion, but during their passage all manner of possibilities – often decisive and sometimes revolutionary – stood to be both uncovered and achieved.[45]

The perennial difficulty of avant-gardes is that they interpret the world for others, assuming that others do not or cannot interpret it for themselves; thus to lead the mass public to a new dawn leaves the power-relations of the dominant society unaffected. Perhaps it is worth recalling Joseph Beuys' idea that everyone is an artist, by which I think he meant that everyone has an ability to re-imagine the world.

BS: Well, as far as I'm concerned very interesting, and really beautifully delivered so, thank you. And I've got three, quite rambling questions and I'll do my best to articulate them, as clearly as I can and then we'll turn to the audience for questions.

I was really interested to hear you talk about citizenship; you talk about this word as a wholly positive thing. I feel like I'm now one of Blair's children, my vision of citizenship and my understanding of the word to me has negative overtones because I feel uncomfortable by how the word is now used in contemporary politics. And I wonder if you could talk about how your vision relates to how it's used now.

MM: I am really old – I was born in 1950 and I can't remember when the regimes changed, but I might technically be one of Attlee's children, I'm not sure. And there was, in that post-war period a real kind of utopianism actually, there had been a reawakening of society, the war was over, fascism was ended and there would be new kinds of freedom and with it prosperity and growth. Now the growth has become an enormous problem, because it's responsible for enormous destruction, environmentally and in lots of other ways, so that we kind of have to rethink completely.

I suppose I would also put myself very much within a European modernity of thought, if I could put it in that slightly odd way. Some of the ideas that we get in the sixteenth century, which in ordinary history are taken as being modern times, not like in art history where you take around 1880 as being modern, are actually very important and the idea of the subject, the citizen, begins at this point. It doesn't really exist before then. But the idea of the subject who organizes his or her own life is mirrored in the way that drama changes through the Jacobean period. The plots are written so that people actually make choices about what's going to happen next. There is a script that the actors use, but the audience kind of tags along with this notion of wondering what will be next, and they decide it. For Bauman, the next step is in cinema and you can kind of imagine the plot yourself. Perhaps now you could actually make film yourself because the equipment is a lot cheaper and easier to carry, so these things move along.

But one of the things that changes is and I have to be slightly wary here because its quite complex and I don't want to dumb it down ever so much – is what is sometimes called the disenchantment of the world. Suzi Gablik in her book *The Re-enchantment of Art* in 1981, talks about rationality which comes at that time in the sixteenth century onwards through the seventeenth particularly, and then in the enlightenment in the eighteenth century, as somehow de-enchanting the work and she looks for things like shamanism and so on as a way of getting beyond that. Now, I have enough respect for Gablik, whom I've met and had some discussion with that I'm not going to attack her ideas, and I think she writes quite beautifully, but for me, that's aggressive – that notion of going back into shamanism. We know almost nothing about it, because it's really difficult to appropriate other people's cultures from another. We are all of us here, white, European, affluent citizens we don't live in societies that actually have shamans. So for me, that disenchantment of the world was a freedom from spells – that old way of using the word enchantment – freedom from the dictates of a mysterious and remote fate over which we have no influence. Its only if you have that understanding that you can get to a Marxist position which is that we can intervene in the conditions that condition us. Marx puts forward this idea that we can intervene. Marx tells us that the philosophers have explained the world but the point is to change it. The way we do that is by affecting those conditions, by challenging the conditions and circumstances by which we are influenced.

The white space of the gallery perhaps is a kind of denial of that in some ways, making a value for aesthetic space. But that's another matter. I think the idea that we can intervene is enormously important; it underpins a lot of my own thinking.

I would see the citizen as growing out of that notion of the subject as a person who shapes the world they live in. But I'd add another thing to it in Hannah Arran's writing, there is a notion that we only get to know ourselves today by what we call identification, through the perceptions of others. And our perceptions of others, others perceptions of us, our perceptions of others perceiving us and this parallel reality could go on as long as you want. That seems again very important, that it's only by being in society that we get a sense of who we are. The hermit, the solitary, probably has very little sense of that – the idea is to abandon that sense of course – but I would see the citizen as the active cultivator of a sense of self in society. And it's difficult, its very hard work.

BS: So, do you see that as the same model that is talked about when our government talks about citizenship – is that the same citizenship they are talking about?

MM: No. I think the rhetoric is utterly false, a total betrayal.

BS: But are they not trying to re-energize the collective?

MM: I think that they are in effect producing increasing exclusivity and elitism; there is a veneer, just like art has this notion of universal value that it's supposed to be good for us, so public art adds an aura to public spaces and urban redevelopment when its really about money.

And now we have some of these other things like citizenship being used as another kind of aura, another kind of veneer, that is supposed to make it all right. What is going on underneath is utterly horrible and extremely violent. But again, let's not be too gloomy because just as capital is globalized so is resistance; through new technologies, through communications, through new kinds of association, through new alliances often between very tiny groups of people in very remote localities with common agendas. In places like the Royal Social Forum and just as there is the G8 and the IMF, there are other structures growing, they are actually there, we don't need to invent

them.

BS: I have got another question, but I want to ask the audience if they have anything they would like to ask Malcolm?

MA1: I was just going to say, a good example of that veneer is an exhibition we went to see recently in the Houses of Parliament in Westminster about democracy. It was a kind of interactive exhibition right in the heart of Parliament, asking people what they thought and encouraging them to have a say in the world's affairs. It felt very worrying; purely a gesture towards notions of what citizenship is about.

MJ: You can't help questioning the context, who has access to that space? Who knows that you can go into the Houses of Parliament let alone have the confidence and knowledge to interact with the exhibition?

MM: For years and years we've had calls, usually from the right, to take the politics out of art, to take the politics out of sport, now from New Labour we have, take the politics out of elections. It's very dangerous. But again I'd have to ask what is actually lost? Because putting the mark of the illiterate on a piece of paper once every four or five years and handing over power isn't really about empowerment. Well, its empowerment of them but not of us, the citizens. I suppose that notion of empowerment is kind of a central one and I would have to argue that power is never given away, it is very rarely even taken and usually that fails in violent revolution. Occasionally it happens. In Lisbon in 1974, when people put carnations in the barrels of soldier's guns, it actually worked, but the dictator Salazar had had a stroke and was gaga and I think they knew the game was up anyway. Other things emerge, you know, there's activism, there's environmentalism, there are lots of different strengths of politics which happened to be outside some of those traditional systems. There are disadvantages to them being outside but that doesn't diminish the power or the quality of the voice or voices.

BS: That's what I was going to ask about. I was thinking, when you were talking

about sites of opposition, how easily commodified, or at least 'lifestyled', they are. For instance there might be an exhibition that describes itself as radical, but actually the type of radicality it possesses is acceptable. In some ways the more difficult questions you ask the more the art world will love it and the more commissions you'll get. Is that not problematic?

MM: Yes. And I have nothing against artists earning a living, money spent on art is infinitely better than on cruise missiles or the war in Iraq or all sorts of other things so I'm not trying to detract in any way from artists getting their slice of the cake. But there's the question of access. And it's not just that the buildings have free entrance, it's who has the vocabulary and the confidence to get in there and mess with it.

MA2: Well, I think that we are more likely to find new challenging ideas within institutions and I keep trying to think about it in a number of ways. Recently at a conference I attended, the architects of this gallery, Caruso St John, were giving a talk about this building and it came across quite radically in their view that what they were building was somehow a beautiful house to protect the independence of art. Now from a tradition of institutional critique, it seems to be strange to think that art once again, in order to be protected, has to come back to the house it fled thirty years ago. So there is always that problematic relationship and I don't know how to solve it.

MM: It may be that we have to think in terms of an access. An access of, on the one hand a kind of critical distancing and on the other, a kind of getting in there. And, simply see that as a creative tension, not solvable, but simply there to work with and at different times moving in different ways: backwards and forwards, along and then it shifting to and fro. Just as I suppose art's aesthetic and social aspects are not alternatives, but that they are probably always both there to some extent and they actually disable each other to some extent as well, but there's a creative tension that is probably the best one's going to get out of the situation, so one can work with that, but one can't solve that, one can't reconcile it. So yes there will be contradictions, it isn't a neat picture. I think though, throughout modernism, from the 1870s onwards, there's been a succession of departures within mainstream art in Europe and North America. So in the 1890s there were successions within Berlin and Vienna and Munich. And in part that was to do with artists taking responsibility for their own futures by organizing their own exhibitions. If you can imagine that there was only the Royal Academy and you had to put your pictures up in front of these people, and after lunch they were probably asleep anyway, to get in the exhibition – I shouldn't be unkind to those gentle people – but, so you say, well OK, we'll do it ourselves. We will be independent, and there's a kind of positive spirit in that, which one can respect. And it leads to departure after departure. In the 1960s with conceptualism and happenings and other non-object ways of working, live art, there's a refusal of the commodification of art. So, the thinking is we won't make objects they can sell in the art market, we will do things that don't exist so they can't sell them. Problem is the market is very good at taking it all back. So instead of trading in objects it can trade in reputations; this is a nothing at all by so and so, this is a totally worthless piece of dust by so and so, and they get round it. According to the American artist Martha Rossler, art is becoming more and more like the entertainment industry, almost a blanche of the entertainment industry. The Turner Prize could be perhaps one aspect of that. So again, you can say what goes out comes back in again. But we have to be careful because not all art is like that all the time there's lots of other stuff going on. We may see less of it for various reasons because the mediation is quite powerful, what gets into the magazines and on the television and so on. But, there is a lot of other more indeterminate stuff going on and it will probably always be like that.

MA2: Another speaker at a conference I was at said "One of my fears is that if everyone abandoned that same sphere where, even some very small meaningless form of intervention can take place, then the official public sphere is deemed as irredeemable." But doesn't this produce the opposite effect of saying well we've completely left the battleground?

MM: I'm going to pick up one thing you said that the public sphere is irredeemable. I would argue it isn't. I would also argue, who would do the redeeming? But isn't that a fairly big question? I think that comes back to that quote from John Roberts, that the transformation is around us all the time. It is limited, it is often stifled, and sometimes it grows. But that's the public sphere, the bits that we might lose are much smaller than that. Certain notions of public space or citizenship and there are difficulties because we have the same words that mean radically different things in some cases because through time the nuances change. But we need to remember that there's that huge part of the public sphere, which is dwelling, that, everybody does. And everybody is expert on. And if you ask, people often tell you quite a lot about it.

BS: Anybody got any more questions?

MA3: Well I have a thought but I'm not quite sure how to make it into a question. The difference between the citizen and individual and we can affect change, who's we? And citizens together is kind of greater than the sum of its parts, and what distinction do you make between the two because different groups of people have different influences and affect change in different ways, often working in opposite directions. And if you are a citizen, what are you a citizen of? Which group do you belong to and so which group should you be a part of?

MM: It's a very good question. Which 'we' do we belong to?, would be one way to start encapsulating it. When I go to conferences in other places, people usually say something about where do you come from, immediately you are required to identify yourself? One tactic I use, I have a little badge that somebody gave me with a red star on a green background that I don't know what it is of, it was given to me by a Russian artist

in New York who was doing a project with a big pantechnicon where if you wrote a message on the side he gave you a badge. I don't know if he had them made specially or if they are from the Soviet Union or what but I wear it because people always ask what it is. There was a conference, in Middlesbrough some years ago, where everyone was speaking and joining in and some one said, "What's your badge?" and lots of people made suggestions and somebody said it's Heineken lager and I don't actually drink that, somebody said it's the arms of the city of Maastricht, well I have been to Maastricht, but I'm not a citizen of Maastricht, then somebody from the back of the room said "It's the Communist Party of Azerbaijan!" Which was so specific that I've used that ever since. Never been to Azerbaijan and not a member of the Communist party, but it's just a nice kind of label that produces very interesting reactions in the person that asks the question. They are usually of complete consternation.

So who's the 'we'? Apart from saying things like I'm a European citizen because I get very pissed off with Englishness and UK society and UK/US society, but I'm not fluent in other European languages so I'm kind of kidding everybody there as well. I suppose it comes down to a lot of very overlapping interest groups. I'm an academic, I get an academic salary, I have a permanent post in the University, if anything is permanent these days, I would within that put myself in certain categories of dealing with knowledge and critique and so on as well. But that doesn't stop me also from being someone who has a garden for example. So there would be other times when that would be the function. I have a son who is eight who is very into railways so some weekends we go on steam train rides, so I'm part of a community of riders of steam railways. These have nothing to do with each other a lot of the time, but they just happen to coincide and intercept. I think most of us probably have a number of these different bits and we don't have to see them as compartments, but we don't have to say they all fit. We don't have to look for coherence in the pattern. So, perhaps there are lots of interest groups and we can be members of lots of them and we can choose not to be members of some of them as well. And we kind of refine as we go on, where we fit on the map and we'll be in more than one place at once usually.

Who is the 'we' that shapes society? Well, that's where the democratic answer would have to be everyone because of social equality and inclusion. I don't like the term social inclusion that's one of these Blairite jargons. But, yeah I would hold to the notion of a participatory society, I'm not sure what scale that's possible on, it's interesting going to some very small scale like micro-societies, places like eco-villages where there is a quite direct participation deciding most things that happen. Sometimes it gets tedious, in one place in Germany for example they had a very long, very, very difficult meeting about changing the time of dinner by half an hour, and you think, excuse me! You know, the world may dissolve into some kind of toxic soup any minute, but you have to learn self-organization.

As a society it's not easy, you've had thousands of years of power and those self-powered are just beginning to grapple with what you actually do. And we don't have answers and we don't know, but I suppose we can try and have the confidence to say that we are part of the 'we'. Remembering that of course I don't have the right to everyone else's voice, there are other voices that are radically different from mine, which I can't pretend to speak for. But I can argue that they should have a space to speak. That's getting a bit rhetorical, but it's a very good question. What do you think is the answer to your question?

MA3: Well I don't know really. It's kind of the difference from what you are saying about being part of being different subsets. I think it's more when you get a number of people together and all their different complexities that make them, whatever this group of people is, all of them together, it becomes something else. And that joint voice may not be an accurate representation of what all those people think. So, it's a product of ten people and I don't quite know, but just the way that there becomes a group monster that is a thing that you can't do by yourself.

MM: Yeah, that gets depicted in different

ways. It's the crowd or it's the mob or its solidarity.

MA3: Yeah. Well, you seem such an optimistic person about community in general.

MM: No, that's only because I'm deeply pessimistic and terrified underneath! There's this huge black chasm, with which one could be permanently, utterly depressed and I have to not simply accept that as a kind of helplessness. I have a responsibility to do something with it which is to try and imagine something else.

MJ: Yes, that's what I got from what you've talked about. Otherwise you could just quite easily get yourself in a position where you think you can't do anything and give up altogether. It is really good to hear you articulate the problems inherent in the dilemmas of affecting change.

MM: They did abolish slavery. Before it happened, most people probably said it would never happen. It's interesting that, there's no logic in history, however, that doesn't mean that all the other bad stuff will get abolished. Marxism says that there is an objective end of history. There's struggle. And I have an immensely comfortable place within that struggle sitting in University, being critical and problematizing things and it's a very privileged place to be. There are also other struggles that go on, some of which are extremely activist, but some are quite slow and quiet and gentle, if you think for example of the way supermarkets compete with each other not to stock GM food – probably the turning point was when someone coined the term Frankenstein Foods. And the narrative suddenly got upturned; this wasn't the benefit of science, it was shit, and we don't want to eat shit! And no one would stock this stuff; now that has had a major impact on companies like Tesco who are pulling back. They'll regroup and they'll do something else, it won't be long, but at least they've had a major set back. And here again is the 'we', the we who are very diverse indeed. It's probably more middle class than anything – it's the shoppers in Waitrose and Marks and Spencer's and the more affluent supermarkets perhaps, but there is a point of power in consumption

sometimes if you think about it in terms of this example.

MA2: That's interesting that you can have power in consumption. I think that environmental issues are extremely important in the new formation of citizenship. One thing that many people coalesce in is the loss of a certain idea of nature. And so, very often the very battles that have grouped people together have actually had, as ingredients, this idea of the environmental issue. There are plenty of institutions which say 'Come to the countryside, it's out here, it's everyone's!' And recently I was listening to a Radio 4 programme which stated that there was a problem in that there are not many black people visiting the countryside and is that because they don't see it as 'theirs'. Is it because there is something within the way the countryside is organized socially that still maybe makes one think of some social structure to which one hopes to emancipate oneself from.

MJ: I come from East London and I didn't know about nature; the nearest we had was a nature table at school with all sorts of odd things on it like an old birds nest. And when I first started teaching in Sheffield my colleagues said we'll take you out to the country for lunch. We went to the Peak District and on the journey I said, "there's sheep!" They thought it was absolutely hilarious; there are lots of sheep in the Peak District. But you didn't see sheep in Hackney.

MA2: Yeah. Unless you go down to the city farm, which is near where I live.

MJ: But also they had this idea of rambling and walking which I couldn't understand. I thought why don't you get the bus, you will get there quicker. This was so alien to me. I didn't know about the pleasure in walking. I think this is probably a class issue connected with leisure, for the working class you don't have time to spare doing something that tires you out, because work does that.

MM: You're right in two ways. One is that you can reclaim this pleasurable activity – it's interesting in Sweden, I think in Scotland too, there's this notion of the common right to walk on any land. As long as you don't

damage things, it's OK. In England we don't have that, it's privately owned and there are keep out signs. But you are also accurate in pointing out that there is a particular, in England, a nineteenth century history of the upper middle classes doing long country walks. And it's almost the way they earn their right to a voice; if you walk all day in the lake district, preferably in the most appalling weather, through this arduousness, you earn your voice in society and people like Wordsworth and Ruskin would be examples of that. I think there may still be an element of that although it's probably more democratized now, but people still actually make it quite a business and they buy all this expensive gear to walk in.

MJ: But it is access again, it's the thought that you could do it, nobody said to me, 'Wouldn't it be good to go for a nice walk!' Walking was always seen as a chore, as a horrible thing to have to do.

BS: But in that there's almost the implication that we all agree that it's good for you and I'm not sure that that's right actually. I think that's moral, somehow.

MA2: But that's a way of saying that the environment is currently used as the new social 'glue' in the sense that it pulls people together. It's scary because it is also potentially one of the only ways to enforce a certain kind of legislation, which we all might act on.

MM: But also notably, the highest levels of bio-diversity are often found in suburban gardens; industrialized agriculture has destroyed virtually everything in the countryside. And the landscape that we ramble in is man-made, a cultural artefact and has been for thousands of years. There are very, very few wild places in the British Isles now.

BS: Is there any more questions form the audience?

MA2: I think it is astonishing, having gone through the whole of the twentieth century that we don't see science as the greatest force for good and the greatest force for change in the last few years and you have a sort of a, shrinking away, a fear of all these developments. You talk about the eco-communities, which are mostly retrogressive and conservative.

MM: No they're not. I really disagree with you there. There are a very large number of these communities and there is a lot of diversity within them and some are fairly regressive yes, many are certainly rural, but there are urban cases too, urban enclaves which try to be sustainable too. Many engage with new technologies of energy, solar, wind and so on. These are technologies, they are often called intermediate or appropriate technologies, but they are still relatively new, still developing technologies and these I don't

shrink away from. I don't actually shrink away from nuclear fission by the way, but you know, I know very little about it. I would worry about nuclear waste from nuclear fission, but I think most people worry about that, I realize there is a certain corruption going on in places like Sellafield. I'm just more interested in the way that in some cases people are attempting to find new ways of working together, as groups of people, to deal with simply how we live together and to find methods of dealing with conflict, which inevitably rises with diversity of interest. If you live in a community of fifty-to-a-hundred, people are inescapable because they are always in your face, they're right there; they're next door to you. It seems to be quite important to develop technologies dealing with how we manage these relationships in a non-violent way and a non-impositional, non-aggressive way. I don't know much about this, but I have visited one or two places where people live in this way and I'm actually quite impressed, I'm still at the very early days of that research. Incidentally I have nothing against science, I actually have nothing against industry it's achieved all sorts of benefits – I have an electric light in my house.

MJ: That's it then. Well I'd just like to thank Malcolm Miles for speaking to us and Becky Shaw for chairing the questions, and thank you all for coming along today.

ENDNOTES

1. This text is an extended and revised version of the talk delivered at The New Art Gallery, Walsall on August 11th, 2004 in the project *Futurology*. I have added the section on subjectivity, and incorporated some ideas, which emerged on the day.

2. This alludes to Adorno's essay, 'The schema of mass culture', Adorno T W, 1991, 'The Culture Industry: Selected Essays on Mass Culture,' London, Routledge, p.84

3. Ressler O, 2004, 'Alternative Economics, Alternative Societies, Alternative Art Practices', interview with Anna Liv Ahistrand, www.republicart.net/art/concept/alternativeinto01_en.htm

4. The inference here is borrowed from Adorno T.W. and Horkheimer M [1947, 1997 Dialectic of Enlightenment, London, Verso, p. 208.

5. Bauman Z, 1998, 'Globalization: the Human Consequences', Cambridge, Polity, p.85.

6. Lodziak C , 2003 ' The Myth of Consumerism, London, Pluto, p.95.

7. Lodziak C , 2003, The Myth of Consumerism, London, Pluto, p.98.

8. Wilson E, 1991, 'The Sphinx in the City', Berkeley, University of California Wirth L [1938] ('Urbanism as a Way of Life', in LeGates and Stout, 2003, pp98-104 [first published in the American Journal of Sociology XLIV, 1] p.103.

9. Zukin S, 1995 'The Cultures of Cities', Oxford, Blackwell p.9.

10. Wilson E, 1991, 'The Sphinx in the City', Berkeley, University of California, p84, Wirth L [1938] 'Urbanism as a Way of Life', in LeGates and Stout (2003) pp98-104 [first published in the American Journal of Sociology XLIV, 1] p.103

11. Broeckmann A, 2004, e-mail 10th June re 'public-media-space festival' Yerevan.

12. Rosler M, 1994, 'Place, Position, Power, Politics', in Becker, p.57.

13. Leslie E (2001) 'Tate Modern' A Year of Sweet Success', Radical Philosophy 109, pp.2-5

14. Doherty C, 2004, 'The Institution is Dead! Long Live the Institution! Contemporary Art and New Institutionalism', Engage, #15, pp.6-13

15. Potrc M, 2000, exhibition catalogue, Berlin, K¸nstlerhaus Bethanien and Munich, Philip Morris Kunstf¨rderung, p.23

16.Hill G, 1968, 'Funeral Music, 8', in King Log, London, Deutsch, p.32

17. Belsey C, 1985, 'The Subject of Tragedy: Identity and Difference' in Renaissance Drama, London, Methuen, p.33

18. ibid p.41.

19. ibid. pp.41-2.

20. ibid. pp.125.

21.ibid pp.125.

22. The inference here is borrowed from Adorno and Horkheimer [1947], 1997 p.208.

23. Auge M ,1995, 'Non-places: introduction to an anthropology of supermodernity', London, Verso. p.60.

24. Zukin S, 1995, 'The Cultures of Citie's, Oxford, Blackwell, p.36.

25. Zukin S, 1995, 'The Cultures of Citie's, Oxford, Blackwell, pp.36-7.

26. Girardet H, 1992, 'The Gaia Atlas of Cities', p.118.

27. Betina Drew, 1998, p.174.

28. Sennett R , 1995, 'Flesh and Stone', London, Faber and Faber, p.196

29. Soja E, 2000, p.249.

30. ibid

31. Sennett R, 1970, 'The Uses of Disorder', New York, Norton, p.45.

32. Jacobs J, 1961, 'The Death and Life of Great American Cities', New York, Random House, p.57

33. ibid, p.373.

34. Curtis K, 1999, 'Our Sense of the Real: Aesthetic Experience and Arendtian Politics', Ithaca, Cornell University Pres, p.31

34. ibid, p.36

36. Arendt H, 1990, 'On Revolution', Harmondsworth, Penguin (Arendt 1990, 69, cited in Curtis 1999, 67)

37. Young I M ,2000, 'Inclusion and Democracy', Oxford, Oxford University Press, p.22.

38. Belsey C, 1985, 'The Subject of Tragedy: Identity and Difference in Renaissance Drama', London, Methuen.

p.33 and p.149.

39. Sandercock L, 1998, 'Towards Cosmopolis', Chichester, Wiley, p.110.

40. Compare with Marcuse: "If the remembrance of things past would become a motive power in the struggle for changing the world, the struggle would be waged for a revolution hitherto suppressed in the previous historical revolutions" (1978: 73).

41. Freshman P, ed. 1993, 'Public Address: Krzysztov Wodiczko', Minneapolis, Walker Art Centre, p.115.

42. Lefebvre H, 1991, 'The Production of Space', Oxford, Blackwell, p.21.

43. Lisboa Capital do nada, 2002, Extra]muros[, p.152.

44. Roberts J, 2001, 'Art, Politics and Provincialism', Radical Philosophy 106, pp.2-6

45. Shields R, 1999, 'Lefebvre, Love & Struggle', London, Routledge p.58, citing Harvey, 1991, p. 429.

REFERENCES

Barker F, 1984, 'The Tremulous Private Body: Essays on Subjection', London, Methuen

Beardsley J, 1989, 'Earthworks and Beyond', New York, Abbeville

Becker C, ed., 1994, 'The Subversive Imagination: artists, society, and social responsibility', London, Routledge

Davis M, 1990, 'City of Quartz', London, Verso

Freire P, 1972), 'Pedagogy of the Oppressed', Harmondsworth, Penguin

Le Gates R T and Stout F, eds. 2003, 'The City Reader', 3rd edition, London, Routledge

Marcuse H, 1978, 'The Aesthetic Dimension', Boston, Beacon Press

Massey D, 1994, 'Space, Place and Gender', Cambridge, Polity

Veblen T [1899], 1970, 'The Theory of the Leisure Class', London, Unwin

Wodiczko K, 1986, 'Memorial Projection', October 38, pp.4-10

The Geography of Gentrification
Tim Butler

Transcript of a talk and paper
given by Tim Butler with questions
from Andy Hewitt
and Mel Jordan

Contributors

Tim Butler (TB)
Alberto Duman (AD)
Andy Hewitt (AH)
Mel Jordan (MJ)
Member of the Audience
(MA1, MA2, MA3)
Becky Shaw (BS)

TB: Thank you very much for inviting me. I'm very pleased to come and see this gallery, which I've heard much about over the years and I will try include it at the end of the talk. I'm a bit unclear really as to quite how to pitch this, I hope I've got it more or less right but maybe I haven't so let me know. I really want to do just six things and I've been told I can talk for about 45 minutes. I have heard that after about 40 minutes you go to sleep but in these chairs you probably won't be able to.

Firstly, I want to say a bit about the concept of gentrification. The term was first invented about 40 years ago by an urban sociologist called Ruth Glass. Following that, I want to give you a short overview of the gentrification process that's taken place in London. Thirdly, I want to present my own argument about what I have called an emerging 'geography of gentrification' in London and the notion of a, and I apologize for the term, of a 'metropolitan habitus' and my views to try and explain it. Following that, I want to think about some of the problems associated with the concept of gentrification – and it seems to me in particular the fact that its highly ethnocentric and highly London centric; it seems to me, that the London centric issue is quite relevant as we're sitting here in Walsall thinking about the issue of gentrification. Fifthly, I want to question the extent to which gentrification and regeneration are able to co-exist in a meaningful relationship or is it rather a kind of abusive marriage, I mean, what is the relationship between gentrification and regeneration? And finally, and

I'm sorry it's at the end, I wanted to say something about the role of artists in all of this; there is at least one major study which talks about the role of art and artistic mode of production, in terms of gentrification in New York. I think actually there are some quite interesting things here and at least if I put it on the agenda you can pick it up in terms of questions. I've only got two slides, one of which is a quote and the other of which is a map.

Ruth Glass first coined the term gentrification about 40 years ago in what has now become one of the most quoted definitions in urban sociology. She says,

One by one, many of the working class quarters of London have been invaded by the middle-class – upper and lower – shabby modest mews and cottages have been taken over when their leases expired, and have become elegant, expensive residences. Larger Victorian houses, downgraded in an earlier or recent period – which were used as lodging houses or were, otherwise in multiple occupation – have been upgraded once again. Once this process of 'gentrification' starts in a district it goes on rapidly until all or most of the working class occupiers are displaced and the whole social character of the district is changed.

Glass wrote that in 1964. I think perhaps the first thing to say is about the term gentrification; it is that notion of the gentry, which I guess implies – particularly to the British – the middle class. The gentry is also a kind of non-urban group; the assumption is that it's a rural group. Therefore it refers to those people of middle rank who had largely disappeared from our cities in the post war game of, my term, 'urban leapfrog', in which the middle classes were leapfrogged out of city centres, out to the suburbs. Glass's description was highly prescient in terms of the subsequent academic career of the term. Gentrification has always been partnered with displacement. Middle class incomers have displaced working class natives from their homes and often the area. In London, at least, the displacement was often in the early days both tenurial and spatial. The middle classes moved into districts and often moved into houses that had been subdivided into flats. Therefore up to six households would be displaced, so clearly we can see the mathematics of what that means in terms of the rental population movement. They were often moved from private rented tenure into council rented accommodation; this coincided with the decline of private rented tenure and the rise, in the 70s and 80s at least, of public sector, council accommodation. Perhaps I should just say, we now live in a society where something like two thirds of homes are owned by…. I was going to say people own their homes – but of course mortgage companies own their homes. But in 1945 something like two thirds of those houses were owned by private landlords so, there has been a massive social revolution in that sense over the last 50 years. In other cases, people moved out of London altogether, and I think there is something quite interesting here in relation to displacement. The work that I have done shows that often these people upgraded themselves into owner occupation and into managerial occupations. So, to some extent I think, displacement was not always a process in which there were winners and losers; for some people, many white middle class people, it actually offered an opportunity for upward social mobility so spatial mobility equalled social mobility. Generally however, it was a class process in which the inner city became polarized between two forms of housing tenure: owner occupation and social housing. The great problem, of course though, in researching this, has been of identifying the displacees who by definition disperse. So much of the research on gentrification has focused on the incoming gentrifiers,

who are, by their very nature, highly visible and able to remake the area in which they are often in a numerical minority, after their own image. So there is a real problem with gentrification research; it focuses on 'winners' and almost by definition, it's very difficult to identify where the 'losers' go. You can do it – you can use census research but actually tracking it down, doing individual research, is really very, very difficult. Many of the areas of London in which I have undertaken research are examples – in Stoke Newington for example, and the area of Hackney. In estate agents speak, East Islington! The middle class have been able to transform Clissold Park into an essentially middle class space. I mean its quite interesting the way that's actually happened over the last 20 or 30 years. This is through the deployment of what the French Sociologist, Pierre Bourdieu, would call symbolic cultural capital. Bourdieu describes three kinds of capital: economic capital, social capital, and cultural capital – this could take up a whole lecture but that's for another time! But essentially if we can just take the term 'cultural capital' he defines it as having two forms which express, 'embodied dispositions and resources of the habitus' – we'll come back to the habitus – 'namely incorporated and symbolic'. The latter, 'symbolic', he sees as the ability to define and legitimize cultural, moral and aesthetic values, standards and styles. And it seems to me in a way, this is what gentrification does – it transforms an area, in which the middle class incomers are nearly always in a numerical minority, into the image of those who are able to define its 'shape and feel'. So, right from the start, gentrification has been about the process of urban social change and the changing class structure. More recently, it has been questioned whether this is as much of an urban process as has been assumed and there has been plenty of research linking it to the countryside (Barn conversions for example or the doing up of old mill towns), and also about whether it is something confined to financial centres such as London and Edinburgh. I will return to this later and the increasing frequency with which gentrification is now being spotted around the country. I think there's a real

problem about seeing it simply as an urban phenomenon. It seems to me it's actually about the way the different social classes are using space. I think the big question is whether it is something that is confined to financial centres such as London and Edinburgh or New York etc, which we can talk about in the discussion. But, by and large, most of the work on gentrification has been confined to large financial centres mainly in the Anglophone world.

I will return to this later and the increasing frequency with which gentrification is now being spotted around the country; there is the gentrification of Cardiff Bay for example and most towns

now identify some form of gentrification.

One other general point that needs to be made about gentrification is how we explain it. Is it something that is done by 'the system' or is it a 'people-led' process? These two competing explanations have dogged the debate, although most commentators would now agree that it is somehow a mixture of the two. I'm simplifying like mad but I think what is agreed is that it is not a 'return to the city process' so much as one of not leaving the city when it is time to put down roots, establish more stable household units and start breeding. Initially, people thought somehow it was about people who had left the city and were coming back. Now I think that's not the case. It's more a case of people not leaving the city when they used to, there was this idea when people had had their fun and it was time to settle down they would move out now they stay for good. In that sense, gentrification is no longer something that is restricted to the single or the 'dual incomes no kids yet', the DINKY's. In terms of the two competing explanations, the supply siders who are mainly of a Marxist persuasion have argued that capital continually seeks to create profitable outlets and one of the ways in which it squares the capitalist circle is through what the Marxist economist, David Harvey has termed the 'spatial fix' – Harvey has this notion of capitalism actually being a bit like a dog that's continually chasing its tail. In the immediate post-war years, capital in Britain, Australasia, North America and to a lesser degree Europe suburbanized and sought out undervalued non urban land this process was aided by subsidized public and private transportation systems – in Europe, subsidized public transport, in the US, the Interstate Highway System. The Interstate Highway System was largely built in the post-war period, exclusively with Tax Dollars, in order to aid the suburbanization process.

More recently, i.e. since the 1970s, this process has reversed and what has happened is that capital has moved back into the now devalued inner-city areas and the Docklands is a good, (maybe only) UK example. So what is happening is that capital seeks out these forms of undervalued land and of course this is the land that in previous rounds were devalued by the active process of disinvestment. Maybe this is why we're now seeing new processes of gentrification in these devalued rural areas, non-metropolitan cities, these were the areas that were disinvested in the 80s and 90s with the industrialization.

As the leading proponent of this view, Neil Smith, says, 'this is a movement back to the city by capital, not people'. The contrary view saw gentrification as being demand-led by the expansion, by the creation of a 'new class' in North American

terms and the expansion of the quaternary sector of advanced services coupled with the decline in the industrial economy. Here I am talking about financial services, legal services and the whole development planner thing if you like – of a post-industrial economy. And the expansion of these services is coupled very much with the decline of the industrial economy. This created what has been called a new class of 'urban seeking' rather than 'urban fleeing' middle class folk, who sought the excitement and cultural milieu of the city rather than the security, and boredom, it seemed to them at least, of the suburbs and the act of catching the last train home after a night out in town. To some extent, the first approach, concentrates on the malign effects of gentrification, of its displacement of working class people from employment and homes whilst the latter identified a more radical, socially inclusive middle class who wanted to flee from the one-class suburbs they'd been brought up in.

Neil Smith referred to the process of what he'd termed 'revanchism' in New York City in which the newly conquering middle classes were retaking the city almost block by block. It is a reference, 'revanchism', to the process whereby Louis Napoleon, and his supporters, regained Paris after the commune of the 1870s. And then declared that the working class were never going to take it again. Smith sees, very much, this as a kind of process that has been taking place in New York, this process from the 1980s onwards particularly in the 1990s he sees, as I say, as one of 'revanchism', of literally a retaking of the city.

David Ley, who has led the other demand led approach, has tended to focus on the cultural politics of the new class of gentrifiers and sees in them the making of progressive political alliances in his native Canada; the kind of people who have, been arguing for a new form of urban politics, a new form of urban development which is much more inclusive than the traditional form of growth coalitions that ran Canadian politics. In reality I think both Ley and Smith accept elements of each other's arguments. I think it is helpful to look at the two debates about

gentrification, the system-led and the people-led approach.

More recently, others, and I include myself in this, have laid stress on issues of gender and culture. As the post-war baby boomers went through the education system a cohort of highly trained young women gained educational qualifications – these were the kind of people who went to university in the 1960s – they gained educational qualifications that permitted them to compete in the professional labour market. For a bundle of reasons the occupations that were most open to women tended to be located in major cities like London and two income households then found that it was not only culturally congenial but altogether more rational to live in a large professional labour market where it was not necessary for them to move home when making a career move. Whereas this was possible when there was only one breadwinner, this became the source of much dispute when the household contained two such people – and commuting made no sense when children arrived and women chose, or were forced by economic circumstance, to remain economically active. In addition, the inner city with its mixed class structure was far more likely to provide childcare and other domestic workers than the single class suburbs. The advantage of somewhere like London is you can actually, again, find a degree of labour market mobility without moving. The labour market is sufficient enough, it's also pretty irrational for two members of the family to get on a train each day to go into the centre, do their business and then go home again. So, I think the increasing extent to which women participating in the professional labour market has been very important. But in particular, I mean commuting made no sense, when children arrived and women either chose or were forced by economic circumstances to remain economically inactive. In addition, I think this is an important point, the inner city with its mixed-class structures was far more likely to provide childcare and other domestic workers than the single class suburbs were able to provide. There has also been a huge increase in recent years of the employment of domestic labour by middle class households.

So how has this all impacted on London? In my next section I am really talking about the gentrification of London. Now, at the risk of gross generalization, one can argue that the origins of London's gentrification can be traced back to Islington. Whilst this was being commented on, really that's what Ruth Glass was commenting on in that slide that I showed you, and other academics from the 1960s, it was also the subject of much media comment and hilarity. I don't know if any of you remember Marc Boxer's cartoons in The Times about the *Stringalongs*. I think is was called *Life and Times in One, the Trendy Ape*. But the *Stringalongs* were the kind of epitome of, if you like, the gentrifying media types who were moving into areas like N1 in the 1960s. And in fact the *Stringalongs* were widely based, it was alleged, around the life of the journalist Nicholas Tomalin who invented the term 'conspicuous thrift' which I think is actually a rather good description of their lifestyle, at an age where middle class life was about keeping up with 'the Jones', about conspicuous consumption and so on and so forth.

It was further elaborated, if we're going to stick with the kind of cultural media, by Jonathan Rabin in his book *Soft City*, which some of you may be familiar with, in which he gave practical hints on how you spot the process. I mean damp patches left in the road by the mixing of concrete. Skips, windows with no lace curtains giving onto living rooms which had been knocked through from back to front and left with stripped pine floors adorned by a single dead sheep. This isn't a direct quote this is from memory. The media characterization was continued in similar vein, somewhat later in the Guardian by Posy Simmonds who retold the trials and tribulations of *George and Wendy Webber* and their family. As ever, these cultural representations had a cruel truth to them and are largely confirmed by the work undertaken on the gentrification of London over the last thirty years by people like myself, colleagues like Chris Hannett and Loretta Lees at King's College, Gary Bridge, Michael Lyons and a guy called Peter Williams who did much of the initial work on Islington and Barnsbury in the early 1970s. I think, these media stereotypes were a new kind of cultural class they were different from the mainstream middle classes.

Over the years, I mean London's gentrification has spread West and East from its base in Barnsbury and Canonbury to Camden and Hackney and from Wandsworth in South West London to include much of Lambeth and parts of Lewisham, Southwark and Greenwich. Interestingly, and I wouldn't want to be a determinist on this, but much of this can initially be explained by the building of new tube or light rail lines. The building of the Victoria line (started in 1962, completed in 1970) connected Canonbury to the centre of government in St James Park and Victoria. The Jubilee Line extension opened up whole areas of Southwark and most recently the Dockland Light Railway has previously put inaccessible parts of Greenwich within 12 minutes of the Bank of England. I discovered this the other day a colleague of mine living in, so he thought, non-gentrified Greenwich now takes 12 minutes; it will have a wonderful effect on property prices which he feels a bit bitter-sweet about! These transportation changes have made enormous changes to London. Now most London boroughs are home to great swathes of gentrified private housing, done up by individual families or small developers. The only exceptions are those areas of South London with their monolithic council estates. If this process of gentrification was undertaken by what might be termed collective social action along the lines of the *Stringalongs* or the *Webbers* acting as pioneers opening up the new urban frontiers – these analogies are again quite important. This was how the West was opened up in the States, the pioneers pushing the frontier forward. The opposite to that then is the Docklands; it has really witnessed the Neil Smith type deployment of large-scale capital revalorising cheap and contaminated industrial sites. More recently however, parts of the city fringe such as Shoreditch, Clerkenwell and Spitalfields have been the object of similar moves by developers wishing to capitalize on spaces and old

buildings within walking distance of the City of London and the telephone number salary men there. I don't know if anyone here knows Spitalfields but it is within two or three hundred metres of the centre of the financial district. There are £500,000 houses with Porsche's outside, it's a very rapidly changing area.

Now I mean the result of this has been, and this is no great insight, but has been a major polarization between those able to afford the huge cost of private housing in the old inner suburban ring and those who are able, or have no option other than to access social housing in this area. What has been squeezed I think is the middle in a situation where even a one bedroom flat will require a household income of maybe £100,000 a year. It is not just teachers, police officers, nurses and fire fighters, so called essential workers, who cannot afford to live in inner London but also university lecturers, many doctors, most civil servants or other highly qualified professional workers. It is really only those with access to private capital, or huge salaries in the City's business services such as solicitors, bankers, marketing people, barristers and others who can afford the £750,000 for a modest family house in Barnsbury or between the commons in Wandsworth, it may be even higher than that now.

Of course, it is never this black and white; many people do find the money, others moved in before price rises became so high and public sector salaries so derisory, others have high earning partners. However, the dividing line between the public and private sectors has become more blurred. It is probably more likely that many of these people, this is just an observation really, will vote for New Labour than the Conservatives which never used to be the case with bankers, stockbrokers and solicitors. The point I am trying to make here is that that we're also talking about a change in our conception of the middle class. The notion of what middle class work is has changed tremendously this has changed along with the process of gentrification.

Coming on to my fourth point, which is about the creation of the so-called metropolitan habitus; what I'm not really trying to argue is that all this has been driven by housing prices because what we have here is a process, which is significantly social in content. Many of the rich and powerful of the city of London can still be found every morning and evening at Liverpool Street station, Victoria or Waterloo getting in and out of their chauffeured Mercedes, BMW's or Lexus limousines. Large numbers of people still commute into London there is no doubt about that. Many others have a *pied a´ terre* perhaps in the Barbican or other such central location. Many however have chosen, and that's the word I want to underline, chosen to live not only in what were previously inner London suburbs – Barnsbury, Notting Hill, Battersea – or further out in Hackney, Brixton or Telegraph Hill, because they are attracted to what I term the 'metropolitan habitus'. A habitus is associated with, Pierre Bourdieu the late French sociologist. Habitus, as he suggests is a social environment which people find comfortable and fits them like an old cloak and as such not only welcomes them but fashions them into its ways. So that's the kind of way I see a habitus, you know monks wore habits – this notion of a kind of close fitting coat which you feel comfortable in but also gives you a kind of look and feel. Others still prefer the suburban, single class commuting life style – the urban fleeing members of the middle classes. For the urban seeking middle classes it is in many cases the memories of a childhood brought up in the 'burbs' and their experiences then subsequently of life at university which has convinced them to remain in the city, even when they begin to take on all the classic responsibilities of family and home ownership which used, as it were, to force the 'reality check' which led to the commute for him and coffee klatch for her. But many of these people will remember that, as a child, life was very boring out there, more than one person has said to me it was living death in the suburbs.

If the post-war middle classes were seeking security in the suburbs then their children were after the vicarious pleasures of the urban existence. Gentrification was about risk taking, living in a 'working class' borough like Hackney or a multicultural one like Brixton. More often than not in fact, the former Hackney is associated with a kind of radicalism (although many of you may remember that actually Hackney for many years was run by Peter Mandelson's grandfather Herbert Morrison who shared a lot with his grandson and he was anything but radical, in fact it was the kind of epitome of safe municipal socialism.) But nevertheless, I think the idea of Hackney is one of class radicalism and working classness. And the 'frisson' of Brixton is often commented on. It's amazing how many people talk about Brixton and tell you it's about the 'frisson' of living there, a kind of living on the edge. And I think that's a very appealing notion of gentrification.

What the original pioneers in Islington focused on was what we might now term social inclusion – sending their kids to iconic schools like William Tyndale or Islington Green led by head teachers with a national reputation. The head teacher at Islington Green School was one of the pioneers of the comprehensive education system at a time when many teachers could actually afford to live in the area as well, forget that now if they want to own their own homes. So this was living, if you like, on the urban frontier in which there was minimal spatial distance from other social groups, particularly in the early days. Increasingly of course, streets became more middle class and their inhabitants learned to manage social and spatial distance in ways, which made the others largely invisible, except when they were wanted to do cleaning or to add local colour (literally in the case of Brixton). This is a process, which I refer to as 'social tectonics' in which the different groups live largely self-contained lives and move past each other in ways that only involve minimal contact yet manage any potential for social conflict. So, in fact, it is very important for many people, in terms of gentrification, to live amongst the working classes, amongst different kinds of people. But in fact in terms of any real contact it is, I would argue, very, very minimal. I think this kind of notion of 'social tectonics' is quite a useful way of describing urban life where there's only actually minimal spatial distance but actually huge social distance and as I say many people made invisible to the middle class who have taken over the area.

At the same time, as the above account has indicated, whilst the main contrast is between the urban seeking and the urban fleeing middle classes, there are also important social and spatial differences within the urban seeking middle class. I think it is important now that we talk about the middle classes in the plural rather than as one middle class as it's increasingly difficult to see it as a hegemonic group. The metropolitan habitus in a large city like London fragments into a series of mini habituses, which represent significant differences of background, outlook and affiliation amongst the London middle classes that are not simply reducible to occupation or income, to take the two most obvious indicators. In other words, what I'm arguing is the way you actually understand this differentiation in London's middle classes is not simply by saying well we understand it in terms of how much they earn, but it's a much more nuanced phenomenon where it goes back to ideologies, politics, and cultural values for example.

In my most recent research this can be illustrated by looking at these areas. In this piece of research I looked at a number of gentrified areas in inner London. We looked at three areas; the Docklands and five areas around London: Telegraph Hill, Brixton, and Battersea in South London, Barnsbury and Hackney in North London. In all these cases, except for Docklands which is seriously different, what people are essentially looking for is an urban community which enables them to build relationships which are seen as sadly missing in a world where, if you like, the long term is systematically being engineered out of the supply chain.

And I don't know if anyone's familiar with the work of Richard Sennett, he wrote a book called *The Corrosion of Character* and I draw very heavily on this. Basically what Sennett argues in *The Corrosion of Character* is that what's happening is the very people who are, if you like, responsible for re-engineering the contemporary capital, for taking the long term out and for finding new ways of making more profits, are suddenly taking fright at what the consequences are for their own personal lives. That in a sense, their kids are becoming kind of mall rats and that actually there's no time for their children,

there's no time for personal relationships and that the personal consequences of this life are now beginning to impact on their household. And many of those living and working in London are precisely these denizens of the new economy but are scared stiff by what it is doing to their relationship with their children which they compare unfavourably with their own upbringing – which of course at the time they wished to escape! The fact that their parents knew exactly when they were going to retire, they had little ways of doing things, they had routines, all that kind of thing if you like about suburban post-war middle class life which was so boring, which they couldn't wait to get away from, they couldn't wait to go to university. They went to university and they made it and they were upwardly mobile and they got the job in consultancy, you know they write the reports, they turn left when they get through the aircraft door, but actually they've got nothing to pass on to their children. This is one of the things that came across more than almost anything else in terms of interviewing people; there is a fear about what's actually happening to their children, a lack of values to pass on. What I'm arguing is that what many of these people are trying to do is to recreate in the city precisely the kind of communities in which they can actually pass something on.

So taking my five research areas, they can all be shown to reflect if you like, different takes on this and to some extent they act as their own housing markets in which people move up when they can. Most people moved to an area and stayed there. As they became more affluent they would buy a bigger property in the same area rather than moving to a more expensive part of London. In nearly all cases, they moved there shortly after coming to London and they often moved there with people they had known at university and with whom they had remained longstanding friends. We ask people – "Could you tell us who your three best friends are?" Almost always at least one of them was someone they had known at university. What was interesting was some of those university friends, had for whatever reasons, tended to move to the same areas themselves. Therefore the area remained highly attractive and socialized them into living in London, and coping with its downsides. I think the notion of friendship, is a very un-researched area, but in a sense friendship is now replacing the notion of community and kin and I think that's very important in terms of actually understanding the way these processes work.

What I want to do now is give you a very brief thumbnail sketch of the various areas that we looked at.

Barnsbury: respondents were all highly educated, and at one stage it seemed like everyone had been to Oxbridge, everyone works as a lawyer, almost universally household incomes were over £150, 000 a year, this was five years ago. What seemed attractive about Barnsbury, was its social capital rich past and the idea of a socially inclusive mix. If you like, it was the first generation of gentrification. It was an area where it seemed that you could, as it were, have the best of both worlds but there was some kind of notion of social obligation and I think that was terribly important. The fact that not one person we talked to educated their children at its secondary schools showed the extent to which idea and reality were at odds, but nevertheless I think in all these cases what we're talking about is a script. What the idea for living there was, seems to be, ideal social inclusion. This was a very important notion of what tied people to Barnsbury.

If you then take Battersea, almost in many senses the polar opposite of Barnsbury. In Barnsbury people had lots of economic capital, but what really mattered to them was the social capital. Whereas those who lived in Battersea, what was important to them was eating out rather than the joining in. Battersea, North Road is called Nappy Valley – littered with every restaurant you can think of, eating out was a major activity. And I think therefore what really mattered about Battersea was that you could actually deploy economic capital in order to maintain a particular way of life in the city. Most of these people, when you actually asked them, said 'we'd really like to live in Wiltshire or we'd really want to live in Dorset'. It was also strongly connected via the M3 to the idea of life in the country, although this was probably never realizable except for the weekends and holidays. What they

were into was shooting, sports etc, but they worked in the financial services industry, it simply wasn't possible. But what Battersea enabled them to do, because of its council and the Thatcherite policies associated with Wandsworth, was to buy particular forms of private services – education, health etc which meant that they could exist in the city without actually having to interact with it.

Brixton: The attraction of Brixton was its multicultural past as the centre for London's African Caribbean settlement. If you like in this sense it was the idea of Brixton and almost everyone we talked to said 'it's the multiculturalism, it's the frisson of living there'. Brixton has a particular kind of multiculturalism a kind of alternative oppositional multiculturalism. It was also a kind of alternative in nighttime economy, with the Fridge and the Ritzy cinema. When we actually asked people, what their interactions were with people from other social groups they admitted it was almost non-existent. Actually the two groups move completely past each other in Brixton and have almost nothing to do with each other. But nevertheless, it was that idea of multiculturalism that was so important about moving to and living in Brixton and that kind of idealness.

If these three places have anything in common, it is to celebrate London's status as a global urban icon – guiltily in the case of Islington possibly, unashamedly in the case of Wandsworth or oppositional in the case of Brixton.

What the other two areas I want to talk about had in common was that they in fact represented a retreat from the city, unlike the first three there was no consumption infrastructure and that was their attraction. In both Telegraph Hill and in London Fields there are no restaurants. There are no bars and they do not have that kind of consumption infrastructure, which gives these other places their attraction. This was part of the attractiveness to those people about being able to live in the city, and in the case of Telegraph Hill it was the epitome of the urban village. The village, in which everyone knew each other, met at the school gate, looked after each other. The kinds of people they knew were exactly like themselves and the shutters

were very much up against the local area which contained some of the most unreconstructed areas of working class life in South London – New Cross, Millwall and North Peckham. The local school was the centre of the social networks, and the middle classes worked assiduously to maintain it as a middle class school and to maintain the relative advantage of their children. In other words, they used what you would see as their social capital in networks to compensate for their relative lack of economic capital. They were unable to afford the kind of private means of the people in Wandsworth but actually didn't want to either; it was the idea of creating a kind of urban village, a village in the mind.

And finally London Fields which was different yet again. The appeal of London Fields as I have already mentioned was the idea of living in Hackney. What was interesting about those people living in London Fields is that they were both either most likely more upwardly or downwardly mobile, in comparison to their parents' social position, than any other group. Many of them had come from very posh professional backgrounds. Top silver service, doctors as parents or they'd been upwardly mobile but to both groups, what actually appealed was that notion of living in a kind of, in your face working class borough with allegedly rampant class background. It was that kind of idea of Hackney that appealed. They were actually very different from the people in Telegraph Hill because, unlike the people in Telegraph Hill, they were not actually prepared to try and change the area or to use their social capital to change it, but rather to adapt to work and find their own particular private solutions to education, to dog shit, or whatever. The two things that come out of this are parks and dog shit; they are very important things if you get really stuck for something to talk about you can talk about them.

I just want to say one very quick note about the Docklands – it was completely and utterly different. Docklands was like suburbia in the city. What appealed to people about Docklands was you could actually go and live somewhere, which was totally low maintenance. UPVC windows you didn't have to paint, but also neighbours you didn't have to talk to. You'd come, you could go out and almost entirely the people kind of living there had existences elsewhere. They had *pied a terre's*, they had just divorced, they had families living in the country and this was kind of urban living, you know, which was constructed with the cranes and everything there but actually required minimal social involvement, unlike all the other places.

I now want to talk about some of the problems with this approach. I would argue that this approach to the gentrification of inner London therefore identifies a number of geographies of gentrification, which accommodate the variety of difference within the middle class. That when we are talking about the middle class and middle classes now, we are talking about multiple identities and I think that's been one of the changes associated with industrialization and globalization. And you simply cannot reduce these differences to occupation or income; you need to take into account the choices that people make. It also takes into account as I say the changes that have taken place globally, nationally and in London over recent decades. The vast pull of London both nationally and internationally, to young upwardly mobile people has been tremendous. I think it also takes into account the massive consequences of gender for middle class families and the employment patterns that implies. However, I think there are three major weaknesses in terms of the work that I have been doing, which again I think reflect some of the things we might want to talk about.

Firstly, gentrification in this account remains a massively white process. In all the areas, in which I undertook research, over 95% of my respondents were white. I don't think this was a problem with the sampling process, more it was a problem of where I looked. I looked in areas where the white middle classes settled. But I know that there is a large non-white professional middle class in London now. For example, I work for Kings College London which is the biggest medical trainer in the country, Europe, the world over, well over half the entrants to the medical school are now non-white. What

is also interesting is what has not changed; the ethnic compositions changed, what's not changed is the class background. They come from professional families they just happened to be non-white families. This is a huge change. But where are these people living? What doesn't work for, let us say, Asian kids, are the kind of cultural capital of Victorian or Edwardian houses. It doesn't have the same sort of meaning that it might have to me, in terms of the kind of history of what happened during those eras. I think much more what we will find is that new buildings, post-war housing tend to be part of their cultural heritage. However, I think it also may be that in some ways, and I can't really get my head quite round this, that white professional middle classes are using part of their cultural capital almost as a kind of form of social exclusion despite their vehemently multicultural rhetoric. Anyway, I think there's a big issue and a big problem here about the fact that there's huge numbers, especially in London of non-white members of the professional middle classes, but they are not living in many of these classic gentrified areas. So that raises a number of interesting issues about where they are living, but also I think it raises the notions about the role ethnicity plays in terms of the construction of these middle classes. I've recently received some funding from the ESRC to investigate these phenomena so I hope to have some answers as a result of the research that we are mainly going to conduct in East London, which is a traditionally non-gentrified area.

The second problem is that the analysis is largely confined to London. Apart from longstanding work on Edinburgh, which is Britain's second financial city, there has until recently been little work done on the gentrification of areas outside London. I think this is partly an issue of scale but what we are beginning to see in other major cities in the UK is a gentrification of the city centre into what is often a kind of 24/7 entertainment zone by empty nesters – young singles or childless couples including a significant element of gentrification by gay men. I think that may be a different form of gentrification but nevertheless people have now begun to write about the gentrification of Leeds, Bristol and Manchester. It makes us ask

questions about what we are actually talking about, when we talk about gentrification there is definitely a big hole in the literature.

And thirdly, there's a big gap here, which is that this work neglects inter-class interactions; it has focused too much on the intra middle class activities rather than looking at relations with other social classes. It has neglected what was a long-standing strand in sociology – that of the community study which examined the nature of 'local social systems'. My colleague Loretta Lees is undertaking a study which will look at these interactions and will hopefully prove to be a useful corrective to these studies that have simply looked at one, albeit powerful, class in isolation.

The last two things I want to talk about are gentrification and regeneration and art and gentrification. I want to ask if it is possible to build a regeneration strategy on gentrification? Will the middle class prove to be a power for good whose activities will benefit the whole community? i.e. the 'trickle-down' approach – if we can attract the middle classes the benefits of this will trickle down. It might be argued, for those of you who know the Rogers Report (Urban Renaissance), with its aim of inclusive regeneration was predicated on the benefits of a café culture which its members had experienced on their forays to landmark or benchmark European cities. Stuttgart, Barcelona etc seemed cities at ease with themselves and which offered a model of dense city living in which good design could promote social cohesion. However, gentrification, in its short history, has been associated with displacement and it has been assumed that it is in some ways incompatible with the notion of regeneration, which it is assumed (although I'm not quite sure why), that it will be of benefit for all i.e. socially inclusive. Certainly in Britain, gentrification has been exclusively about owner occupation whereas in North America it has also included rented accommodation. However, in both, it seems to be coupled with both physical and social displacement and increasingly polarization. The increased rhetoric on choice in public services,

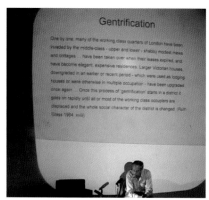

notably education, suggests its going to be hard to construct socially inclusive neighbourhoods in which competition for scarce resources is built in, although possibly the new city academies may help promote alternative approaches. The experience of London, however, where gentrification is rooted in a socially exclusive housing market has been that, at best, it leads to a kind of socially tectonic situation in which not only inhabitants, but I think sadly their children live in almost entirely sealed life worlds from each other.

And finally, I apologize for leaving it until the end, art and gentrification. It does seem to me relevant to talk about given the way art and culture more generally are now seen as part of any regeneration strategy. It used to be the case that a cultural infrastructure was evidence of a strong urban economy – one can think of Manchester in the nineteenth century, its' philharmonic orchestra etc, its' art galleries were indicative that it had a strong economy. Now a cultural strategy has to be at the centre of any economic regeneration strategy. Walsall and its new art gallery is an oft-quoted example of this, it's easy to think of others. Colchester where I live is now commissioning a similar gallery designed by an architect called Rafael Viñoli in partnership with the university to house its collection of Latin American art in order to regenerate the eastern end of the town. You could therefore take quite a benign view that actually art and culture is leading to

regeneration. However, Sharon Zukin's work on the SoHo district of New York city could offer a rather more malign view of the role of gentrification in *Block Busting*. She argues that there is what she terms an 'Artistic Mode of Production' in New York and that this was invoked to allow change of use to old industrial buildings. The south of Houston area was basically small manufacturer sweatshops. The textile and garment industries began to move out and the developers wanted to convert it. Very strict zoning regulations in New York said no that area was to be for industrial use. In the beginning artists were allowed to use them as workspaces, they needed large spaces with 24/7 access. They needed places where they could build things, spaces which had the properly strengthened floors etc. Artists were seen as different, an exception to this rule, also art is an important part of the New York economy. So dispensation was given for them to live and work in these places, hence, the live/work spaces that we're now hearing about all the time. Slowly this transformed the nature of the area, galleries moved in to sell the stuff. This in turn attracted a kind of culturally capital rich group of well off people who wanted to emulate the live/work style, the so-called 'loft livers'.

It became increasingly hard to hold the line that you had to be a practising artist to live there. The end result was that the area became transformed, the artists could no longer afford the rents, and the lawyers and so forth started 'loft living'. There is a

similar story in East London where many of the areas used by artists are now beyond their means. I am not, of course, arguing that artists are somehow the cultural lieutenants of property development, but I think it does point to how we need to take a broad view of gentrification as regeneration. We also need to look at the other side, my memory of Hackney in the 1970s was of hundreds of abandoned houses with LEB, (these initials stood for London Electricity Board), LEB-off written on their outsides and their toilets smashed by councils to stop them being squatted in. To some extent this was the antithesis to gentrification it was thought that no one is going to live there.

I just want to put forward a final thought before we get too het-up about the evils of gentrification ? It is that London, New York and many other cities prior to gentrification led regeneration were suffering from massive disinvestments.

AH: Thanks very much Tim, that was a really interesting presentation. I suppose it might seem to you peculiar that we asked you along to speak as part of this project, but I think that one of our key interests is to do with the question of function and functionality and the way that art can be instrumentalized through the regeneration and gentrification process. Our understanding of these processes has been acquired through our experiences of working in the public realm, working with planners, and commissioners.

I am interested in the way that you have plotted London and you made it clear that we can see particular areas growing, both in cultural capital, and in economic capital. I wanted to ask the question, what do you foresee the future of these areas becoming? Do they continue to grow outwards? Or do they reach a natural conclusion? Are we looking at new areas growing as perhaps the original areas become too expensive to move to and new middle class communities emerge in places that are perhaps not the most obvious places within London? I suppose it's a question of, what is the future of gentrification?

TB: I don't know, it's futurology. One of the things that is certainly happening in London is, middle London in particular, is now increasingly a middle class city. The 2001 census shows that whilst at the same time something like 45% of the male population of Hackney are now what is termed economically inactive. That hides a variety of sins including quite a lot of people who are students, so there is this kind of polarization. Now particularly in South London, there are very large swathes of pre-war and post-war housing estates that are, if you like, still kind of no-go areas in terms of gentrification although many housing blocks that have been done up, intercom phones etc put in. So I think you can see the continuing pressure on inner London. But I want to make a general point, which is that really what we're seeing is a kind of Los Angelization of South East England, the whole of South East England is now essentially London. Daniel Dawling and Bedford Thomas have just produced this wonderful atlas for the 2001 census and essentially what they are arguing is that there are two Britain's. There is a Britain that runs somewhere from the Wash line which is London, which is dominated by the pull of London and there are a series of independent states as it were, which are the rest of the United Kingdom. Dawling and Thomas say we're talking about a nation that was united by history but it is now divided by geography. People have two houses, weekend houses, they work in the city and what we're seeing is a whole process of gentrification which is now taking place from Basingstoke to Colchester, from Canterbury to High Wycombe, it is now one large travel to work area within which people move, gentrify, do things up etc. But we can't forget that the greatest areas of deprivation in Britain are still in London, the top three are Hackney, Tower Hamlet's and Newham, these are always the top three of the most deprived boroughs on the deputy prime ministers ranking.

So I'm not sure if that answers your question but I think one needs to expand the scale of it, one needs to look at these things slightly wider than simply as one particular city.

MJ: I wanted to ask a question it is a bit anecdotal and sorry about this, anyway I was born in Smithfield and I went to school in Hackney and I come from a working class family who had, and I don't think this is unusual, an aspiration to move East. East to Romford or Essex or even Southend-on- Sea. There was a sense of social mobility and I am not sure that still exists? I don't think poorer people have the same social mobility today as they had in the 60s and 70s. I wondered if you had any thoughts on this? I am also interested in what you say is a tectonic relationship; I went to a very ordinary school it was multicultural, I had black and Asian friends, I didn't even know they were black and Asian if you get what I mean. I didn't see them outside school because my parents didn't mix with their parents. I saw white working class kids outside school. This doesn't allow for much mixing of social groups.

TB: Well, what we're also trying to do is look at how people, 'transients' the geography term, moved out towards Southend and Essex, there will always be an extension of East London – I remember interviewing someone who said, 'well my parents kind of followed the central line out'! People continually moved, those that could moved out. Now, where it gets much more complex, than its assumed is when it becomes tied up with 'white flight'. I refer to the fact that work that I did do on the census that was a longitudinal study to track individuals, certainly showed that many of those families that left Hackney between 1971 and 1981, had moved from private rented or council accommodation into owner occupation. They often moved from being skilled manual workers into managerial occupations this enabled some form of individual upward mobility. But clearly there were those that didn't have the resources – financial, cultural, intellectual, human or whatever to move out. Many of them, are trapped increasingly, the elderly and so forth.

I don't know whether this is an answer, but clearly what we're talking about I guess is the notion of dynamics. John Urry, a sociologist in Lancaster, increasingly argued that sociology is kind of stuck in the past, which saw the census that took place every ten years giving you a kind of map of society, of social structure, into which you then slotted people. He's got this argument, what he sees as mobile sociology, which is actually that if you look at society now it is almost entirely based around mobility. Mobile phones are one example of a more mobile existence maybe we haven't yet introduced the kind of ways of tracking that, of thinking about it. But it is not a question of measuring it every ten years and seeing where things have moved to, it's much, much more fluid. And I guess that's part of the answer as well, is that we have to begin to think much more about it in terms of these kinds of changes.

MJ: I suppose I'm just concerned about the working classes in London that come from London. Where do they go? And as they get less and less able to be mobile because I don't think they have the sort of luxury of the mobility that me and my family might have had in the 1970s. I think it comes back to your question about polarization, are we looking at increasing social exclusion and polarization in the city?

TB: I don't totally buy John Urry's view really, if you do have a kind of view about an increasingly mobile society, those who are unable to be mobile are massively disappointed in ways that previously people might not have been.

MA1: You've got to be mobile, you know, because there's so much investment in that part of the country, in London and the South East. I'm from the North but I find

it very difficult because all the industries in computer software are concentrated in London. I think there was once talk of building a science park in the North West, which would address the balance slightly because there's an infrastructure there, that's not being used but there wasn't sufficient political backing for it so you're kind of constrained to moving to London for work.

MA2: Do you think gentrification actually increases social capital in general - does it affect that sort of dynamic?

TB: It's a tricky one, I mean one of the problems is there's at least two major definitions of social capital, and they tend to be used inter-changeably which I think is part of the problem. And certainly the current government is a great believer in social capital. I suppose you'd have to ask the question, social capital for who? I mean the argument is that you would increase it for the community as a whole.

If you take the example of Telegraph Hill, if you argued such a capital within that particular social network which is pretty class bound, I think it does increase it. So I would argue it's cultural capital gets memorized in the social network.

Also I wanted to just respond to the previous question, I agree with what you said. A guy called Tony Fielding, once referred to the South East as an escalator region: where people went then moved off of it; they gained their skills etc. I interviewed a lawyer who made me feel old, she was half my age and earned about four times as much as I do. But the only way she could actually have a life was to take a partnership in Leeds where she's in the second financial centre – probably take a drop in salary but then she could actually consider having a family, which simply was not possible in London. You can argue counter to this, for example Manchester takes pride in the fact that its not London it knows the benchmark for London is New York, the benchmark for Manchester is actually that other plethora of European regional cities. Of which we are now highly connected, by regional airports.

BS: I've got a question and it is related to what you were saying. I'm really interested

in the way you talked about and emphasized choice and the movement of individuals. I wondered how does planning and the strategic decisions about London intersect with this kind of movement of people that seems far more about individuals, what role does planning play in this process?

TB: Well, a very good question. One of the problems with London is that, like most major cities, its transport networks are radial I would argue that a global city like London should provide ways of enabling people to move around the city. The argument is that if you enable that level of infrastructure then lots of other things can and will happen.

However much we understand about planning it becomes retractable at the level of things like education because certainly the middle classes treat London as one large education market – we are made to talk about education now as a market. You simply can't plan it because people find ways to get round the planning. I have heard stories where people can only go to a school near where they live so in order to get access to a better school they will rent a flat – just opposite the school!

BS: But, say for example, in terms of one of your research areas do you also take into account, the population of Dalston? How does the council attempt to plan or have control of how this gentrification happens?

TB: There's not a lot they can do. If we take the example of Dalston we can come back to the big issue of transport, they are now extending the East London line, to Dalston. Education and housing is also another massive issue its one of the things that will bring London to a halt. If the people who work for the middle classes, dog walking and things like that haven't got anywhere to live then London will stop being a desirable place to live for others because they won't be able to get things done there.

MA3: It's true it's very difficult for those sorts of workers to afford to live near enough to where they work. I'm interested in this in relation to the artistic community; for example in New York where they went to SoHo and got priced out, then moved to Chelsea and have been priced out there too. What will the future hold for London in terms of their key workers and the cultural industry when people literally can't afford to live there? Are they going to commute in? I doubt it. So I wonder if other cities in the country will become these centres instead?

TB: Interesting question. I've worked in East London for 30 years but I've now started working in the centre of London and it's a completely different experience in many ways but one of the things I have noticed is there are ten coffee shops – Pret a Manger's, Cafe Nero's etc within three minutes of work. Nobody in those shops speaks English as a first language; this demonstrates the extent to which London depends upon migrant labour and those people clearly have to live somewhere. I think there has been enormous ingenuity in terms of finding housing spaces that previously did not exist. East London is the last ungentrified area of London. My suspicion is that what's going to happen is increasingly the white middle class will start moving there and suddenly there will be this struggle and the age of professionalism will take over. Again coming back to transport, one of the things that has improved is the night bus service it's actually amazing now.

MA3: I was also thinking about artists who've had a traditional practice of using spaces, which are usually empty warehouses. As they disappear I wonder if artistic practice will change in its nature or whether indeed artists will just move to somewhere where they have space that enables them that kind of lifestyle of working like that?

TB: London borough apparently, I can't remember what they called it now, but it does look a bit like it has changed towards artists. They are encouraging and making available space for people to live and work. The trouble is as soon as you've got successful you're out on your own. If you go out to Stratford, which is eight minutes from Liverpool Street there's a big warehouse, which somebody's taken over, an entrepreneur who lets stuff out, still in a relatively reasonable way. It does seem to me that artists need clusters I think its quite difficult to sit on your own, you can write your novel like that but I think artists

do require other people.

But I think there is some recognition that a city like London will only work if it is fairly culturally attractive and I think that it is important that there are a range of artists, that it doesn't become gentrified in the kind of way that culture became gentrified in Edinburgh which, as I understand, is a problem for Edinburgh.

AH: I think it is useful to ask the question 'who are artists'? I think for the most part a lot of them do come from the middle classes themselves and in some respects perhaps they are part of a gentrifying class.

In your book *London Calling* you talk about areas in which artists can be edged out; we know that artists have got an excess of cultural capital but of course some of them have also got economic capital because of their background. I think artists are like any other professional class of people, they may have the same aspirations and the same desire to change the environments in which they are living in, I mean they are part of it. They can be an active part of gentrification like any other middle class person.

I just wondered whether you thought the activities of artists are perhaps, within gentrification, are over-played or exaggerated. And some of this gentrification would take place never mind what artists were doing and the activities of artists were actually really quite useful just for perhaps packaging or marketing an area and that's simply what its all about really. A little added glamour perhaps.

TB: Well I don't want to put myself out of a job, but you know, to some extent I think gentrification's a bit kind of over played as well! I think we're moving through a period at the moment of just such massive change it's a bit like, what happened between 1780 and 1820 when Britain became an industrial society. Well now we're seeing the same sort of changes in this transformation to post-industrialism and presumably we still need washing machines and things like that, we must have standards! So as I've tried to indicate I think this process of gentrification which is always seen in terms of the city and one or two cities, is now something that's much,

much more widespread that we're seeing taking place over a much wider area.

To try to answer your question I think, if you go back to the kind of language that saw gentrification in terms of frontiers, pushing the frontiers back, the brave pioneers that did it. These kinds of people, clearly as you put it, have an excess of cultural capital, if it is possible to have an excess of cultural capital. They were very important in terms of those alternative lifestyles, those ways of doing things and that kind of conception that then enabled others to come on their coat tails and I think we're talking about a process that's now becoming much more mobilized. I think we are talking about a kind of cultural new class for whom, art or culture in the broadest sense is actually incredibly important because that was one of the problems with suburbs there wasn't any, you had to go up to London then you rely on getting the last train back. Sometimes you missed the last act because you were worrying about missing your train. I'm exaggerating but now I think, culture and art is part and parcel of what we actually do in a place of industry. It's about science and symbolism isn't it?

AD: I just want to thank you first of all because your talk has given me so many triggers for potential questions which mostly comes from the fact that I live in

London and my studio is in Dalston and I live just around the corner from London Fields in what was an old shoe factory, so I know these areas very well. I did feel a bit like a pioneer when I found my shoe factory and, on the basis of a six year lease, we've spent a year just working on it to make it into a house because it meant we could afford a reasonable rent in an area which seemed to offer enough for us to work and to do all the things we need to do.

We had no funds that could have enabled us to change many things around the area, but we have certainly noticed that every other building around us has changed and been turned into a so-called 'loft space'. When you actually go and see these places as a prospective buyer, I haven't got a spare penny to do that, but it's interesting to just go and see, you can find maybe one wall surface with exposed bricks which gives it enough clout to be a loft!

So, I wanted to ask what studies are conducted, that identifies areas prior to them becoming gentrified, to identify places that might offer potential for change? And incidentally talking about Stratford I think that anything about Stratford is short-lived if the London bid to the Olympics goes through because I'm also trying to find places there too.

TB: I suppose the short answer to your question is if I knew, and if I'd invested I would probably be worth $20,000 a day! But I don't. There is the so-called rent gap model, where you look at the average returns and so forth.

One of the best indicators of gentrification is actually the number of people, with degrees in an area. The census happens every ten years and can determine the social composition of an area. I'm possibly getting involved in a project that's looking at studentification (terrible word); students that move into an area do appear to be areas which become gentrified areas for all sorts of reasons because students then attract coffee shops and bookstores, as well as other sorts of things.

I would do the financial working out and I would also start looking at where there are students and if there is what I would term an appropriate infrastructure; student quarter, café culture, or of a developing middle class presence however alternative it might be.

MJ: I think it is about time to round up then. I'd just like to say thank you again to Tim for his great presentation.

The Creative City
Charles Landry

CL: Thanks a lot for inviting me along today. A rather sunny day and this guy, (referring to slide) you might think, is completely irrelevant to Walsall but about a couple of months ago there was a world tea party event and I met up with him in Vancouver for the second time, so that shows you that art travels and that's one of my themes today; mobility and the good and bad side of it. I want to talk to you about the 'creative city' and I'm going to ask questions like; how do you become a creative place? What are the dynamics of a creative place? And how do you think about making a place more pleasant to live in?

In order to create change we've really got to think differently – there's an expression by Einstein, 'if you try to address a problem with the same sort of thinking that went before you, you're going to get the same sort of answer.' So if we really do believe that the places that we live in could be better in one way or another, then we do need to shift our way of thinking about them. The conclusion to that is that if you think differently, you do things differently and I think artists have a contribution to make in terms of helping us think differently about problems. When we talk about creativity or the 'creative city', we mean supporting

invention; it's about developing a place, a cultural place. I think one of the problems we have when we think about cities is we think of them in a linear way. I mean if you could just do a survey now and ask people what a city is, the answer would be formed out of straight-line thinking, and I believe this type of thinking is a problem. The regeneration process takes a hell of a long time and what's really very interesting is what occurs between having an idea and making it happen. What do you do in that interim stage? It could be six or seven years, and that's where the artist is the key to keeping us creative. The issue is that when one is thinking about the city, to identify the hard infrastructure, but we have to remember it is also about the soft infrastructure; change has got to happen in an ethical way so it is not just creativity for its own sake, as I believe creativity can have negative effects as well.

The culture of the place and the confidence of the occupants really discern whether a capacity for imagination can be released or not. So, a culture of a place could take the whole place backwards or push it forwards, so in that sense it's the pivot point around which everything happens. The other important thing is that culture can generate value. In terms of a city's regeneration, what one

Transcript of a paper delivered by Charles Landry with questions from Dave Beech

Contributors
Charles Landry (CL)
Dave Beech (DB)
Andy Hewitt (AH)
Becky Shaw (BS)
Gavin Wade (GW)

is trying to do is combine something that generates value in a broad sense, but also value in a more tangible, perhaps a more economical and social sense. And that is quite a difficult thing to do; an example would be a project in Leeds where a group of youths self-managed a recycling project – recycling waste and turning it into money. In a project like this you can see a number of processes are happening at the same time. The youths became more involved in their community generating social value as well as the economic value from the recycling.

So, why do cities need to be creative? Well maybe it's obvious; the world is changing, maybe that's a dramatic thing to say and some people might disagree, but cities need to adapt and Walsall is the same and in principle we have to use our imagination to solve seemingly intractable problems. I argue that the use of creative thinking in relation to problems is a method that often allows us to identify the connections between seemingly disparate things. A project, I think, is created when it does more than one thing with the same action; like the project that I just described in Leeds, it is 'creative' when you are trying to do one thing that has a series of spin-offs. The other thing that I think is important to creativity is that it implies that definitions change over the course of time. I believe it's about thinking about the edge of the competence rather than the centre of it. When one talks about urban creativity and inter-organization creativity it is incredibly difficult to defend, because in a city, a place or a town, there are a number of different cultures which are often contradictory; people don't necessary like each other or love each other, or whatever. There are also different languages spoken, different professional heights etc, for example an engineer might approach a problem differently to an artist.

As we are talking about something as complex as a place I would argue that the capacity to think in an integrated way, to see these different perspectives at the same time is really the most interesting challenge of creativity, we could call it holistic thinking. So, if you have the sparkle of creativity that you need in a city, in a place, this is the capacity and

openness that you need in order to have an idea and realize it. There are many places in which the conditions won't allow you to have an idea and then turn it into some sort of reality. We all know places and offices and organizations that are the 'but' places, in my experience, they don't seem to get anywhere. Even if you look at the old production processes they tend to start with ideas; a company, a factory etc but we now need to look at the world and think about creativity differently from the manufacture of a product. In my organization there are four people and a dog, [the company is called Commedia] we project ourselves to the outside world and our networks as if we are much bigger. The image I've just pictured here is much more how reality works in places and cities which requires a completely different way of operating it is less than global and requires a basis of trust.

I spoke the other day in the Arctic Circle in what was an old warehouse building where all they do now is hold conferences and meetings. This change of use demonstrates a shift in the economy which is a global thing and people are producing and manufacturing products somewhere, but less so here in the UK. Indeed our predication is that there are 150, 000 manufacturing firms in Britain at the moment, small to large, but over the next 15 years or so, three quarters of those will go.

So, what you have is situations like this in factories; this is a bicycle factory in Slovenia (referring to slide), but this is about to change as bicycles are coming to you from China because of the difference in cost. Now if you just look at harbours and at the names on the back of those lorries that are driving around the country. Evergreen for example, you might think is British company but it is in fact a Chinese company. Where once Britain and Europe was the workshop of the world, that has declined dramatically and the Far East is where all these things are being produced, these are the new workshops of the world.

This is one of the major reasons why we do need to ask ourselves what can we do? Many companies in these regions will collapse, full stop; the difference in labour costs is 20:1 and Indian companies are using incredibly well educated people who can speak very good English. Many of the services, even services we used to think that we would capture and keep forever are migrating; all the call centres, lots of sophisticated accountants are going to places like India. So, when you see cities, towns or areas like the Black Country you have to ask what will we survive on? This is the real issue that we have got to address in terms of what being creative is about in regeneration terms. It is very stark that we have to ask what do we survive on? Here in the UK some of the answers are, numerical, clerical and educational.

I am not going to go into this in detail right now, we don't have the time, but if you are thinking about creativity at a deeper level you need to look at the big fault lines in the world, changes that are happening, that are so deep that we are not going to feel the impact in the next hundred years. One of which is about economic rationality, that we can decide everything in terms of how much its worth versus environmental ethics. This is one of the major fault lines in the world, which literally I think its not going to be solvable overnight, but you can see those battles already happening.

I think that in the 'old world' people believed, for example, that the key thing was to have a cheap, competitive business. What I'm really trying to say is that it's all about quality, attracting people, people with interests, stimulating people to work together creatively rather than adopt the straight-line thinking that I described earlier.

So, a 'creative city' is obviously a place, which allows you to think about creativity, and generates a culture of creativity. And the key thing is talent. Well, there is an issue there, the dilemma is that everybody is wanting to get this talent, this young talent, but we can't forget that we have to also think in terms of older people, and address the issue of making places that are usable. Like lots of places in Britain, Tyneside and Blackburn, are losing their own people who are leaving and going to the hub points around the country.

So, it is really about a shift in the pattern, we are trying to identify these resources, we are valuing assets maps, essentially we measure what capital is or can be. We are trying to be proactive but I believe if we do it the old way we just

end up with some sheds, and our towns and cities will all look the same. And people won't be able to really deal with what we will call the 'Chinese threat'. We should adapt by looking for potential, lots of potential is blurred within the arts you know, for fifteen years different disciplines have been blurred; music, the visual, and whatever else.

So, when we 'map the flow' it is just a way of describing lots of these creative things are happening in different places, and demonstrates that the creative people may not be in the obvious spaces within a city. I don't see why it can't happen. It's not true that all the creative people are in the centre of town. So often it's about getting rid of stereotypes like capital obviously, social capital, then reconnecting and learning. Is the University of Wolverhampton really connected to the places where people live or is it just an isolated island, this is important as we know students often regenerate places.

So when we think about the creative industries we have to make sure that we don't overlook sectors. And then there's also the opening of museums and art galleries to consider.

We must try to think of planning in a much more participatory way; allowing ourselves the conception of where we want to go, determining and looking at the roots of a place. Policies and strategies should be determined this way round. It might mean in this whole process you are forced to be uncomfortable because you're telling the story of a place and I think Walsall needs to now rebuild the story that connects with leather in some sort of way. I support this approach rather than those distribution logistics which I've just seen about 500 of, its not really much of a future if all you've got is sheds and you distribute stuff from the sheds, and that's what Walsall is known for, just a place that your driving through.

When you adjust your thinking and think culturally, everything is a resource water, ice, nature, trekking, history, industry, craft, colour etc. When one asks is this a cultural thing? You have got to think about the past, present and future and then you can imagine intellectual traditions; all of these things are then

part of this cultural thinking which could include local skills, talents, enthusiasms and so on, and of course the attitude must be confident.

Has a place got the energy and determination within itself to actually change? That's really what regeneration is but regeneration isn't only about the physical change of a place. So thinking artistically, seems to be a different way of looking at it; it is a subset of thinking culturally and we always blur these things and mix them up, clearly artistic thinking increases imagination. Music or a television programme often does that too. So, is culture the definition of creative?

This is a restaurant called Arts, (referring to slide) is it by definition creative? This could be any sort of restaurant, there are lots of restaurants called Arts, this happens to be a Chinese restaurant.

I took these slides in Oslo in half an hour – 35 shots of different Coca-Cola advertising this could be in any city. This makes me want to ask is globalization by definition creative?

Is technology by definition creative? Is factory by definition creative? Is graffiti by definition creative? These are the questions we have to ask to enable us to understand our cities and find ways for cities to develop along with the needs of the people who live and work in them.

This is Calcutta (referring to slide) where graffiti is tidy. So is that creative? – organized graffiti? I don't know, it's a quite difficult question to answer. This is another place that squatters took over and regenerated, they were allowed by the state to leave their graffiti as a symbol of what they had achieved; they didn't want this little spot in the USA to be regenerated without a share in it.

How much art is seen as creative? This is a place in Italy (referring to slide) that regenerated itself by just deciding to paint the front doors of houses and it seems to work. This is Argentina, this 'shanty town look' is now desirable, you can go to the posh interior design shops and see how to create this 'look', and I'm sure there are no profits going through these shops back into the places the 'look' originates from. This is an example of creativity, which has

been absorbed by someone else, and it doesn't directly benefit the creator.

I want us to think about whether architecture, by definition, is creative? This is a sewage works in Japan (referring to slide), this is an example of how public infrastructure can look different. This is a sewage works, we don't have to visualize sewage in a particular way – here the architecture changes our perception of it.

Our own cultural institutes need to be creative because that's why they exist. We did some work about ten years ago, on budgets that institutions like this have (The New Art Gallery Walsall). First we asked what the maintenance costs were, and then what were the remaining outgoings. Often the maintenance budget was far higher than the content budget. So, how do we work towards establishing the institution that gets beyond this problem? That actually does work financially for both upkeep and content? These places look great, they're an inspiration and they work in relation to a creative economy.

When we are discussing the creative city we cannot forget public art and the artist role in gentrification. This is Boston (referring to slide) where there are many warehouses and something called the Fort

Point Alliance, there are 400 apartments in this area, which are all owned by artists. The artist's contracts are such that they can only sell according to the value increases of the standard of living. This is quite a complicated contract, but what that means is once the area has gentrified, you don't get to push out the artists. The gentrification of New York has suffered from the classic model of artists moving in to cheap areas, making them desirable and then being pushed out as rents increase.

This is Albania (referring to slide). There are about 5, 000 billion apartments like this and they are all grey. The artist who had a public art commission for these buildings said he decided to spend five percent of the regeneration budget on colour. So they just started painting these grey buildings. Now you may like them or dislike them, but there's a pattern. You could say that if you just change the way the place looks you have a completely different relationship to it.

Anyway I am going to end on that point, thank you very much.

DB: Thank you Charles. I am going to start with a few questions and then

we will open the discussion up to the audience. The first thing I wanted to say is that as a contemporary artist, I'm not as comfortable as you seem to be, with the way that you use the word 'creative'. Within contemporary art the word 'creative' is kind of taboo; it's treated as something kind of stupid, the word 'creative' is almost like a myth word that you use as a cover up. So, if you don't want to actually explain what you do, you say you made a 'creative' decision. So, creativity seems to have no content whatsoever within contemporary art, of course that might be different in other areas. From the point of view of an artist to hear the word 'creative' keep coming back to you like this, when you feel like you understand modernism is uncomfortable. One positive thing that modernism achieved was at least artists aren't talked about as 'creative' any more.

CL: Well, I completely agree with you I mean I try to use the word imaginative or some other adjective. When I first got involved in this area, in terms of the city and the link between creativity and the city, it was about 13-14 years ago and that seemed fine then, the combination of the word 'creative' and 'city'. At the same time, the business world was also talking about creativity a lot and saying what was more important in investment is less having the money and more the ideas. And, people pick up on the words and in a sense hollow them out so there has been a hollowing out process of what that original idea, at least in my mind, was. To me the 'creative city' is, just to repeat, a place that has the conditions where we can think about things, plan things and do things in different ways, that's my definition of a 'creative city', that's how I describe it in the book, *The Creative City*.

DB: One of the other words that keeps coming up as well is another taboo word, not in the same way, not in the sense that it is regarded in art as a stupid word. The word 'culture' always raises, within art, as many problems as it seems to solve. The word 'culture' for people within contemporary art is almost too much trouble than its worth because as soon as you start talking about culture then people want to know do you mean culture with a capital 'C'? Do you mean culture with a small 'c'? Do you mean culture as an anthropological thing, where everything is culture including how you hold your pen or how you comb your hair? Or do you mean culture in the sense of high art as being culture and everything else as not being culture? Do you mean culture as opposed to anarchy? As in the kind of early 20th century theories of culture? And so culture seems to be...

CL: Nearly taboo.

DB: Yes, but it is always going to be, its always going to lead to confusion and to problems that the word itself can never deal with. In a sense the word has got such a history now, such a loaded history especially with elitist writers of the 19th and 20th century who wanted to preserve culture, who wanted to save culture, who wanted culture to be protected from, for instance industry. And what you end up doing within that tradition is separating culture off from life. So people like Roger Fry would say, 'when you walk into a gallery you leave the world behind' and that was his separation of culture from everything else that we do. And so culture

for an artist, especially an artist today who is interested in breaking down the barriers between art and everything else, culture becomes one of the obstacles that you need to get over. What culture has become as a concept becomes one other thing that artists have to get over in order to make their art more usable within everyday life for everybody else.

CL: Yes, I can see where you're coming from I mean obviously I'm coming from a different position and a connection. When we got involved in cities, which really properly happened in the early 80s, the problem was, as is still today, that, lets call it the non-physical side of the world, was completely not seen as important and somehow places, what they were like and their personality, and I'm using the city as having a personality and a psychology, was so completely off the beam. So we grabbed that word, when I say we, I mean the other people involved in that process, partly because it was a way of trying to make a very serious point, or trying to separate ourselves off from the traditions that existed up to that point which is to think of cities and places basically just as physical constructs. So, at the time, using the word culture with all its confusions was actually quite helpful, and it was also quite helpful to advocate for the arts because one didn't have to define, I mean you were saying culture is difficult to define, the arts were also quite difficult, you just sort of grabbed arts within culture and somehow this whole debate about culture-led regeneration emerged which I think to some extent was helpful. So, initially I think it was helpful, partly because it was vague, the reason why I now try to make distinctions like creative city, creative class, creative economy, is because I think we now need to be more precise.

DB: I can't comment on whether the language that you use or the strategies that you use will work in another sphere. The list of questions that I've got here, are in a sense questions about how contemporary art or art in general or culture in general, the stuff that I'm involved in all the time, is being represented at the level where you are working, with the people you are working with. Maybe it works in the situation in which *you* use the word 'culture' or when

you use the word 'creative'. I just wanted to ask questions about how that represents what we do, or how that affects what we do as artists. For instance there is another issue to do with culture which Pierre Bourdieu has analyzed very carefully in his sociological work, that culture is often treated as a positive, creative, inspirational thing but in fact underneath all of that, what we're actually looking at is forms of social distinction. And at one point you were talking about culture and of encouraging creativity and by which you mean, or you said, encouraging educated people to get involved in these things. You said you wanted to encourage, or you wanted systems that encouraged more educated people.

CL: Or people to become more educated.

DB: Yeah OK, but even for people to become more educated, again within that sort of sociological tradition would already set off alarm bells in terms of social distinction.

CL: Yeah I see what you mean.

DB: When you're talking about a cultural city and cultural changes, what you're talking about is cultural capital and you are talking about a city generating for itself more cultural capital and through that cultural capital it will regenerate itself economically and so on and so forth. And as artists cultural capital is a problem for us, because we are obviously seen as the ones with cultural capital, we are the artists. And because of that, you get into all kinds of difficult situations that you don't want to be in because people are presupposing before you talked to them that because you are an artist you have got cultural capital and you will talk in a particular way because of that. Do you see what I mean? So, we are assumed to have cultural capital because of the role that we have as artists while, on a daily basis, as artists what we are trying to do is to overcome cultural capital, to operate within the real world, rather than take advantage of that cultural capital and move in and about the world in a privileged way, because we are 'artists' in inverted comma's. What we are trying to do as artists is to say 'artists are just like everybody else'. We don't want to be privileged by this cultural capital we want to use what we have learnt and what we have experienced in order to relate to people in ordinary kinds of ways. So, again that element of education, of people wanting to be educated is about them wanting to be distinguished from other people, and that's what artists are trying to break down they don't want to be distinguished from other people.

CL: Right, I hope I didn't say those words you said. I certainly didn't mean them in the way that you seemed to think I did. I wouldn't exclude myself from needing more education. What I am talking about in the context of the bigger picture and if you look at what we, we collectively, will survive on, I'm saying we in general, and that includes me, we all need to be more skilled more educated etc, etc, that's the context in which I meant it.

In terms of creativity, something I didn't mention here, which I believe in, is that the creativity I'm talking about doesn't only apply to artists. For example, social work can be creative – so what I'm interested in, and I haven't necessarily found the answer – what is the distinctive form of creativity or use of imagination that artists have that adds value to things? So, that's in a sense my quest. In terms of the cultural capital thing, I know what you are talking about. What I am interested in and what I do believe is true in regeneration processes is that you have to raise expectations and aspirations and I am interested in that process of raising aspiration and sense of self which is why I

kept on talking about motivation.

DB: There was one more point that came up which I thought was another classic, problematic situation for an artist to be in. When you used the phrase, I wrote it down, you said, but you might not have wanted to say it exactly like this, 'Art creates value for property.'

Now what does that mean from an artists' point of view – well you kind of worry about that – you ask yourself, is it really my job as an artist to create value for private property? Is it my job to move into an area where there is cheap property, set up a gallery, transform the area and then when the property value has gone up, I get kicked out to another poor area. I actually don't benefit from this process, somebody else will, the person that owns the property. If that is my job it doesn't seem like a very useful job for me.

CL: That's why I gave the example of Fort Point in Boston, that is the general tendency. I said that regeneration is a property development process. Unfortunately that is what regeneration is. Sorry. I have reached the conclusion that this is at its essence. I gave the example of Fort Point in Boston; it's the only example I know where it's a very comprehensive example to buck the trend, there are very few examples where that happens. Loft living, 20 years ago described the process of artists gentrifying areas in New York which we can see everywhere else now. So, the role of the artist is not to do that, the role of the artist is just to get on with their art. But a side effect of being an artist is often that they

lead to those processes.

DB: But, what I'm interested in here is whether artists are being sold to town planners, businessmen and so forth on that basis. Because that's sort of distasteful really isn't it?

CL: They are, they are. The difficult challenge for artists if we are talking about a new phase of regeneration is really their critical capacity, which is part of the element of art as far as I understand it. The general logic of course is that the artist makes the area safe, which then the solicitors and etc move in and in a sense gives a bit of 'pizzazz' for the property developer but that is the general thing. Yeah, artists are being used if that's your question.

DB: OK, maybe that is a good point to go to the floor.

GW: I missed the start of the talk so I'm sorry about that. I just wanted to clarify whether you were operating as an observer; kind of offering critical, theoretical positions, or whether you are 'brought in' to practice your ideas – in terms of consultancy and effectiveness?

CL: In both of those things what I try to do is reflect on what they are doing and to some extent this conversation is a reflection of that, of a particular book that Dave is referring to that I wrote called *The Creative City*. I would say its a reflection on the failure to be imaginative in the planing process And basically in crude terms what I do most of the time is work in cites, is the

answer to your question. However, I sometimes write something down about it.

GW: I mean are you brought in as a 'creative'?

CL: I don't think I'm brought in as a creative person, I don't think, some people may or may not say I'm creative. I don't really know. I'm brought in to solve a problem, whatever that problem might be. In the first 20 years of Commedia's existence it was very difficult because the sort of things we have been talking about here were regarded as completely insane, it was difficult even getting these kinds of issues on the agenda. The last years have been easier but now one's had to sort of reverse one's tack because where as initially we might have said for example, artists can help you in a sort of instrumental way, now that's had to sort of go in reverse and take a sort of slightly more critical position.

GW: There's a line where you said about planners needing to think more artistically and I mean in a way that just struck me as being, wrong! That it is not a planners job to think artistically but it should be a necessity for a planner perhaps to work directly with an artist and in a sense that is where the education lies. The education lies in the role of involving somebody who can apply art. And so a planner, the only way he can think artistically is by knowing, perhaps when you should involve an artist in the process.

CL: Well, I'm not sure. I mean I'm doing some work at the moment about the mind set of people who deal with regeneration problems and I'm looking at the way engineers think, social workers think, artists think, not that I know but I certainly agree that a planner should appreciate an artists way of thinking.

BS: Please God, never send me to work with a planner! I don't think artists should go and work with planners. I think the issue for planners is that they are juggling capitals and there is a need to make profit. You used a quote and again, I hope I quoted you right, you said 'thinking culturally means everything as a resource.' But I don't believe this vision you painted is actually any different than the world

I live in already. It just seems to me all these things are ways to make profit more creatively. I don't understand how they address the balance and make the world we live in better. I still think they make profit from people.

CL: The 'they' being who?

BS: The people who hold means to make profit in the first place.

CL: When I say, seeing everything as a resource, its just looking at that panorama, if you want to call it that for the moment, and just saying what are the beginnings from which you can build up something that regenerates both physically, economically, mentally, socially, whatever. So, that's how I am using that word.

I do disagree with what you just said about planners, I think that's part of the problem. I'm not saying that you, as an artist, should change in anyway, but the problem is the communication within. So, I think its not a good idea to be like that about planners or business people or property developers I could name you 15, who are very interesting people...

BS: I never suggested that they weren't interesting I'm suggesting that I'm not sure I can help.

GW: My concern is not that all artists should have to do it, but there should be opportunities where an artist could be brought in to be part of a team, I'm not saying an artist is going to solve the problems but having an artist as part of the team could be beneficial in most situations.

DB: I think what Becky is saying is that it shouldn't be an artist it should be a communist. All planners should by law have to work with a communist in order to design a new city!

CL: I think one of the key issues that is emerging, which seems to be a general issue is whether one operates within a box, or in an insular way.

BS: So, is it about doing something rather than nothing?

CL: Usually it's about trying to achieve

something or other. I'm not saying that every artist has to be socially engaged, I'm just saying that we've got choices here, we've got a set of things, we've got a problem, a deprived area for instance, it's a good idea that different mind sets look at the problem and explores solutions.

DB: One thing that strikes me about the use of culture and creativity, in the regeneration process and in some of the things that you showed us in the slide presentation. I am thinking of, for instance, the project in which five percent of the budget was used to add colour to grey buildings, here nothing else was improved, and you said that it was the addition of colour that gave the citizens more confidence. In other words, it made them feel better about a life that hasn't changed.

CL: Correct. Broadly it hasn't changed.

DB: Well that seems to me to be almost a classic description of ideology. Ideology makes you feel good, despite the fact that you're in a shitty situation. And in a sense you're saying, what do we do with a shitty place? We paint it.

CL: That was one solution.

DB: That's not regeneration is it?

CL: But it's the beginnings of regeneration. When I said it is a long-term process, in this specific example, Tirana was the pits. Have you ever been there? It lives on selling drugs, there's no industry, nothing, the place is like that first picture I showed you, the guy who became the mayor says 'where do I start?' And the reason I talked about this, in terms of the world I operate in, is that would be the last place to bloody start! You'd start with the bathroom, you'd make sure the bathroom works, or you'd go to the inside of the building if you were working with the building, or you'd say where are the jobs coming from? Now all of those issues the mayor knows about, so taking everything into consideration he decided to let them paint the buildings, I think that was interesting because it triggered off some get-up-and-go.

DB: One of your key terms, which you use a lot in the book anyway, is 'confidence'. And one of the aims of regeneration is to build confidence within a city and to make that city feel good about itself and that seems to be related to that example in my mind. It's about making people feel better. I mean I know that if people feel better, they feel better and that's better! If people feel better then, you can't say that they only think that they feel better if they feel better then they do. I'm not trying to knock that but what I'm worried about is the possibility that some people are making people feel better despite the fact that nothing significant has changed in their lives.

CL: That could well be the case. Yes, every particular point I've made and every example I've made oscillates between being a solution and setting out another problem.

DB: I can imagine a businessman, or business woman, being very taken by the idea or having a confident city, because they're going to imagine that their workers are going to be happier when they're working, to be more productive, so on and so forth. That it becomes in effect a kind of economic booster. For producing their profits, that's what I'm talking about. Because what we're not talking about is raising their wages, we're talking about making them feel better.

CL: Well, for me, we just use the words 'feel better' or 'confident' which is perhaps a better word for me. What I'm trying to do is generate, I suppose because a lot of the time I'm working with people who feel nothing is possible, I'm trying to create a setting within which more people believe they can do things that they didn't believe they could achieve. That's what it's about.

I mean I'm aware of the logic of capital, but within that, you know, there are hundreds and thousands of people who are setting up in a sense their own micro-entities or whatever, and doing things and surviving in their own terms, and for me their doing it in their own terms they feel freer etc, etc. So, that's the purpose of the 'feel better' factor.

DB: There's a question over here.

AH: It is a quick question just to bring it back to the *Futurology* project. In the project the artists have been working in the Black Country, and as we are thinking ahead to the year 2024, and I just wondered if you had any thoughts about how the Black Country might stand in 2024? I mean if the sort of spectre of China had really come into play then?

CL: I think it definitely will, it might not be China, it might be India.

AH: Do you think we'll be worse off?

CL: Yes. Unless people find a way of using brain power to generate stuff to work on which is why this thing about aspiration is so important as well as their expectations of themselves and the place that they live in. The predication as I said is that 60% of all manufacturing companies will go, perhaps I'm being a bit too Doomsday-ish but you just need to look at the facts. Indian people are incredibly intelligent, often far more educated than us and taking over many of the things that we thought were safe forever, what are we going to survive on? That's the question I ask myself.

DB: Thank you very much Charles.

Education and Social Change
Claire Fox

CF: Well it's great to be here, this is my first time in Walsall. I think I should state for the record that I am involved in politics and that I am not an artist. I have absolutely no expertize on visual arts at all! I'm an art enthusiast and an art lover. But, despite the fact that I have absolutely no knowledge about the arts, over the last few years The Institute of Ideas [Claire is the director of The Institute of Ideas] has found itself talking and writing a lot about art and politics. And the reason for this is because the arts have become politicized as never before mainly through what I consider to be excessive government intervention into the arts. The Department of Culture, Media and Sport (DCMS) has to be the most hyper-active department around with policy upon policy which you are undoubtedly all familiar with and now worse than that, the department for Education and Skills have now got in on the act and jumped onto the arts bandwagon so I think we can expect to see at lot more government intervention.

I think all of this politicization of the arts is bad for the arts and actually bad for politics. I want to explore this in a couple of ways. First of all I want to look at the problem of the new instrumental demands that are being placed on the arts by government, the demands that the arts should have an explicit social role whether its accessibility or social inclusion or indeed the idea that the arts should contribute to social change. Secondly, I want to look at the politics surrounding the contemporary theories about the concept of creativity, which I think are rather problematic. A word of warning, there is a whole set of orthodoxies around these theories, if one opposes social inclusion, the social inclusion agenda in relation to art galleries one tends to be accused of wanting to socially exclude ordinary people from going to galleries and preventing socially disadvantaged people from seeing the arts. Or when it comes to creativity, if you argue as I do that everybody isn't creative one is immediately accused of elitism. I think that these kinds of arguments are moralistic, prescriptive and censorious and they don't help or aid debate. So, I am appealing to you to be offended with good grace, basically, because I'm bound to offend some of you some of the time.

On the first question. I think the demand that art should be socially useful or socially worthy is just as dangerous

Transcript of a paper delivered by Claire Fox with questions from Simon Poulter

Contributors
Claire Fox (CF)
Mel Jordan (MJ)
Members of the Audience (MA1, MA2, MA3, MA4, MA5, MA6, MA7, MA8)
Simon Poulter (SP)

for the arts as the kind of bean counting approach that Thatcherism employed in relation to the arts all those years ago. You might not personally remember but the Tories attack on the arts was that the arts for their own sake were no longer a valid excuse. Thatcher demanded that everything be judged in terms of its value for money and there was a kind of attempt at saying 'what economic value does the arts play for society?' If we are going to subsidize you we want to know what you do. And this was a kind of explicit philistinism that most of us rejected and believed that we have moved on from. But, I would say that we have an exactly mirrored approach from the present political administration. They have simply taken the language of economic value for money and cloaked it in the radical language of social justice, but I think it's just as damaging. So now the arts can no longer be the arts for their own sake, they have to be socially inclusive, accessible, multi-cultural, and I think that this is having the impact of unhooking art from its artistic moorings. In fact, art for arts sake is no longer an accepted justification and I think we should reclaim it.

These days all arts institutions are rated and indeed funded by their commitment not to art for its own sake, or to the quality of the creative output, but rather they are rated by access, their out reach activity and so on. The creation of great art, which I think is the core activity of art, is now side lined by introducing considerations that are extraneous to that activity. The arts are increasingly judged by whether they deliver a set of social products. So theatres and galleries are examined to see if their

programming policy contributes to the elimination of exclusion. Orchestras and concert schedules are scrutinized to see if the music they play will be recognized by or relevant to ethnic minorities or inner city youth. Museums are questioned about whether they display cultural artefacts of excluded groups and so on. I remember when Tessa Blackstone gave her first ever speech as Secretary of Arts, and she asked what she thought was a kind of cutting question. She said, 'Can the arts be more than just frivolous, trivial, irrelevant?' That was her way of asking more of the arts than 'art for arts sake'. And she went on to say and I quote,

I am in no doubt that the arts can contribute to improving health outcomes and there is increasing evidence that the arts can play a role in both crime prevention and reducing re-offending.

Now this seems to me to be utterly ridiculous, bad for the arts and as I said before, bad for politics. When it comes to improving health outcomes for example, one might imagine that was the job of the National Health Service. But oh no! The arts have now got to carry out that job. The NHS fails but we will give the job to the arts. Similarly, there has been a kind of more recent demand on the arts, which is that the arts should create social participation. The DCMS talks about the arts building social cohesion and the arts allowing communities to re-forge and develop social networks. At the launch of the Initiative of Youth Music, one of the many kinds of music initiatives we have seen over the last couple of years, a government spokesman said that the aim was, 'to establish music-making

opportunities as a force of regenerating communities, fostering social inclusion and community cohesion'. A few years ago a government think tank, DEMOS, in a report by Charles Leadbeater and Kate Oakley, made a similar point when they said that, 'The arts and culture create meeting places for people in an increasingly fragmented society.'

I just want to return to this point about social cohesion and social fragmentation, as this is basically a discussion about a political problem, not an artistic one. We know that there is a broad anxiety about isolated individual social fragmentation and I am as concerned about disengagement as anyone else. Disengagement is evident from the low turn out during political elections and there is definitely a sense that communities are falling apart and it's not a very pleasant atmosphere to live in. But, again it seems to me to be incredibly dangerous to burden the arts with the project of social engagement, a project that politicians have singularly failed to resolve. This is what the DCMS is now demanding of cultural institutions. They have almost been hijacked to provide points of contact between the isolated political elite and the public.

I think it goes something like this; they look at the crowds that are flocking into the Tate Modern and The British Museum and they are kind of envious. You know, something is happening. Lots of people buzzing around and seeming to be engaged. Why can't they be like that with us? So they subsequently take the galleries and museums and decide to make them a vehicle for themselves to connect with the public and subsequently galleries and museums that are told to relate to their visitors needs very directly to develop more intimate personal kinds of engagement and so on.

What is interesting in this whole debate is that paintings, I know that that's a rather old fashioned concept, or cultural artefacts of any description, are just props in this process.

The visitors, the audience, the 'connecting with people' are the focus. In fact these 'props', these cultural artefacts sometimes even get in the way and it is quite interesting when you read about the projects that are flagged up in government policy documents, often they don't mention the cultural artefacts at all – they are absolutely irrelevant to the discussion. In other words the desire to connect overrides cultural consideration. Once the demands placed on the arts are non-artistic, the arts themselves often become marginalized. I believe that Charles Landry spoke at the last of these discussions and Charles Landry is a big sort of cultural consultant brought in by the government to advise on various things, and is rebuilding Eastern Europe along 'The Creative Cities' lines as we speak, making far more money than me I have to say! But anyway, I went to a speech that he gave in London and I have kind of debated with him on this topic, where he actually argued with some enthusiasm that the thing that was most exciting about the Tate and the Great Court of the British Museum, was that they were great places as hubs of engagement. He used the illustration of the fact that he had sat in the Great Court of the British Museum and it had been really exciting to see how engaged young people were. He said there were lots of couples who were snogging, but he also said the other exciting thing was people were text-messaging each other and his point was that this was all very exciting. He then suggested, and this is the first time that I came across this, he said you must go to The New Art Gallery in Walsall, Claire, because it's really brilliant; there are all these skateboarders who use the whole outside and they are engaged with the local art gallery because its really popular for skateboarders. And at no point did we talk about what was on in

terms of exhibitions. In other words this whole process of social cohesion and the arts, it seems to me, potentially devalues the art. If you only value a cultural artefact or a painting because it can tackle unemployment or improve self-esteem, then it seems to me you have no idea what it's really worth as art. All it is about is how you are using that painting rather than the painting itself.

There is a cultural diversity project in West Yorkshire, which is about involving 16-25 year olds, working with the museums there and working with the museum's South Asian Art collection. The aim, according to the project officer, Rajed Analva, is not in any way to help these young people to appreciate South Asian art, the project is called *Who am I?* The aim of the project is to use the collection to explore young people's sense of identity. So the consequence is that the group produced a video, rather dubiously not art, talking about how they had bridged their cultural differences and whether they felt they were British or Asian. The aim, according to the project was that, to quote, 'That the youngsters would see themselves reflected in various artefacts.' In other words the artefacts were simply there so people could see themselves reflected. There was no understanding of or attempt to appreciate them as they are, for their own sake. In fact, they were just merely tools. And I think this is one of the things that we have to be wary of, that art is simply being used as a set of tools for social engineering purposes.

Once this politicization of the arts is institutionalized, art itself is no longer judged aesthetically as an end, but only as a means to other instrumental ends. I think using artefacts as simply tools, is a particular problem when it comes to the education debate in relation to the arts. The Department of Education and Science is now joining the DCMS as a government department whose getting involved with the arts. But, when the DfES proclaims that museums and galleries are an ideal way of contributing to literacy and numeracy, you have to be worried that what it is going to amount to is counting the artefacts rather than appreciating them. There's a DfES project called

Museum Fever, which is based in Salford where residents of the Salford Foyer, who effectively are young people with accommodation needs, disadvantaged young people, have become involved with the Salford Gallery. The aim of the project is to reengage these young people through the work of the gallery, but all the literature on this project, emphasizes how the participants have developed their new skills in relation to web design and ICT skills. In none of the reports is there any mention of appreciating the substantial collection of Japanese ivory carvings that the gallery has; I don't think they went anywhere near them, or understanding the iconography of the galleries large collection of Victorian paintings. So, I think that kids are actually losing out, its actually a con this idea that they are being exposed to art, they are just simply having ICT lessons in an art gallery.

Creative Partnerships are worth considering here for a moment. When Creative Partnerships were launched with all that great razzmatazz and millions and millions of pounds of public money, they had a proclaimed mission, and that was to develop long-term partnerships between schools and cultural and creative organizations and artists. I think we have to ask to what end? What's the point of those 'creative partnerships'? Again the literature is full of instrumental, non-artistic reasons. Music, we are told, can give pupils an opportunity to work together and to develop their teamwork skills and of course to develop pupils self esteem. It's as though arts education dare not speak its name. At this year's National Drama Teachers Annual Conference, the emphasis was on the value of the subject in developing pupils skills in, would you believe, 'thinking skills' and also that drama could be used tackle the crisis in behaviour in schools. I'm not quite sure whether it is to keep the pupils busy or what, but there was no mention of theatre, acting skills, performance skills, the writing of plays, the appreciation of theatre – they are just not on the agenda.

The annual arts week at a school in Solihull a couple of years ago again didn't have arts as its focus but it had a political theme. The artist in residence

who was working there was asked to work with the kids on a project on conflict and resolution. The schools arts co-ordinator, Jane Horsewill, said 'Children need to talk about issues to explore a topic, especially something like Afghanistan,' which was the war going on at the time, 'and the arts are a good way to do this.' It is interesting to ask what the kids learn from a project like this and when they did the assessment this is what James Burton, who is eleven, said. He said, 'When America bombed Afghanistan it hit back at the Taliban. At home, if you hit your brothers and sisters they hit you back and then you hit them back.' Apart from the fact that this is rather dubious politically, as a way of understanding rather complex matters of international politics, again at no point was the idea of the arts at the forefront of the project.

So, I think we might wonder why we bother calling it an arts project at all really, I mean it could be any old project it's just like citizenship. Maybe the reason why the arts have been brought on board in this way is a sort of clue given by the fact that David Miliband, the schools standards minister, has now become very interested in the arts. He claims that arts education enhances pupil's attainment across the curriculum and arts educators have actually been and are key to the standards agenda. I'd like to point out that according to the evidence this isn't even true, but there is a great play made on the idea that if we have the arts they will improve standards. It is rarely noted that actually when it comes to standards, the standards of arts GCSE's is below those of many other art forms. It doesn't seem surprising to me because in the end it just seems that the arts are simply being used as I say for non-artistic reasons.

And if you look closely at the DfES agenda, you realize that the aim is not actually about improving education in specific arts at all even though at the moment that is all that they are talking about and it really is quite a big focus. The new agenda is on a more general sense of creativity. Creativity as you will know has become something of a new mantra; David Miliband, when launching *Music for Life*, talked about creativity he

says, 'Creativity spurs higher standards. Creativity in teaching, creativity in the curriculum, creativity in staffing.' I mean, creativity in staffing, what's that about? I suspect it's a bit like creative accounting and that means less staff. When Estelle Morris was at the DfES she suggested that the creativity agenda meant that we could move on from the sterile debate about arts education, and what she called a sort of unhelpful sense of a pecking order of subjects; she said once you've got the creativity agenda, then it doesn't really matter whether its 40 minutes or 60 minutes given to a subject on a curriculum, where there's one or two lessons a week, whether you've got two percent of teacher training places in the arts or whether you've got 22. All that, she said, is old hat because now we've got creativity across the whole of the curriculum – the whole of the agenda. So, effectively she is saying that the fact that arts education is not very central doesn't matter because everything's creative.

Now I would like to unpick this weasel word 'creativity'; I think it's worth taking a step back and just considering what it means when we talk about creativity. The term 'creativity' has become very hip; if the creative process was traditionally associated with the arts, it's got a much broader definition today. I was shocked recently when a friend of mine, who is one of those business consultant types, revealed that he was earning a fortune running what he calls Creative Enrichment Seminars to bank managers so that they can rediscover their creative inner child.

New management theory is full of all these references to creativity and one of my favourites is the web-site becreative.com, which provides advice in creative career planning, where you can get your own personalized creative acronyms for creative management and you can get a creative quotation for every day of the year. I thought I'd share with you today's from Ivy Compton-Bernette, 'Real life seems to have no plot.' Helpful? I don't think so. Needless to say the government who are very keen on it have picked up this kind of absolute gobbledegook management jargon,

and they have incorporated it into their own agenda.

In short 'creativity' has become one of those New Labour buzzwords. Tony Blair says, 'Our future depends on our creativity.' When former culture minister Chris Smith launched *Culture and Creativity: The Next 10 Years*, he mentioned creativity 28 times in the opening few paragraphs and all of them had a variety of meanings and I still don't understand any of them. We know that there is the Creative Industries, there's Creative Cities and of course there's our very own Creative Partnerships with its three C's; Creativity, Culture and Community. This all sounds great but I think this promiscuous use of the term 'creativity' not only renders it meaningless and banal. Although it sounds fairly meaningless and banal and we can kind of laugh at it, I don't think its quite as harmless as it looks. In fact, I think the government are driving home several messages through the creative agenda and I want to challenge it.

Firstly, there is a clear message that creativity is not about the arts, or not *just* about the arts. Creative Partnerships say they want to move beyond art education as

a model of the past and then they suggest that 'creative learning' will produce 'creative employees' in workplaces who will be more agile and flexible, and I quote 'Creative employees adapt proactively to challenge, ensuring business is ready for anything.' This link of creativity with business and the squeezing out of the arts or rather squeezing the arts into business, has become clear in the use of the key phrase Creative Industries. This lumps together the arts with a range of non-artistic activities and treats them as no different from any other economic sector. By rolling up museums and galleries and theatres into the economic category of the Creative Industries, I think you remove what might give the arts a distinctive right to exist, and that is the creative process. It is interesting that a business consultant Dennis Sherwood who advises the government on creativity says, 'You can be just as creative in the cement manufacturing industry as in the music industry.' Therefore, artistic creation is akin to cement-mixing.

It is worth standing back and remembering that for all the hype in relation to jobs in the Creative Industries,

and I suspect you will be more aware of this than many people, there's a lot more spin than substance. The number of creative workers is blown out of proportion. In 2000, the total number of people who actually produced cultural products or needed to think originally in their work who worked in the creative industries, and that includes advertising, was just 5.4% of the workforce. I think the reason why the government can claim so many people work in the creative industries, is because they've adopted a rather 'creative' interpretation of the word creative! It's being applied to an ever-expanding range of industries. It includes IT types, who work on computer games, and then there's pop-stars, no wonder the figures are going up with television programmes like, Pop Idol, Fame Academy, The X Factor. There's also Tourism and the Service Sector, which has now become a creative sphere. I think serving hamburgers at a theme park is hardly most people's idea of creative employment, describing it as such of course, reflects a kind of self flattery about how we are all 'creative' these days.

This leads to my second problem with the new creativity orthodoxy, the idea that we're all creative. Creative Partnerships states that at the heart of the programme is the belief that everyone is inherently creative and in the Government's All Our Futures document, it is stated 'Everyone is creative from the pre-school child to the most distinguished scientist or artist.'

I hate this approach; it relativistically equals out creativity and compares untutored children with adult artists, it insults distinguished artists and it patronizes children. And finally, it reflects today's almost compulsory anti-elitism where nobody can be judged better than anyone else and no work of art better than another.

I also want to challenge the Creative Partnership idea that we are inherently creative from babies upwards. For me creativity is only possible at the end of the learning process, not before it. I think creativity can only be fully realized through mastering disciplines whichever those disciplines might be. Now the idea of mastering a discipline goes against the grain of today's creativity zealots. On the one hand we have the generic use of the term creativity, which plays down the specific demands of a discipline, and empties creativity of any content; the creative manager is just the same as the creative world-class pianist that is just the same as the child creatively banging on a keyboard. There's no essential difference; they're all being creative.

The other way that creativity is used is to undermine disciplines, the application of learning tools to ones trade. In the new music schemes, that are happening in schools, there's an emphasis on creativity over training. In place of teaching children how to master basic techniques, such as reading music or understanding theory and even the rigours of tonal harmony have been removed from A Level, instead there is an emphasis on self-expression.

Again we have this idea of the inherent creativity, but lets take the DCMS, Creative Partnerships' model of the creative pre-school child and ask, how does that creative pre-school child learn to draw? Now its true, every small child wants to draw and every small child tries to draw, but although they are surrounded by a world of visual images and despite parental cries of 'He's a creative genius!' every time they pick up a crayon, in truth, children can't turn what they know from perception or just their subjective desire into creating something really worthwhile. If the child has no literacy of perspective, if a child doesn't practice through, for example, life drawings, still lives, imitation and repetition, then simply they can't develop their artistic ability.

Now the idea is often posed that this kind of mastery and rigour is uncreative and really just amounts to an adherence to the status quo. I disagree, even if an artist's ultimate goal is to transcend the conventions, for example of drawing, rather than to succumb to them, I think everybody needs to have an attitude of respect for the knowledge and skill and discipline. In my opinion, we all stand on the shoulder's of giants. Open-mindedness and individuality and originality, those parts that I consider to be truly creative, demand knowledge of the rules one wants to transcend or to challenge. James Joyce was only able to abandon punctuation in *Ulysses* because he had mastered it. This is not on a par with illiterate ramblings of someone who doesn't understand the use of commas, semi-colons or full stops.

In this new creative world, what overturns artistic conventions? Just think about what it is that's replaced the rigour or the discipline in this new creative world. Its worth noting that in a recent survey of 42 art courses and art colleges in the UK, negotiating skills are compulsory on more courses than life drawing, and a majority of courses teach networking.

To conclude, I think this new inclusive creativity is a real problem. It seems to be based on a fear of making judgements, on a fear of putting anyone under pressure to go beyond the natural limits, and a fear of leaving anyone out. An inclusive creativity in which we all have access to and none are excluded does sound idyllic but actually I think its no more than content-less creativity and no more than dull conformity. My political message then is it's time for the arts to reclaim the creative process back. I think it would be a revolutionary act if it were to happen. I think that the arts should try and unhook arts from politics and proclaim that the arts are valuable for their own sake. To proclaim that the arts can be socially useless, the arts can be socially irresponsible, the arts might even be socially reactionary. It shouldn't matter. It doesn't matter. All that matters is that it's art. The only demands that it should answer to are artistic and the only question I'm worried about is, is it they any good? Thank you very much.

SP: OK, thank you for that. I'm sure that's provoked quite a few questions from the audience. I just wanted to ask you a fairly straightforward question, Claire are you creative?

CF: I did ballet for a long time and I wasn't particularly naturally talented I found it very difficult but I worked very, very hard and practised and did all the things you need to do if you want to be a ballet dancer and in the end I kind of achieved something that might be quite creative in as much as I was able to dance. The only thing was when I didn't practice, when I kind of lobbed around the room, it was kind of ugly. In other words I do think that there is such a thing as dance and I think you have to apply yourself so I don't know whether I'm creative or not, I think you can actually create cultural artefacts of some sort by applying yourself. Obviously in the midst of my ballet class, there were some people who were actually naturally brilliantly talented but even without that initial talent I think that you can become creative.

SP: It is interesting you've answered this question in this way because what underlies your polemic is a sense of an orthodoxy and a sense of classicism; that some people are naturally talented, they are capable and the masses are never going to be the same. Some of the things you were picking up on, like life drawing for instance, you obviously feel that artists should be taught that process, so where does this classicist polemic come from?

CF: Well I think it's rather a peculiarity of today that life drawing has become associated with classicism and some kind of traditional approach. I'm not suggesting that every single art college should have life drawing classes. I made the point, that I don't know anything about visual arts, but I do think that the discipline has to make its own demands of itself, and then things can move on. I was actually talking about how a child might learn to draw though, there are still people who want to draw and want to be able to create in that way. So, I think that you have to be really careful that you don't assume that because somebody is interested in what's being thrown out in the baby-bathwater scenario, that they want to defend some sort of rigid, hierarchical status quo of the past and only believe in classical painting. That's not particularly my point.

SP: But, there is a problem – isn't there? Which you tried to sort of deflect at the beginning of your paper; when one enters into this notion of an elitism and the romantic model of genius it underlies the polemic sitting there in the background.

CF: I don't believe in a romantic notion of genius particularly. What I've just tried to say about the ballet is that, in fact, I think people can acquire artistic excellence of sorts if they're taught it. I think one of the things that we are doing is letting people down because we are not actually giving them access to the arts, either as observers or as listeners. For example, in order to be able to develop as somebody who's going to write music that might be beautiful you have to be taught music. And at the moment children are not being taught music in as much of a way as I'd like them to be. I don't particularly think everybody needs to be a Mozart, but I think that it is necessary to equip people with the tools in order that they can achieve their potential.

I used to be an English teacher and I find it utterly despicable that it is considered to be elitist to want to give everybody access to Shakespeare and to great classic works of literature. There is a kind of deeply patronizing sense in which people say that those texts aren't relevant or they're dead white men or any of these notions, and that we should teach *Trainspotting* instead because our pupils will get it because they're all inner city drug takers.

First of all art should take you into

a world that you're not already in, and secondly, I believe that everybody can access great art. You can have a dispute about what great art is, and as long as that's an artistic dispute, rather than a social dispute, I don't mind. I'm not prepared to argue that a work of art is not great because it offends contemporary sensibilities politically. That's my main point. If it can be justified as great in artistic terms then that's fine.

SP: OK. The other thing I was going to run by you, which is a bit more of a specific question. You will recall that Roosevelt actually set up a kind of 'new deal' programme, a workers programme which enabled lots of artists to be employed at a period of time which was difficult economically in the USA; essentially artists would be off painting murals on public buildings, which is not too dissimilar to some of the orthodoxies that perhaps underlie Creative Partnerships. One of the things that came out of that was a sense that artists at least were doing art, and people like Philip Guston, Jackson Pollock, Diego Rivera, actually pretty much used it parasitically as a means to actually develop their practice. So, even if one is cynical about government programmes, isn't there a kind of counter orthodoxy which says that some of these programmes actually can create waves, enabling artists to come through with things that they really want to do?

CF: Well, I think that there's a number of ways of approaching that. I think that historically, in this country anyway, the arts have been subsidized by the state for sometime, but I don't think that state subsidy of the arts necessarily means state interference in the arts. I think that the model post-war was one which did allow artists to have a certain flexibility. I'm entirely sympathetic to the fact that, if the money's on the table, people are going to want to take it? And I don't blame people for playing the tick-box game you know you want money from the arts council so you say you are going to do a socially inclusive project.

We all know the buzzwords to use, I'm not immune from that myself when I have

to get funds. However, if intellectually you don't resist these trends, and if you actually internalize them and then reproduce them back out intellectually, that's where I see the problem. I think that a lot of artistic institutions, for example, have taken all this on board, not just in the pragmatic sense of just taking the money and running. I think that a lot of people have started to downplay the arts, believing that they are involved in process of social change.

This is slightly different with artists and institutions. I think if you take museums, museums are kind of involved in a process of self-loathing. I mean they are hugely embarrassed by the fact that they own the treasures of Empire; they're really embarrassed about the fact that they come out of a 19th century particular model and they don't really know what to do with themselves. So, they've adopted this new mission with some vigour, but you talk to the directors and heads of museums these days and it's like talking to the head of social services! They're forever telling you what they're doing for unmarried mothers, you know, mentally ill Asian women – it's just remarkable! And they have the treasures of the world stored in those places and that is what I want my peers, ordinary people to have access to. The idea that they're hiding them because they want to make themselves relevant to ordinary people, and they don't think ordinary people would get difficult collections, is just a terrible insult.

SP: Well, my final question is what do you actually think of the *Futurology* project and exhibition? And the process, given that, having worked with Mel and Andy, one of the things that I think the artists who have been involved with it have felt is that we weren't just chosen to meet the criteria.If anything we were actually selected to confront the criteria and Creative Partnerships and many of the dogmas and issues that you talked about.

CF: Well, that's the point that you made earlier, which is that obviously you'd hope that people would try and subvert New Labour's agenda. I'm ever hopeful that people won't just take this on the

chin and roll over and die. I don't know this exhibition properly, I mean, you run round it in two seconds and what I've read about it, it seems to me to know what it's trying to do and it's reasonably ambitious. I know lots of people that have got money from Creative Partnerships who I consider to be doing great things, but I don't think they should need to play the game in order to get those sort of subsidies, that's my point.

SP: Could you just sort of really quickly map out an alternative arts spending model for us?

CF: Yeah, give the money and butt out! I mean, if there is a social commitment, if there is an intellectual and social commitment to the arts from the government, then that's it! That should be it and everyone should stop being defensive and, if they don't support the arts in that way, I'd rather they didn't give the money. I mean, if they don't believe in the arts for their own sake, then even though we might not like to lose the funding, you could say that in a way it would be a less compromising situation.

MA1: What criteria would you use to disseminate the money? How would people get hold of the money?

CF: People would get it on the basis of artistic merit, that's the point. How money is allocated from the government to the arts is obviously highly contentious and has been for a very long time. Some people adopt the strategy, as is done in America of arguing for a kind of libertarian – no state funding of the arts because, once the state funds the arts the state will interfere in them.

The university sector in this country has been funded by the state for many years. But over the last 20 years its had an unprecedented degree of interference by the state into the content of what is taught in universities, into what is researched, into introduction of employability skills and so on and so forth. Before that, there was a broad commitment to the intellectual project of having universities, and they gave money over and the universities had academic freedom and they were allowed

to get on, and now that has changed. That is what has also changed in terms of the arts. Now, when you say what artistic criteria should be used, these things are things of aesthetic judgement and they will undoubtedly change socially, politically over years. I appreciate that one minute representation might be in fashion and the next minute process-based practice might be in and there will be different aesthetic rows held amongst the artistic community. My suggestion is that this government and the administration are not interested in the arts, at all! They are only interested in the arts in as much as it delivers social product. Artists should be very wary of being flattered by getting funding; you might think well I've just got the money so it must be a good arts project. But there are some incredibly naff, terrible, third rate artistic projects that are funded by the state but because they are doing the socially right thing, nobody dares say anything about them. I think one has to be able to have artistic judgement. I think some pieces of art are better than others. And I don't think just because it's given the title art, it deserves to be treated with reverence.

MA2: You say you want to break the link between art and politics, because you don't approve of government politics, but is it possible to have combined good art and good politics? I mean is it a worthwhile thing to do? Should your aim be to produce art, which communicates good politics? Or should we just forget art and just concentrate on politics?

CF: Well, I think that it's accidental if an artist is political, if that makes any sense. I don't want to say that every artist needs to be political; I'm political, and I'm very interested in political art as a consequence. Its not like that I would not like that aspiration to exist, its just that I think it's a very dangerous point of view. I think its easier for me to understand this, in terms of things like theatre, which I'm familiar with. I think that theatre, particularly at the moment, is being misused in terms of funding for political ends. Theatre, particularly theatre in schools, has to be about bullying, has to be about anti-racism, has to be about obesity, has to be about this ,that and the other and sometimes the plays are terrible. It's a slightly peculiar notion. Take literature, which I'm also familiar with, Graham Green is my favourite author, was my favourite author, when I was in my 20s, he's pro-imperialist, Catholic, a misogynist, but he's a brilliant writer. He made me understand Imperialism and Militarism far more subtly than any agitprop play that kind of lectured me about the dangers of American Imperialism. I think you have to be very careful; the political outcome of art isn't actually in the hands of the artist if you see what I mean?

You can't manipulate your audience like that. I love early Renaissance painting; I am as you might have gathered a bit of a traditionalist! I think it's absolutely beautiful but I don't have a religious experience. The reason I love it is because I'm a Humanist. And I'm absolutely fascinated by the emergence of Humanism; isn't it fascinating that that was paid for by rich patrons, it is supposed to be about singing the praises of God, and I look at it and all I can see is human development; its all about the Enlightenment and the emergence of human rationality for me. So, I think you have to be very careful about imagining that art can do a straightforward political job. However, I'm not trying to say of course that, if you're an artist who is interested in politics, you should forget it! Then you are going to try to create art that's going to reflect your interests.

BS: I'm one of the artists involved in the *Futurology* project. I'm also uncomfortable with the instrumental use of art in government policy. What I find confusing, is that although art does have a social worth and a social value, a very important one, when we talk about government agencies harnessing arts agency to deliver on social targets, it starts to look to me like the instrumental use of art. The moment you start talking about the problems of art being used in an instrumental way, people then revert to talking about art that has no connection with society; I think that at least some kind of connecting with society through the current practices is better than a kind of removal of art from society.

SP: I have been involved in a number of projects which have been politically engaged and I have personally witnessed, not just young people but people from a variety of groups be transformed by the process i.e. it's upped their game; it's made the young person think they could be a film director or maybe that they could do some creative writing. I think that somewhere between this orthodoxy and the criticism, that Claire has made of projects like Creative Partnerships, there are points where artist projects do actually go into a location and actually give somebody a break. That's got fuck all to do with Blair-ite politics, that's to do with artists being in a space or with particular people who've got an educational agenda to inspire others. I think there is actually, a sort of an in-between area here where art can be political and transformative, and there is a history of this and it's always been the case.

CF: But I don't know why that's necessarily political. One of the things that Creative Partnerships has done well, that I think has worked, is where kids have gone in and spent time in artists studios. I mean you could say well that's political, it certainly has had an impact on the kids because they've been with an artist who's talked about art. I'm not suggesting that artists should compulsorily lock themselves away from society and not care about future generations' interest in the arts. I think that arts are socially valuable, don't get me wrong. I think they're socially valuable because I think that a world without arts would be disastrous.

SP: But your polemic is black and white on quite a lot of these issues.

CF: I think that the arts are socially valuable because the arts can help people change themselves and change the world, but not in a straightforward way as I was indicating to you. Not always as you'd expect it to happen. I'm the sort of person who thinks that everybody should spend all of their lives watching Shakespeare plays and reading poetry. When I was teaching, I wanted to inspire people; you think 'God if only you could read this sonnet it will change your life.'

SP: So, what is the relationship then between educational practice and artistic practice, because obviously teachers can inspire?

CF: Yeah, but I just made the point that I think a lot of the new arts education policies are sidelining arts. I want people to be taught music, art and drama.

MA3: I'm Adrian Mandel from Born Media Company in Hereford. I'm quite interested to know what you think arts education might actually be. Some of the things you talk about, that you said during your paper, is that art is produced for non-artistic reasons and you see arts as being sidetracked for non-artistic reasons. I think some of these non-artistic reasons are some of the most important reasons to make art. You said that you thought that art only happens at the end of the learning process and I wonder whether you could define what the end of the learning process is? What comes across from your talk is a very traditional approach to teaching art and art education. How would you, instead, think about the education of those people in a more artistic process?

CF: Well I think it's been so many years since state school kids sat round listening to Beethoven in schools, I mean who are we kidding? They haven't had access to that. I wish they had the room in the curriculum. What you get is a situation where it is assumed that state school kids won't get Beethoven.You have a ridiculous notion where music teachers are instructed to make music relevant by finding out about the music of the street; this is basically a real problem. It seems to me that we have abandoned the notion that people can access difficult, challenging art; it doesn't have to be Beethoven, it doesn't matter who it is, because we patronize people by imagining that they can't get it, they won't understand it etc. So when you ask, 'how would you have arts education?'

I would have music lessons and those music lessons might be about listening to music, appreciating music, learning something about music history. If you listen to Beethoven for a long time and you understand something about the history of classical music, and if you decide it's rubbish and then become a rapper, fine. But do not say to kids, Beethoven is a load of traditional old rubbish. Usually the people who are saying it are people who went to private schools, and have got their classical music collection sewn up at home. And then they go out and say, "oh yes it's very elitist, we don't want you to have it, we know you won't get it, but we'll give you street music because you will get that."

SP: So, are you saying then that successful cultural paradigms can't emerge from the street then?

CF: I'm saying that the motives behind the promotion of street music in music education are done in bad faith.

MA4: I'm not sure that education is as black and white as that. I'm just about to start doing a music competition for a film project with three schools in Worcestershire, which have a completely different scoring bill, something entirely different to what they normally do and to achieve this they have to engage creatively with their teacher, with their own ideas.

CF: I'm identifying intellectual trends. I mean, it is true that I'm painting a black and white picture, but they are the intellectual trends. If you look at any debate on English teaching, the trend is to say that we have a real problem; there are problems with how we make this particular form of literature 'relevant' and 'accessible'. The Science Museum recently did a 'relevant' museum for inner city youth; they called it, 'Sport Science'. That's what they think of people, they think the only way you'll get people into the Science Museum is to give them what they already know – Sport!

MA5: I'm the senior officer for Creative Partnerships in the Black Country. I've just got a couple of things to say. Your opinions have been sweeping statements. In terms of art practice in schools, it's all got to be varied. Part of the agenda for Creative Partnerships is to support teachers in moving away from looking at Picasso and Monet, and that's all they are looking at, and to look at contemporary practice and what that can offer. And I'd just like to say, as well, that in my past life I have been on the steering group for Arts

Council National Touring Programme which was to award a significant amount of money to artists, and it was quite easy to judge which ones you were going to give the money to, because there were a lot of mediocre applications. Those artists that have taken their work very seriously – they are the ones that get the grants.

CF: The Creative Partnerships Project, as you will know, produces endless reams of literature that explains itself.

MA5: It's not perfect.

CF: No, it's not that it's not perfect, it's that it has an ideology. Its ideology is public; I have access to that ideology and I have set it out here. That ideology I quoted directly from Creative Partnerships, I haven't made it up. Now you can say, yeah, but in my project we don't really do that, we are not really like that. But if Creative Partnerships isn't really what Creative Partnerships says it is, then actually somebody needs to tell us what Creative Partnerships really is. I have had boringly endless rows with the DCMS and DfES on this, they won't be held to account for what they publicly argue for. They say, you must look at what's really happening. Well if that's what's really happening, then turn that into an ideology and argue for it!

MA5: But there's an enormous amount of anxiety coming out of government about the impact of what is still just a two-year programme, which will have £110 million spend.

SP: Can you just say what you think about the propaganda about the organization that you work for?

MA5: I'm from Creative Partnerships and I'd argue that it's the best thing since sliced bread! I've been working for them since May, and there are all sorts of issues within it, but as far as I'm concerned at the moment, it has just been a two-year programme. It's an action research programme, that's all it has ever been. We're being called to account on the impact of this upon pupil's behaviour, on pupil's self esteem, that's what's being measured.

John Trayner: With regard to these people that are saying you can't have Beethoven because its elitist, and you can have the street music because you understand that. They put this forward saying it's a non-elitist argument but it seems to me that, if you look at what elitism is, this is elitist! It's saying we'll keep this for ourselves you can have the other stuff. It seems to me, that is a very disingenuous bit of the government policy.

This is not the only place we see instrumentalization; we see it in the interpretation of projects that various organizations, like the Tate Modern, put alongside exhibits and exhibition declaring this is what this work is about. It's precluding other possibilities and making you feel like you have to understand the work in the way the interpretation tells you.

MJ: I was just going to say that I think there has been a crisis in fine art education, which for the last 40 years has been based on ideas of self-expression – this is problematic. To address this, I have been attempting to teach students with a content-led approach; asking students to respond to the inputs that I give them, so that their work is based on knowledge, rather than attempts at expressing themselves. I don't want to teach skills like life drawing anymore, because, as well as the inherent ideological issues, I don't want to suggest that art is based on skills and techniques. I do expect to teach students about content, theory and history, all the reasons why art exists. We can't just return to traditional conventional modes and models of learning skills. This whole idea of self-expression is not very useful if students believe that this is the basis of art practice – it's just not true as well as not being thorough enough.

MA6: Have you got a definition that you use for creativity? You spend a lot of time explaining what it isn't, so if you are going to chip away at what it isn't you might like to give us some idea of what you think it is?

CF: Well, I'm noting that the definition of creativity is an ever-shifting one in today's climate. I don't think it was ever

a pinned down definable concept, but it was associated with, until maybe 25 years ago, artistic practice and artistic process. You can certainly say that it's changed in the usage. It has changed exponentially. I mean first of all its exponentially used massively if you look at the literature. I haven't got the figures, but if you check on the number of articles on creativity it was something like 126 in 1976 and there's now 10, 000 just in the first 6 months of this year in UK newspapers. It's everywhere. So, there's an expediential use of it.

If you then read those articles, you discover that the meaning of creativity is ever-shifting. I have tried to illustrate the way that it has become a much broader and fluid concept and I think very unhelpfully it has had quite a damaging impact on some of the things we associate with the creative process. So, I would say, it was more associated with the arts. Indeed the literature makes the point that it was largely associated with the arts, although it states we need to broaden our concept of creativity and realize that everyone is creative and it is rather exclusionary to just associate it with artistic practice.

I think it relates to Mel's point you know. I'm not in any position to know what the arts curriculum of a university is. I can actually come up with a brilliant curriculum for English and Literature because it's my subject, I know about it. And I'm not going to pretend I can do it on every other subject, but I don't think that the way that arts education is going at the moment is the decision of arts teachers. I'm suggesting that there's a whole range

of external focuses that are coming in that are distorting that practice.

SP: We'll move on, but the point is you're defining things through the negative.

CF: I'm trying to assess social trends through the way things are; I'm not trying to define anything. I'm trying to assess what I think is going on socially through the way creativity is used as a phrase in today's climate. I'm trying to look at all these uses of creativity. What does it mean? What might it suggest? etc

MA7: You were saying that music is creative then you were mentioning Pop Idol. In my opinion, some music is creative and some isn't. Its just like saying some artists in some situations are creative and some are less creative. Some artists may have creative days and some artists may have less creative days, and some makers of cement will do things creatively sometimes they won't do them creatively.

SP: OK, thank you. Is there anybody in the room who hasn't asked a question whose burning to?

MA8: I'm head of education at Tate Liverpool and before that I worked in a contemporary art gallery in Bristol for a number of years. I was on the *All Our Futures Committee,* and I can tell you that it wasn't a government agenda.

CF: Sorry, it wasn't a government agenda?

MA8: It wasn't a government agenda and the *All Our Futures* report came out of a

year of consultative meetings with artists, with designers, with architects, with hundreds and hundreds and hundreds of teachers and quite a number of other people. In fact it's all documented so you can find out, and we were observed by OfSTED, TTA, DCMS, DfES, DMD, CMS and DMD actually commissioned it but they were tactfully silent, I have to say; all of those people were observers. Then we had a meeting with Chris Smith and a meeting with David Blunkett and I have to say that they were defensive but they were actually listening. This is an unpopular view, but I was there so I understand the process that we went through, and what came out of it was the *All Our Futures* report which does try to explore and define creativity, out of a whole series of discussions for a whole year with thousands of people who had a vested interest.

When we went to the Labour Party conference and we were asked to present it, the majority of the audience were teachers and creative people or however you want to describe it, and they were gagging for it. They were waiting for that report because they knew they had inputted into the report and they wanted it to impact on their schools; they wanted it to impact upon every area in the curriculum and what my disappointment is that Creative Partnerships are not doing it! You know it isn't doing what it's meant to be doing, in some cases it is, in some cases it isn't.

SP: Can you define, for us, what they should be doing?

MA8: When we put that report together, as a group of people, but also through

consultation, we had big ambitions for what Creative Partnerships should be. Art organizations and schools have been working together for donkey's years on all sorts of different programmes and projects, as well as having artists going into schools. We have had orchestras and dance groups going into schools, and we have also had schools going out. This has been going on for ages and ages, patchy and not consistent but nevertheless going on for a long time. What we hoped for is that there would be some much more innovative, partnerships between science, industry, the arts, music, and all kind of social groups, and that wasn't for a governmental social engineering outcome, the idea was more to do with giving everybody access and validating everybody.

I actually do believe you can be creative when you're making a shirt and that there are different thinking and learning styles and different styles of producing something, but I think to invalidate people is being elitist, I think it's counter-productive.

CF: I think that is a very useful clarification, the thing about it is though, and I think this is something that's peculiar to the way this government works, this government has never actually written an original report in its life. What it does is to commission other people to do the work.

I remember when *All Our Futures* came out, when I read it, I thought it contradicted itself all over the place. I thought parts of it were brilliant. It's a long document. I wrote pages on it. I'm sure you don't really want me to bore you with that now! But there were lots of things in it that were very strong and there were lots of things that I thought were very dangerous and I, as you can see, I disagree with the stuff on creativity.

I then spent a lot of time going to the DCMS events where everybody talked about *All Our Futures* all the time; it then turns up as policy, as a consequence of that report.

A lot of people thought if we can get creativity on the agenda through the report, then we're really going to out arts as a central focus and what I think has happened is that the creativity agenda squeezed the arts out altogether; I think it was an attempt to mainstream the arts to give it priority and I just don't think it's worked.

SP: OK, good. I think we'll take just a couple more quick questions then we'll wrap it up.

MJ: I just wanted to say something about the Partnership part of Creative Partnerships, seeing as we have talked a lot about the Creative bit. I just wanted to really think about 'partnerships' as I believe that the idea of a partnership

is really complex and I'm not sure that anybody has given that enough attention. I think partnerships are delicate things to sustain; both parties need to know what they are getting out of a partnership, they need to know if their own objectives will be met. In all sorts of partnerships I think we've got to be able to put our cards on the table and say, well what are we all going to get out of this? Are the things that we are going to get out of this, the things that we both need? I think there's sort of something problematic here that needs to be considered carefully.

SP: But that's going to take time to establish. Presumably, in your case, with Creative Partnerships, you're going to evaluate the *Futurology* project and the processes that you have had to go through and provide some information, which will inform the next phase.

BS: Self-expression – it's just as Mel said, there is a tradition of teaching in art schools; there is this idea that art is just about a kind of splurge of expressions and its not about something far more disciplined. I would also like that idea of teaching art dead and buried. But the word self-expression is interesting because I think there's something really complex there. We are all against a kind of male, avant-garde genius who just expresses himself, but I think that the use of art, how it's currently being used as a social agenda, is all about getting rid of self–expression and all about negating the artist and saying, you're in-serviceable people. That is just as problematic and, if we try to encourage art schools not to teach self-expression then we lose the idea of communication and the individual.

MJ: I wouldn't denounce autonomy or self-expression. I suppose what I was trying to talk about was how art is currently taught in art schools. I don't think it is rigorous enough and I think that it's based on an aesthetic ideology. My fine art education was, 'there's an easel, go and paint over there in the corner' and you were lucky if you got a tutorial once a week and it all had to come from me and who was I? I was an 18-year-old kid, nothing much had happened to me. The most I understood by the end of it was that I was working class, I hadn't realized that properly before.

I think I am trying to talk about art being based on a set of knowledge that students can then study and then make their own minds up about. I know that some of my recent graduate students can really take me to task about anything because they've read stuff and looked at art; they understand how it helps them think and how much it contributes to understanding the work they want to make.

SP: Any final words from you Claire?

CF: Yes OK. It follows on from the self-expression thing and somebody earlier asked me what I meant when I said that creativity happens at the end of the l earning process.

I was trying to challenge the notion that we're all inherently creative as it's presently being used to effectively argue against inputs in terms of teaching and knowledge, which I am very nervous about. That is why I use the Estelle Morris quote she said 'it doesn't really matter whether you have only 2% of teacher trainers that are doing arts or 22%, or whether it's one lesson a week or two'. Once you go down the route that we are all inherently creative and you can just encourage people to express themselves, you never have to teach anyone anything. Although it's not a conspiracy, its none-the-less a trend that we have seen in relation

to the way art education has gone. At the very time when arts education seems to be at the foremost in the agenda, you talk to anyone who teaches art in schools and they are tearing their hair out with desperation!

I also think that the point about partnerships that was raised is useful. At the Institute of Ideas, we do all our work in partnership with someone; it's part of the nature of what we do. Not through Creative Partnerships, but the Tate Modern or British Museum or Battersea Art Centre or wherever and we work across science, the arts and culture.

In truth you feel its on the one hand very creative, to use that word glibly. It's great having more than yourself to be held to account to but it obviously can be a bureaucratic nightmare and you also feel that your slightly compromising all the time. I think that the idea at the very heart of Creative Partnerships is a good one, although we have to be careful about the partnership aspect. I think people that work in education in galleries and museums are very concerned about the fact that they are being asked to think about exhibitions that will fit in with the curriculum that will actually kind of help achieve the learning outcomes of the DfES; you know this is not quite the same as working in partnership.

I suppose the main thing is to just say something about intellectual trends. I think that it's very important that intellectual trends are discussed and I think that discussions like this are invaluable. If you are on the conference trail of this stuff, there is not a sense of open rigorous debate on these subjects, it just doesn't happen. What happens often is, I say something and people come up to me at the coffee break, and squeeze my arm and say, 'well done, it needed to be said', and then run off! Because they don't want to be seen with me! Now I'm not saying that I've won the argument. These are a minority of people, but the fact that people who work in the arts don't feel that they can have these discussions in the open and that they just don't happen, seems to me to be really problematic and the nice thing about this atmosphere here is that you can actually have a barney, that

you can actually be quite harsh with each other. You can actually, hold each other to account and it is not the end of the world and actually you understand the world a little better afterwards.

The irony is, I think that we're letting young people down because we often don't expose them to that high level of rigour, and one of the things that I most hate about the kind of 'arts and self-esteem movement' is this idea you can kind of improve people's self-esteem, without them having achieved anything. Well, your self-esteem goes up if you have done something good, it can't go up if you haven't done anything. So, I just think that we have to allow this debate to make a greater impact in the world in order, even for the people who would disagree with me, to have any real moral high ground to stand on because at the moment they haven't really won the intellectual arguments; they've simply asserted them. I think everybody who is a bit worried about them really deserves to put them under a lot more pressure because it will help sharpen them up and actually make arts and education a more interesting place to inhabit. OK, that's it. And thanks for inviting me.

SP: That's very good, thank you very much Claire and thanks for all the questions.

Rasheed Araeen is an artist, writer and publisher/editor of *Third Text*. He conceived and founded *Third Text* as a collaborative art project in 1987, which is now continuing in its twenty second year. He is also now directing a project which will produce the most comprehensive and inclusive of history of art in postwar Britain. His latest conceptual art project is *Mediterranea*, an open ended project realized and sustained by the collective will and consciousness of people themselves, in and beyond the life of the artist.

Barby Asante is a London based artist whose practice uses performative strategies that either invite participation or engage with its audiences. She has exhibited widely in Britain and internationally. Her research involves considering diversity within the practice and expanding the knowledge base of what Live Art practice constitutes. As lead artist for their youth project the *Architecture Crew*, along with Architect Nick Edwards, she created and devised a programme of projects which explore regeneration and the built environment.

Dave Beech is a member of the Freee art collective, writer and lecturer at Chelsea College of Art. Freee's recent projects include, *Nought to Sixty*, at the ICA, London, 2008, *How to be Hospitable*, solo exhibition at the Collective Gallery, 2008, *How to Make a Difference*, solo exhibition at International Project Space, 2007 and *Protest is Beautiful*, solo exhibition at 1000000mph Gallery, 2007. He is also a regular writer for *Art Monthly* and other art magazines. He co-authored the book *The Philistine Controversy*, Verso (2002) with John Roberts.

Tim Butler is Professor of Human Geography at King's College London. He has been researching the gentrification of London for the past twenty five years. He has written a number of books and articles on this transformation, notably *Gentrification and the Middle Classes* which was published in 1997 and more recently (with Garry Robson) *London Calling: the middle classes and the remaking of Inner London*.

Nick Crowe and **Ian Rawlinson** have worked collaboratively since 1994. Their work explores issues around urban space and the social, cultural and economic forces that shape our experience of it. Previous projects include architectural adaptations to a bridge in central Manchester, a durational performance work for Lower Manhattan Cultural Council and a planning application for a metal fenced ghetto around the Oval cricket ground, London. Their 2003 film *Two Burning Bushes*, after a tour of the UK, was shown at PS1 MOMA, New York.

Claire Fox is the director of the *Institute of Ideas* (IoI), which she established to create a public space where ideas can be contested without constraint. Claire initiated the IoI while co-publisher of *LM* magazine (formerly Living Marxism). Claire is a passionate supporter of the arts and argues that efforts to dilute the arts for the benefit of 'the socially excluded' are patronizing rather than democratic. Claire is a co-convener of the yearly *Battle of Ideas* festival and is a panellist on BBC Radio 4's *The Moral Maze* and is regularly invited to comment on developments in culture, education and the media on programmes such as *Question Time*, *Any Questions?* and *BBC Breakfast*. Claire writes regularly for national newspapers and a range of specialist journals.

Andy Hewitt is a member of the Freee art collective and lecturer at University of Wolverhampton. He is also undertaking a PhD at Chelsea College of Art. Freee's recent projects include, *Nought to Sixty*, at the ICA, London, 2008, *How to be Hospitable*, solo exhibition at the Collective Gallery, 2008, *How to Make a Difference*, solo exhibition at International Project Space, 2007 and *Protest is Beautiful*, solo exhibition at 1000000mph Gallery, 2007.

Mark Hutchinson is an artist. Recent projects include, *Being Outside*, solo exhibition for The Negative, London, *(tape runs out)*, exhibition with Paul O'Neill at The Arts Institute, Bournemouth, *Escape*, solo exhibition at Vamiali's gallery, Athens, writer and participant for *Metropolis Rise*, a touring exhibition in Shanghai and Beijing, a co-author of the collective text by the Analysis group, *Analysis 1: On Collectivity*, co-organizer of, and participant in, the touring exhibition, publication and symposium *There is Always an Alternative: possibilities for art in the early nineties*, with Dave Beech, *Escape From Studio Voltaire*, solo exhibition at Studio Voltaire, London and *Contaminant*, an installation for the Collective gallery, Edinburgh. He has written catalogue essays for Ayling & Conroy, Beagles and Ramsay, the Freee art collective, Caroline McCarthy, Paul O'Neill, and Lindsay Seers.

Mel Jordan is a member of the Freee art collective and teaches at Loughborough University. Freee's recent projects include, *Nought to Sixty*, at the ICA, London, 2008, *How to be Hospitable*, solo exhibition at the Collective Gallery, 2008, *How to Make a Difference*, solo exhibition at International Project Space, 2007 and *Protest is Beautiful*, solo exhibition at 1000000mph Gallery, 2007.

Charles Landry founded Comedia, Europe's leading cultural planning consultancy, in 1978. His books include, *The Art of City Making* (2006), *The Creative City: A toolkit for Urban Innovators* (2000), *Riding the Rapids: Urban Life in an Age of Complexity* (2004) and, with Marc Pachter, *Culture @ the Crossroads* (2001). He has presented over 150 keynote addresses on topics including *Risk and creativity*, *Creative cities and beyond*, *Art and its role in city life*, *Complexity and city making*, and *Diverse cultures, diverse creativities*.

Esther Leslie is Professor of Political Aesthetics at Birkbeck, University of London. She is the author of *Synthetic Worlds: Nature, Art and the Chemical Industry* (Reaktion, 2005), *Hollywood Flatlands: Animation, Critical Theory and the Avant Garde* (Verso, 2002) and *Walter Benjamin: Overpowering Conformism* (Pluto, 2000). She is on the editorial boards of the journals *Historical Materialism, Radical Philosophy and Revolutionary History*. Together with Ben Watson, she runs a website of polemics, rants and pictures called *Militant Esthetix*. www. militantesthetix.co.uk

Malcolm Miles is Professor in Cultural Theory at the University of Plymouth, UK. His current research is in a field triangulated by contemporary art, critical theory, and aspects of the social sciences dealing with social transformation. He is author of *Urban Utopias* (2008), *Cities & Cultures* (2007), *Urban Avant-Gardes* (2004) and *Art Space & the City* (1997), co-author of *Consuming Cities* (2004, with Steven Miles), and co-editor of the *City Cultures Reader* (2nd edition 2003, with Tim Hall and Iain Borden). www.malcolmmiles.org.uk

Simon Poulter is a founder member of PVA Media Lab he has devised and delivers the *LabCulture* programme which enables and supports artists to work with new technologies. He has worked with Hull Time Based Arts, to produce *UK Ltd* running a fake privatization company and he also produced *Counter Marketing* unveiling the worlds earliest known scratchcard.

John Roberts is Professor of Art & Aesthetics at the University of Wolverhampton. His recent books include, *Philosophizing the Everyday Revolutionary Praxis and the Fate of Cultural Theory* (Pluto Press, 2006) and *The Intangibilities of Form: Skill and Deskilling in Art, After the Readymade* (Verso, 2007).

Deborah Robinson is Senior Exhibitions Curator at The New Art Gallery Walsall. She has worked for the Museums and Galleries service in Walsall since 1991. Exhibitions curated include *Copper Jubilee* by Gavin Turk, In Memoriam (featuring the work of Jananne Al-Ani, Echolalia, Darryl Georgiou, Susan Hiller, Alastair Maclennan, Kenny Hunter, Gavin Turk and Felix Gonzalez-Torres) and solo exhibitions by Hew Locke and Conrad Shawcross.

Ruth Robinson is an artist contesting the status and role of the 'creative' within contemporary art practice and arts relationship to its assumed audiences. Her critique of the role of art and its systems examines the right to autonomy for artists and citizens alike, in a domain where difference and diversity are only accepted on the terms of the elite. Robinson has a commitment to expanding the radical possibilities of art aiming to increase awareness and instigate debate and action. Her work is research and documentary led- the outcome intervention, event and critical text.

Becky Shaw uses live, photographic and written methods to explore contemporary materiality. Current work includes a response to Firstsite, Colchester's new gallery, and a print series, *Local Colour for Incertainplaces*, Preston. She was Research Fellow at ICIA, University of Bath, 2007-2008, exploring the contemporary relationship between objectivity and subjectivity, and in September 2008 became MA Contemporary Fine Art leader at Sheffield Hallam University. She was co-director of Static Gallery, Liverpool between 2000 and 2006, developing projects including: *Exit Review*, an examination of critical writing and art education, *Press Corps*, a response to Liverpool Biennial 2004, and participating in Cork Caucus.

Charlotte Smith is an artist and writer currently living and working in Los Angeles, California where she is completing her MFA Interdisciplinary Studio at UCLA. Exhibitions include solo show *Occupation* at Bankley House Studios Gallery, Manchester, and *Toy Challenge Perform* at the Custard Factory, Digbeth. Her practice is an investigation of spatial occupation, appropriation and function. Smith is part of [insertspace], a curatorial group based in Birmingham UK, facilitating projects across a realm of public sites with other members Cheryl Jones and Matt Westbrook (see www. insertspace.org.uk)

Freee make two main kinds of artwork: large billboard sized photographs of performances in which the artists present texts; and slogan texts works displayed directly onto gallery walls. They have also produced text-based performances such as a 'bed-in', 14 mini protests and a makeshift spoken choir. They have shown at the Venice Biennale, the Guangzhou Triennial and had solo exhibitions at 1,000,000mph, London, International Project Space, Birmingham, The Collective Gallery, Edinburgh and have been commissioned by the BBC, Hull Time Based Media, and ARC.

How to Make a Difference, solo exhibition, gallery view, 2007, International Project Space, Bournville Centre for Visual Arts, Birmingham, UK

How to Talk to Public Art, Video stills, 2006, BBC and Arts Council England commission for the Power of Art BBC in conjunction with International 3, Manchester, UK

Protest is Beautiful, billboard poster, solo exhibition, 2007, *Protest is Beautiful* 1000000mph Gallery, London, UK

Bring Me Sunshine, performance, group exhibition, 2006, *Peace Camp*, The Brick Lane Gallery, London, UK

The Economic Function of Public Art is to Increase the Value of Private Property, billboard, Freee, 2006, *EAST International 2006*, Selectors Dirk Snauwaert & Jeremy Deller, Norwich Gallery, UK

Fight Against Multiculturalism Commodifying Your Difference, billboard, gallery view, Freee, 2008, *How to be Hospitable*, solo exhibition, Collective Gallery Edinburgh.

Don't Let the Media Have the Monopoly on the Freedom of Speech, billboard, Freee, 2007, solo exhibition *Protest is Beautiful*, 1000,000 mph Gallery, London. Also shown, *How to Make a Difference*, IPS, Birmingham, 2007 and *Terms of Use*, Montehermoso, Vitoria, Spain 2008

I am a Foreign Citizen, I am a Migrant Worker, I am a Local Outsider. billboard, Freee, 2008, *How to be Hospitable*, solo exhibition, Collective Gallery Edinburgh.

Protest Drives History, billboard, Freee, 2008, Commissioned for ICA bar for *Nought to Sixty* exhibition.

The First Condition of an Ecological Politics is that it Halts the Commodification of the Planet by Putting all Landowners, Exploiters, Entrepreneurs and Bureaucrats out of Business. Freee, 2007, *Fusion Now! More Light, More Power, More People*, The Rokeby Gallery, London.